T0073818

Enterprise Strategy
for Blockchain

Management on the Cutting Edge series

Robert Holland, series editor

Published in cooperation with *MIT Sloan Management Review*

MITSloan
Management Review

Enterprise Strategy for Blockchain

Lessons in Disruption from Fintech, Supply Chains, and Consumer Industries

Ravi Sarathy

The MIT Press
Cambridge, Massachusetts
London, England

© 2022 Massachusetts Institute of Technology

All rights reserved. No part of this book may be reproduced in any form by any electronic or mechanical means (including photocopying, recording, or information storage and retrieval) without permission in writing from the publisher.

The MIT Press would like to thank the anonymous peer reviewers who provided comments on drafts of this book. The generous work of academic experts is essential for establishing the authority and quality of our publications. We acknowledge with gratitude the contributions of these otherwise uncredited readers.

This book was set in ITC Stone Serif Std and ITC Stone Sans Std by New Best-set Typesetters Ltd. Printed and bound in the United States of America.

Library of Congress Cataloging-in-Publication Data

Names: Sarathy, Ravi, author.
Title: Enterprise strategy for blockchain : lessons in disruption from fintech, supply
    chains, and consumer industries / Ravi Sarathy.
Description: Cambridge, Massachusetts : The MIT Press, [2022] | Series:
    Management on the cutting edge | Includes bibliographical references and index.
Identifiers: LCCN 2022000700 (print) | LCCN 2022000701 (ebook) |
    ISBN 9780262047166 (hardcover) | ISBN 9780262370851 (epub) |
    ISBN 9780262370868 (pdf)
Subjects: LCSH: Strategic planning. | Blockchains (Databases) | Business
    enterprises—Technological innovations. | Business logistics—Technological
    innovations. | Finance—Technological innovations. | Electronic funds transfers.
Classification: LCC HD30.28 .S268 2022 (print) | LCC HD30.28 (ebook) |
    DDC 658.4/012—dc23/eng/20220310
LC record available at https://lccn.loc.gov/2022000700
LC ebook record available at https://lccn.loc.gov/2022000701

10 9 8 7 6 5 4 3 2 1

Contents

Series Foreword

The world does not lack for management ideas. Thousands of research-ers, practitioners, and other experts produce tens of thousands of arti-cles, books, papers, posts, and podcasts each year. But only a scant few promise to truly move the needle on practice, and fewer still dare to reach into the future of what management will become. It is this rare breed of idea—meaningful to practice, grounded in evidence, and *built for the future*—that we seek to present in this series.

Robert Holland

Managing Director

MIT Sloan Management Review

Preface

Books are written by reflecting and building on the wisdom and work of other scholars, and this book is no different. I have benefited enormously from reading and following the writings and opinions of a large number of blockchain researchers and entrepreneurs. Blockchain has been sometimes referred to as the bedrock on which Web 3.0 will be built, a new version of the internet that draws on decentralized peer-to-peer interaction. For many, cryptocurrency is the starting point for their voyage into the intricacies of blockchain. And although blockchain has been extensively deployed in gestating Bitcoin and other cryptocurrencies, I highlight the extensive application potential of blockchain and the underlying distributed ledger technology for enterprises and across society.

Blockchain is a fast-changing field at a stage where there are new developments every week, and as I researched and wrote this book, I was constantly rewriting to reflect this continually morphing space. Hence, writing this book—and reading it—is the beginning of a journey. I hope this book stimulates your interest and leaves you wanting to learn more.

My thanks to Emily Taber, Acquisitions Editor at the MIT Press, for her thoughtful assessments, her continuing involvement, and encouragement in the writing of this book. My thanks to the several anonymous reviewers who took the time to offer insightful comments on draft versions of this book. Thanks to Abigail Holstein, development editor, who wrestled with and competently clarified my draft manuscript, and to David Weinberger, who offered perceptive comments on the introduction. I want to thank the D'Amore-McKim School of Business at Northeastern University and Acting Dean Emery Trahan for creating a supportive environment during the research and writing phases. And a special thanks to my wife Beth for her patience and support during the long period I was wrapped up in researching and writing this manuscript.

Introduction: Blockchain's Disruptive Potential

In 2021, a group of hackers broke into a computer system containing software applications governing pipeline operations at the Colonial Pipeline Company. They encrypted data and locked access to the system critical to the pipeline's functioning and demanded ransom payments to release the data.[1] Colonial's 5,500-mile gasoline and diesel fuel infrastructure links refineries on the Texas Gulf Coast with most of the eastern seaboard, supplying 45 percent of the fuel consumed by individuals and enterprises in major metropolitan areas and states such as New York, Virginia, North and South Carolina, and Georgia. Such ransomware attacks are commonplace—and costly—for enterprises of all kinds. The attack forced Colonial to temporarily halt its pipeline operations, leading to regional gas shortages, long lines, price increases, and gas hoarding. It also revealed (again) the vulnerability of critical US infrastructure operations to cyberattacks. Colonial paid a ransom of around $5 million to be able to decrypt its data and regain access to computer systems.[2] And in addition to paying the ransom, the company had to contend with lost revenue and reputational damage.

Whether for a pipeline or a financial institution, it is essential for a company to protect itself and its operations and databases against adversarial, ill-intentioned economic actors. A solution lies in distributed ledger technology (DLT), popularly referred to as blockchain. DLT was designed with the assumption that firms will be faced with untrustworthy counterparties who will attempt to exploit online transactions for private gain. In the case of Colonial, with its use of sensors, valves, and leak detection systems in controlling its pipelines, blockchain-based multitier cybersecurity protection in a smart metering environment could have provided protection.[3] An alternative would be using distributed data storage for critical data, linked to a permissioned blockchain.[4]

Granted, legacy solutions to prevent these kind of ransomware attacks already exist, such as air-gapped systems,[5] offline cold backups, and a tested IT disaster recovery plan. In air-gapped systems (where the network is disconnected from outside networks, both wired and wireless, with WiFi transceivers prevented from being in the vicinity of the air-gapped systems), the only way to transfer data is to copy the information to a physical peripheral such as a tape backup or a hard drive and then connect it to a recipient system. Offline cold backups, done with all users offline, ensure that files cannot be changed during backup and are protected from live viruses and hacking attempts, with the backup data stored offline. Blockchain offers an alternative but must prove its superior effectiveness over legacy solutions to justify making the transition. While blockchain has existed for more than a decade, only in recent years has it matured to the point of becoming a potentially disruptive innovation. This book explores the opportunities blockchain makes possible, while also defining the limits of current blockchain applications, to provide leaders of legacy enterprises with strategies to leverage blockchain for maximum competitive advantage.

What Is DLT and Blockchain?

DLT relies on three interconnected concepts—distributed peer-to-peer (P2P) networks, robust cryptography, and game theory–derived incentives known as tokens. Tokens are digital assets that have value and can be used as rewards to motivate desired behavior and as a means of payment within the DLT for services rendered by a participant, such as verifying authenticity or transferring asset ownership. Blockchain is one application of DLT and is perhaps the best known, and it specifically groups exchange transactions between counterparties into blocks and then cryptographically chains the blocks together, hence "blockchain." Blockchain is the technology underlying Bitcoin creation and exchange, and since then its applicability has rapidly reached far beyond cryptocurrency. DLT uses robust encryption so that data is secure and available only to intended recipients. Copies of the data are distributed across nodes so that hacking data would require breaking into the multiple nodes and altering each copy, making tampering increasingly evident as well as increasingly difficult.

How Can Blockchain Be Used?

Blockchain's superiority goes beyond value exchange and data security. Blockchain can help avoid intermediaries that add costs and introduce inefficiencies and incremental risks. Here are some brief case studies— some happening now, some in the near future—that illustrate blockchain's reach.

Global Supply Chains

Global supply chains are an arena plagued by delays, fraud, unethical worker treatment, and data inconsistencies between counterparties. Supply chain fraud, for example, from using the same invoice to obtain financing from multiple credit sources can cost $600 billion a year. With heavy reliance on paper-based processes, stored in data silos at multiple locations, administrative costs can run up to 20 percent of shipment value. Delays due to lost or damaged documents, or data inconsistencies between supply chain partners, make it difficult to predict when shipments might arrive at their destination while increasing the amount of inventory in transit in the supply chain.

In 2017 IBM and Maersk teamed up to develop and offer TradeLens,[6] a blockchain platform designed to resolve the chronic challenges facing global supply chains described above. First deployed as a global trade digitization platform, TradeLens connects the large variety of supply chain actors—disparate entities, ranging from customers and their suppliers to transportation and container shipping firms, customs agencies, ports, and software developers—to a "single source of truth." The several supply chain entities can thus obtain the same information about a transaction, avoiding disputes, delays, and the need to reconcile inconsistencies. TradeLens also offers a digital bill of lading facility, allowing supply chain entities to securely issue, transfer, and deliver bills of lading.

TradeLens is not only good for the businesses it serves but also good business for IBM and Maersk. In exchange for a fee, shippers receive continuously updated data on their shipments, enabling them to monitor goods' movements around the globe and to increase their efficiency all while keeping data secure from hackers. After two years in the marketplace, TradeLens tracked 30 million container shipments, 1.5 billion events, and 13 million documents across ten ocean carriers and more than six hundred ports. And TradeLens's value only increases as more supply chain entities become members.

Cross-Border Payments

Cross-border payments can be frustrating and costly for payers and recipients. That is a problem because cross-border payments are expected to total around $30 trillion in 2022, incurring fees as high as 6–7 percent of the transfer amount, which could total over $2 trillion. Payments can take several days, and when a sending agent does not have a presence in the receiving country, they must rely on a local financial institution to complete the transfer. Those transfers can be opaque to clients who may not know in advance when the transaction will be completed and the specific exchange rate used for conversion, leaving them facing financial risks while the transfer is in process.

This problem plays to blockchain's strength as a trustworthy and transparent ledger. It can help fulfill cross-border transactions faster, at lower costs, and with less risk to the transacting parties. That is why central banks from the United Kingdom, Canada, and Singapore are joining together on pilots to offer faster payments at lower cost with central bank digital currencies (CBDCs).[7]

Blockchain's scalability means that its utility in cross-border payments can also be useful in managing small retail transfers, such as remittances by migrant workers sent home across national borders.

These transactions are subject to high fees and a lack of transparency. The total addressable market for such remittances was estimated at $548 billion in 2019.[8]

Such wide blockchain applicability has led start-ups such as Ripple to offer alternatives to the long-dominant SWIFT messaging system standard that is at heart of the global correspondent banking network infrastructure for remittances. In doing so, Ripple offers speedy, low-cost, reliable payments and access to a broad range of countries and currencies. Banks such as Santander partnered with the company to offer low-cost, one-day cross-border payment using their mobile app One Pay FX starting in 2018.

Protecting Digital Data: Music, Video, and Digital Art

For the past few decades, musicians, video game designers, and other artists—as well as their industries—have struggled to protect the digital files of their work from being copied and/or stolen. Creators and companies primarily reach consumers through intermediaries whose fees can be a significant portion of the total transaction revenue. Music streaming services provided by Spotify, Apple, Amazon, Google, and the like pay musicians relatively small amounts for their art, with the bulk of profits from membership fees and purchases of music files going to global music recording companies and producers. If musicians made their music available on a blockchain, listeners could connect to that blockchain using an app. They could then pay with microtransactions in return for varying levels of access, for example, one-time listening, repeated listens over a certain duration, and sampling rights. This would help musicians cut out the streaming services as an intermediary and keep more revenue for themselves, disrupting Spotify, Apple, and others, just as those streamers once disrupted older music distribution businesses. Berklee College of Music launched its Open Music Initiative with this goal in mind, making its RAIDAR licensing platform available in 2020. RAIDAR incorporates smart contracts and musician identity verification, enabling them to license their artistic endeavors for a fee, with low transaction costs.[9]

The video game industry could experience the same sort of disruption as the music industry. Currently, producers such as Epic Games—the maker of Fortnite, a game that had 350 million users worldwide—are charged a 30 percent commission for sales in Apple's App Store and Google Play. Epic Games sued Apple and Google[10] to force the two firms to lower their commission rates, claiming they were abusing their monopoly positions. Facilitating access to video games through blockchain-based applications could ensure secure access and channel payments to game creators while avoiding commissions paid to distribution platforms such as those controlled by Apple and Google.

The first such game was *CryptoKitties*, launched in 2017 on Ethereum, with the game's goal of breeding, buying, and selling virtual cats. The goal is perhaps laughable except that the game's popularity overwhelmed and slowed down the Ethereum blockchain, with some virtual felines selling for over $100,000. A newer game, Ubisoft's *Hash*, allows players to build new environments and create challenges for other players, charging other players a fee for access to these new "chapters," thus using blockchain to facilitate decentralized game development, with developers compensation shaped by the popularity of the environments they create.[11] Similarly, *Axie Infinity*, from game studio Sky Mavis, whose co-founder and CEO Trung Nguyen hails from Vietnam, is built on Ethereum, and enables gamers to earn SLP tokens (native to the game) while competing, which can be then converted into cryptocurrencies on exchanges.[12] Further, *Axie Infinity*, derived from classic games such as *Pokémon*, allows gamers to build monsters called Axies and then have them battle other Axies, with these Axies and the terrain that form part of the game, becoming NFTs, that can be traded. Gamers need to buy an initial supply of Axies to start playing, and a round of venture capital funding in October 2021 valued *Axie Infinity* at nearly $3 billion.[13]

In the visual art world, blockchain's nonfungible token (NFT) capability allows one-of-a-kind digital files to be created and traded. Files are encrypted with a key that only its legitimate user can unlock and access (public–private key pairs). NFTs thus offer an ownership title to a digital asset. The ability to create them has given rise to a whole new market for digital data, such as Sotheby's sale of digital art by Beeple for $69 million, with vast numbers of NFTs created, sold, and traded at accessible prices in the mass market through entities such as NBA Top Shot and Hashmasks.

While a screenshot can copy digital art from a display, NFTs provide proof of ownership and allow digital art to be collected and traded. Zurich's Suum Cuique Labs brought together seventy artists to create a set of 16,000 pieces—Hashmasks. Each piece is distinguished by unique features, such as a distinctive mask, eye color, skin tone, background, characters, and a hidden message (e.g., a royal flush scattered across multiple pieces).[14] Upon its release, buyers paid around $9 million in Ether (the Ethereum-based cryptocurrency) for the entire collection. A market quickly developed, and pieces deemed rarer or more desirable sold at higher prices—one sold for $650,000.

Credit Bureaus and Credit Scores

Credit agencies, like Equifax, aggregate individual financial and other personal information to develop credit scores and credit profiles. These agencies continue to earn significant profits despite their security lapses. Equifax is a telling example—in 2017, hackers compromised 140 million personal information records, with the company agreeing to pay $700 million in fines and customer restitution in 2019 and incurring a loss of $400 million that year.

With blockchain-based identity verification, consumers could store and control their personal financial information on a blockchain and monetize such information, deciding how much of it to share and with whom. They could also restrict access to their personal information, sharing only the barest details necessary to meet requester needs. Such a development would not only merely undercut the business model but would also reduce the need for companies like TransUnion, Experian, and Equifax.

Why the Growing Interest in Blockchain?

These select applications are just a handful of the numerous—and increasingly successful—pilots and applications that are built on blockchain. While the ever-broadening reach of the technology is remarkable, the size, power, and commitment of the entities embracing blockchain is telling. They are positioning themselves to be first in their fields and to meet competition from rising start-ups and late-to-the-game incumbent peers. Why? Blockchain threatens disintermediation, dislodging incumbents in their role as intermediaries. It allows transacting parties to interact directly, cutting out a middleman, such as a bank, thus lowering fees and reducing the costs of doing business.

Blockchain's advanced encryption and decentralized storage of copies across nodes also makes it almost impossible for hackers to intrude and alter or extract information. Compared to centralized databases, blockchain offers greater protection from hackers, allowing economic actors to trust transaction information generated and stored on it. The chaining of transactions into tamper-resistant blocks allows counterparties to trace a transaction back to its course and thus pinpoint when a problem or error occurred. And with blockchain's decentralized secure network, a transaction can be completed simultaneously with the finalization of a payment.

Roadblocks to Blockchain Adoption

Blockchain technology, though innovative, is immature and needs continuing development to overcome its performance gaps relative to mainstream legacy solutions, especially in areas such as processing speed, scalability, security, and user friendliness. It is generally opaque to the mass market; few mainstream users have experience using blockchain, and experience with private and public keys to protect security. For such reasons, blockchain lags in matching the enterprise-level service quality standards that legacy applications offer. However, while immature in some aspects, it is fast developing and rapidly overcoming its deficiencies.

Technological obstacles are only part of the reason why enterprises have not embraced blockchain beyond pilot efforts and limited trials. Blockchain adoption faces two additional challenges—organizational and economic. First, blockchain applications often require organizations to change and collaborate more extensively with independent entities, suppliers, regulators—and often competitors—to reap the benefits blockchain has to offer. Enterprises must contend with attenuated organizational boundaries and develop cooperative strategies for innovation and customer service, a step they may not be ready for. Enterprises also have to prepare their organizations to accept and successfully use it. Developing such organizational readiness involves recruiting specialized personnel, gaining more education, onboarding technical and managerial staff, and overcoming resistance to change.

Second, blockchain application development and implementation requires capital, human resources, and time. Upper management—hardheaded chief financial officers and boards—might be unwilling to approve budgets requiring such significant investments without clear evidence from positive cost–benefit analysis and return on investment estimates, which is difficult to obtain at blockchain's nascent stage. These additional obstacles contribute to incumbents' unwillingness to persist with blockchain, delaying widespread use. Economic challenges also extend to finding and addressing appropriate market opportunities and overcoming legal and regulatory uncertainties.[15]

Responding to Potential Disruption from Blockchain

Given that blockchain can offer potential disruptive impacts but also faces these hurdles, will incumbents be successful with an attitude of watchfulness? If a more immediate response is advisable, how quickly should they respond? What tools and capabilities do they need to launch a response before the disruption starts destroying incumbent franchises? And how should incumbents respond?

The answer is not wait and see. Blockchain challengers can build a significant lead in the incumbent's market space, and a belated response will likely be inadequate. How other incumbents respond, specifically one's competitors, is also important. These other incumbents, by taking the blockchain threat seriously, can become "superfast followers."[16] They will be ready to launch blockchain solutions at scale while one's own firm is still preparing its initial response. Hence, incumbents are better off experimenting with blockchain expeditiously to minimize risk from subsequent industry-wide disruption. They need to ready themselves to exploit blockchain's full potential because blockchain will gradually overcome its technology limitations and achieve its full value.

Incumbents have an ecosystem advantage over disrupters—they are part of the business ecosystems that blockchains seek to disrupt.[17] For example, an investment bank seeking to implement the entire bond life cycle in a blockchain can draw on existing business relationships and trust established with market makers, issuance syndicates, securities custodial agents and regulators, and others to persuade all of them to participate in a bond life cycle blockchain pilot. Their feedback and insights will be critical to assessing the feasibility and advantages of managing corporate bonds through blockchains. And the timely response of third-party pilot participants allows incumbents to leverage their ecosystem presence to ward off their challengers.

Incumbents also have the unique advantage of investigating blockchain through several measured approaches, limiting risk and interruptions to regular business.[18] They can acquire or partner with blockchain upstarts, leveraging the challenger's capabilities. Incumbents also gain access to a larger talent pool and to pioneering blockchain technology while incorporating new customers. If the incumbent firm chooses an alliance, it can put in place learning mechanisms and knowledge transfer processes to capture and feed blockchain-specific learning back to its core operations. Knowledge transfer from alliances can be complemented with internal blockchain skills development and education, fostering a ready pool of managerial and technological talent who are ready to step in when blockchain efforts take off. Education also helps reduce resistance to change, making for better alignment and rollout.

Incumbents can also adopt a venture capital role, providing seed capital to blockchain start-ups. While gaining exposure to new technology and product/service offerings, incumbents can assess how best to integrate blockchain advances into their business models. Alternatively, they can participate in external venture capital funds that specialize in blockchain innovation and still get a clear view into blockchain development.

Incumbent firms can (and should) launch pilot projects to familiarize themselves with blockchain. The pilots can draw on existing capital and customers and skilled personnel (in-house and newly recruited) as well as an incumbent's ability to take on risk. Ideally, incumbent firms will begin pilots in multiple areas, launching a swarm of blockchain innovations so they can ultimately spot the best performers. DLT involves decentralized ledgers—multiple copies of the same records, held by the various members of the decentralized network. Hence, firms could experiment with collaborating with network members of organizations outside their own organizational boundaries to determine the relative benefits of ceding decision-making to a decentralized network.

Incumbents can then use such pilot projects to develop cost–benefit estimates supporting approval for commercial scale rollout. Through these projects, firms can leverage blockchain's capabilities to offer improved customer solutions, such as with new products. Pilot projects can also prepare firms for making necessary pivots while maintaining existing customer relationships and offering greater privacy protection, instant settlement, and an overall better experience. Incumbents can also integrate their relevant legacy capabilities and solutions with newer blockchain solutions to ameliorate pain points that customers and partners complain about, offering immediate answers without having to wait for blockchain to mature further.

Blockchain disruption is inevitable, and incumbents must respond with a variety of options, summarized below in figure 0.1. Taken together, the broad objective incumbents need to pursue is steady growth in their blockchain skills and knowledge. Whether that occurs

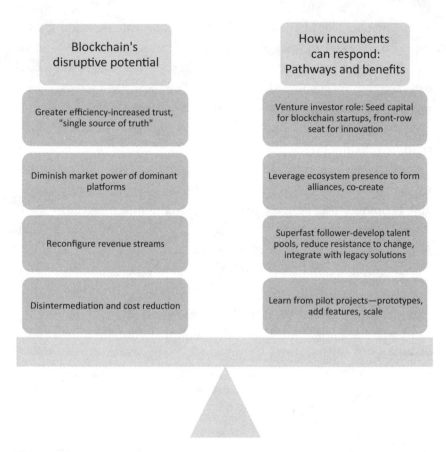

Figure 0.1
Combating blockchain disruption: Pathways for incumbents and benefits

initially through acquisition or investment, successive pilot projects of increasing complexity will put this objective within reach.

In Clayton Christensen's formulation of the disruptive innovation concept,[19] new entrants with limited resources challenge an established industry and its incumbents with an innovative solution that has rough edges: it does not match the performance of incumbents' product and service offerings. Paradoxically, incumbents might be offering a level of performance that overshoots the requirements of some portion of the market, and the overperformance may come with a price tag that deters consumption. New entrants attempt to bridge this gap, targeting market segments where performance exceeds their needs as well as market segments whose willingness to accept lower functionality has been disregarded.

Disruptive innovation challengers target these underserved or overlooked segments, realizing that these customers might welcome an "inferior," low-end product, with poorer performance and deliberately limited functionality at a likely reduced price. Incumbents may not find such new entrant strategy threatening because the customer segments targeted are low-profit customers or "nonconsumers," that is, not their current customers. Nonconsumers are essentially a new market, created by a combination of innovation and price. If entrants are successful with this low-end strategy, they can move on to target mainstream customers. Entrants gradually catch up to the price and performance profiles and value propositions of incumbents, recognizing that innovation alone might be insufficient to close the deal. Mainstream customers would consider the total value from switching, including innovation benefits, lower cost, comparability (or superiority) to existing solutions, ease of use, and dependability in solving their specific problems.

It is precisely this path that blockchain challengers are following. Right now, they are targeting customers with solutions when the underlying blockchain technology is still immature but evolving and improving. It is only as the technology improves that blockchain challengers can target mainstream market segments. This improvement path is a slow process—which is why incumbents have time to develop opportune and successful responses.

At this point in their evolution, many blockchain start-ups are primarily targeting nonconsumers and customer segments with limited spending power and small order sizes. These customer segments have margins and profit contributions that might be insufficient to cover the costs of customer acquisition and customer servicing. Using blockchain does not automatically result in disruption because the resulting product or service offered, as well as the segments targeted, may be judged unimportant by the incumbents being challenged. As such, these blockchain-based organizations do not represent an immediate threat to established incumbents. Instead, it is the longer-term consequences that should worry incumbents.

For example, Filecoin, a system of blockchain-enabled decentralized data storage, initially targeted customers with a low volume of storage needs or unwillingness to use large, centralized storage services where contractual terms did not offer sufficient privacy or defense against data loss to hackers.[20] The company seeks to challenge centralized storage providers such as Amazon Web Services. It uses the complementary IPFS P2P decentralized file transfer and storage network to offer secure decentralized file storage, encrypting and storing client data at multiple nodes. The company uses tokens to motivate storage providers and to ensure that its clients can access storage capacity as desired, guarantee that the data has been stored for the contracted duration and is accessible at any time for retrieval, and guarantee that longer-term data storage is available if desired.

Another intriguing blockchain-based start-up is Plastic Bank, which seeks to prevent unrecycled plastic, a significant portion of which emanates from emerging markets, from ending up in the ocean. Plastic Bank created an asset-based token that individuals can receive on their smartphones when they collect and turn in waste plastic. Tokens are used instead of cash payment to be able to provide proof of the provenance of the recycled plastic to potential buyers as well as to reduce the user's burden of storing and safeguarding against the theft of cash. The tokens are exchangeable for cash, solar-powered smartphone charging, cooking fuel, school tuition, utility bill payment, and health insurance, thus also addressing poverty alleviation. Plastic Bank offers waste collectors a bank savings account and an opportunity to earn credit ratings, enhancing financial inclusion. This system requires forging connections between individual plastic collectors, waste collection centers, manufacturers using recycled plastic, and shippers.

Nebula Genomics, a genetic testing firm, uses blockchain to give customers control over their data and protect their privacy. Using blockchain helps Nebula's customers to remain anonymous, and in turn customers can submit samples and receive genetic reports without identifying themselves, ensuring their personal data is not linked to the encrypted genomic information stored off-chain. Companies offering genome sequencing can profit by sharing their customers' data with third parties, and Nebula's point of differentiation is that it allows its customers to decide whether to give permissioned access to their data to outside entities such as pharmaceutical companies or academic medical researchers. This allows customers to earn fees for their data while also contributing to medical research and without compromising their privacy. Nebula can protect privacy and guard against data misuse by restricting researcher data analysis to trusted execution environments (TEEs), wherein researchers can analyze data on Nebula's computing equipment and storage devices, which anonymize individual data.[21]

As the disruptive innovation process unfolds, these organizations will build additional functionality and expand their ecosystems to create and deliver robust solutions. Promoting the development of ecosystems around the initial innovation allows blockchain-based customer solutions to be developed collaboratively across firms and industries, disrupting intermediary profit streams further still. Thus, in Filecoin's case, third party apps such as Codefi's Filecoin Storage app, provide additional capabilities, which allows potential users to search the Filecoin storage marketplace and compare prices, storage capacity and their reputation score.

When mainstream customers adopt disruptive entrant solutions in significant numbers, leading to significant shifts in market share, disruption is complete. However, we are not yet at the stage where any blockchain disruptor is showing a sign of breaking into the mainstream. Initially, blockchain primarily appeals to technologically savvy users comfortable conducting mobile e-commerce transactions on smartphones and using distributed apps (Dapps). Dapps are specific to blockchain in that they run on P2P networks with transactions recorded on nodes across the distributed network. This contrasts with traditional apps that run in a client server mode, with the app transacting with a centralized server, possibly in the cloud. In the case of an app, information is centralized at the server and can be hacked. Dapps are designed to take advantage of the tamper-evident and tamperproof nature of transaction validation and recording across distributed nodes in the P2P blockchain network.

Furthermore, blockchain features may not be attractive to mainstream market customers. Changing standard blockchain architecture to entice mainstream market customers may come at the price of some of blockchain's innovative edge. In the case of financial applications, for example, incumbent enterprises would want to improve transaction processing speed while limiting the reproduction of transaction details at every node. "Permissioned blockchains," which use permissioned nodes that grant read-and-write privileges to fewer nodes, may meet both needs. Restricting write privileges increases transaction processing speed, while limiting read access helps keep transaction details private and known only to the permissioned nodes, favoring their enterprise use.

As a result, transaction information would be reproduced only at the permissioned nodes, reducing visibility of transactions at every node. However, controlling the right to join the blockchain and specifically grant read-and-write privileges preserves the centrality of incumbent intermediaries, who would be able to exercise control and governance authority. In other words, intermediaries would be able to control access to the blockchain, set performance standards, and continue to charge intermediary fees, albeit at a lower level. This, of course, undoes one of blockchain's signature innovations—disintermediation—raising costs and increasing network vulnerability if the central incumbent nodes are hacked and compromised.

New challengers will need to match the performance standards currently offered by incumbents. Blockchain, as discussed in the next chapter, needs to overcome various obstacles that currently make it less capable of satisfying the needs of large enterprises. As challengers upgrade their applications, incumbents will have the time and opportunity to learn from start-up missteps, which will allow them to study the underperformance of their challengers and to develop business use cases that can benefit from blockchain applications. Incumbents may then have a better understanding of their customers' needs and frustrations. They can draw on longer-duration customer relationships and accumulated customer interaction data.

Incumbents can also identify pain points that led to lower customer satisfaction and use such information to address product and service limitations. This backdrop allows them to combine customer data with advances in blockchain methodology to launch pilot projects and test how a blockchain application can improve customer outcomes. Of course, they might conclude that moving to blockchain is unnecessary and that challengers could be fought off with improvements to legacy applications that overcome their deficiencies. But for incumbents who find use in blockchain, their depth of knowledge and experience in their own arenas will empower them to head off possible inroads by challengers while taking the lead in enterprise blockchain implementation.

Blockchain Unbound: Chapter Highlights

In this book, I examine blockchain's disruptive potential—how that potential is being and will be realized, obstacles in the way of disruption, and, for incumbent enterprises, the critical advantage inherent in investing, exploring, and experimenting with blockchain now. I draw on lessons from blockchain application experiences to offer strategies for enterprise scale blockchain deployment. Figure 0.2 shows the progression through the chapters that follow.

Chapter 1 begins with the technological features of blockchain that power its disruptive capabilities. I show how these features can be leveraged to resolve long-standing problems affecting enterprises and their customers. I then highlight blockchain benefits for enterprises, discussing internal applications and customer-facing and ecosystem-wide applications, illustrating these application directions with examples. Internal applications are easier to develop and use, likely resulting in accurate, widely available data and transaction records (a single source of truth) and efficiency gains. Such lower hanging fruit can lay

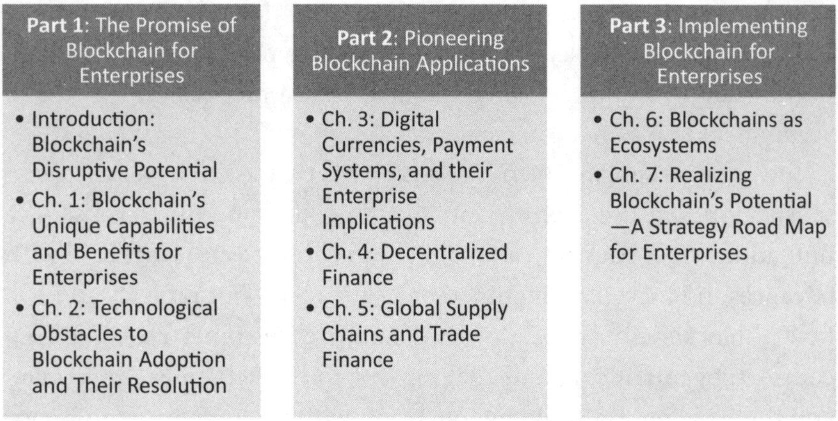

Part 1: The Promise of Blockchain for Enterprises	Part 2: Pioneering Blockchain Applications	Part 3: Implementing Blockchain for Enterprises
• Introduction: Blockchain's Disruptive Potential • Ch. 1: Blockchain's Unique Capabilities and Benefits for Enterprises • Ch. 2: Technological Obstacles to Blockchain Adoption and Their Resolution	• Ch. 3: Digital Currencies, Payment Systems, and their Enterprise Implications • Ch. 4: Decentralized Finance • Ch. 5: Global Supply Chains and Trade Finance	• Ch. 6: Blockchains as Ecosystems • Ch. 7: Realizing Blockchain's Potential —A Strategy Road Map for Enterprises

Figure 0.2

Blockchain unbound: Enterprise strategy for harnessing its disruption potential

the groundwork for more complex external applications, which are likely to provide better customer solutions and a possible competitive advantage.

In chapter 2, I look at technological obstacles to blockchain adoption and how they are being resolved. I examine blockchain start-ups and how they are resolving technological barriers to blockchain application, particularly the blockchain trilemma: simultaneously maximizing the security, scalability, and speed, influenced by the extent of decentralization. Disruptive technologies are often brought to market and continuously improved by new entrants. This continuous improvement process helps harden and improve the technology, overcome performance gaps, and improve competitiveness with legacy systems. I review several such blockchain start-ups and their business models and the customer needs they are attempting to satisfy. Only 10 percent of blockchain trials have made it into production, and blockchain projects are "progressing faster" in other markets outside the US, especially in Asia-Pacific.[22] Technological advances from these start-ups are essential to the realization of blockchain's disruptive potential and eventual blockchain acceptance in enterprises. The various examples highlighted in this chapter point to a wide range of innovative activity in the blockchain arena. Their experience offers pointers for formulating blockchain strategy, and I draw lessons from their choices regarding problems addressed, vertical market focus, industry-specific solutions, and complementing key applications to jointly offer an ecosystem of solutions.

A major development in the blockchain world is the growing promise of digital currencies as a means of payment. Chapter 3 considers various facets of the payments revolution, highlighting the role of digital currency payment systems, private stablecoins, CBDCs, and their enterprise implications.

Blockchain deployment in tandem with the rise of digital currencies raises the possibility of disrupting the financial services market. A set of emerging alternatives, collectively described as decentralized finance, is discussed in chapter 4. Financial services cover a range of offerings, such as payments, savings, credit and lending, remittances, trading and settlement, exchanges and derivatives markets, and insurance. These many facets of financial services are marked by the need for intermediaries to manage counterparty risk, obtain legal compliance with regulations, and provide access to the services. Intermediaries in the financial world maintain control over assets (on behalf of customers), assume systemic risk, and have access to aspects of transaction data. Incumbents offer trusted service across multiple integrated services in return for intermediary fees, which can be a significant portion of transaction amounts or assets. The several decentralized finance applications discussed in this chapter represent a surge of innovation, with each major category of decentralized finance innovation building on previous advances in earlier decentralized finance apps, gradually creating a complete decentralized finance ecosystem that has the potential to make decentralized finance the "killer app" in blockchain.

Another area of industry activity that is well suited to blockchain's advantages is the global supply chain and trade finance complex, which is discussed in chapter 5. Global supply chains function ponderously because of their reliance on paper-based processes and electronic data interchange (EDI) for transmitting documents. Conflicting information and lost documents lead to errors and slow down transaction approval, resulting in long lead times, lack of transparency concerning status and location of a specific shipment, and inefficient capital allocation. Chapter 5 discusses several supply chain blockchain pilots gaining traction. The discussion in this chapter spans the interconnection of supply chains, cross-border payments, trade financing, and marketplaces matching buyers and sellers. I discuss blockchain benefits for supply chain performance, from data consolidation and visibility to shipment tracking, enhancing transparency and trust in supply chain network data, monitoring shipments, and solving problems in real time.

The various examples discussed, across industries and in start-ups, underline the progress in deploying blockchains for tailored vertical industry applications and highlights the particular aptness of blockchain for developing cooperative, interorganizational customer solutions. Hence, in chapter 6, I focus on the value of applying a strategic ecosystem framework to blockchain deployment in enterprises. I consider the benefits of adopting an ecosystem perspective, and issues that arise in thinking about blockchains as ecosystems, including cultivating ecosystem membership, coordinating cocreation, fair sharing of rewards among members, ecosystem governance, and evolution. I then discuss how blockchains can be used in an ecosystems framework, discussing three industry examples: health care, supply chains, and autonomous (driverless) vehicles.

I conclude, in chapter 7, by drawing together the lessons learned from the various industry applications and adopting an ecosystem perspective to outline strategic steps for successfully using blockchain in enterprises. I trace a path forward for incumbent enterprises, from establishing a business case for applying blockchain to evaluating enterprise cost–benefits to preparing the organization to develop the requisite knowledge and people skills and overcome resistance to change.

Not every business problem requires a blockchain-based solution. Alternatives such as distributed databases and a control tower/ dashboard might work, and the discussion in this final chapter highlights when blockchain deployment is the best approach. Blockchain applications, at their heart, involve democratizing access and offering autonomy and control over decision making, risk taking, and sharing rewards. Together, these traits represent a departure for an enterprise accustomed to exercising centralized control in hierarchically structured organizations and solutions. The analysis and discussion in this final chapter, along with the strategy road map, can help enterprises prepare for the rise of a disruptive technology, one that will impose a radical shift in almost all ways of doing business.

1 Blockchain's Unique Capabilities and Benefits for Enterprises

I began by surveying blockchain's disruptive possibilities, pointing out that for all the benefits it can deliver, large enterprises have been slow to adopt the technology. In this chapter, I dig deeper into blockchain's unique capabilities and the architecture that underpins its potential and shapes its ability to resolve chronic problems with digital transactions. Like other potentially disruptive technologies in their early stages, blockchain better meets the needs of nonconsumers and narrow customer segments who find legacy solutions on offer overly complex and perhaps unaffordable.[1] Blockchain is still evolving, and I highlight technological drawbacks to using it. Nonetheless, we can see a future in which its these drawbacks are resolved and it becomes a commonplace feature of enterprise business. Blockchain start-ups, discussed in chapter 2, are at the forefront of efforts to gradually overcome these drawbacks. In chapter 7, when I discuss enterprise blockchain strategy and implementation, I address how firms can address economic and organizational impediments to blockchain rollout.

What Makes Blockchain Unique?

Blockchain's unique value stems from its distinctive design and architecture, which offer powerful advantages and benefits to enterprises. Digital transactions remain vulnerable to several persistent problems, exposing enterprises to delays, fraud, and other additional costs.

Blockchain provides solutions to the following persistent and costly challenges, which are discussed in more detail below:

- identity verification
- trusting counterparties in a transaction
- reliable transactions and provenance assurance
- disputes and delays arising from inconsistent information
- integrating transaction with payments
- safeguarding digital assets
- dangers of excessive centralization
- interorganizational collaboration

Identity Verification

In digital transactions, how can a merchant be sure of the identity of the party on the other side of a transaction? Identities can be hard to detect, leaving the firm vulnerable to hacking, fraud, and financial harm. Misidentification can also prejudice the firm's compliance with regulatory requirements such as know your customer (KYC) and anti-money laundering (AML) provisions.

Blockchain Solution: Self-Sovereign Identity Blockchain, using private and public keys and zero-knowledge proofs (ZKPs), creates simplified, decentralized identifiers controlled by the individual, called self-sovereign identity (SSI). Public key-private key pairs are unique to each individual. As the terminology suggests, an individual can make the public key widely available, while the private key is only known to that individual. When two individuals—the *sender* and the *receiver*—seek to conduct a transaction, such as exchanging value or transferring data, the sender can encrypt a transaction with the receiver's public key. The recipient can only decrypt the information using their own private key while also verifying that the information is from the sender with the sender's public key. Both sender and receiver keep their private keys secure.

SSI uses ZKPs to verify information while disclosing as little detail as possible so that individuals and entities can validate their identity without disclosing additional details.[2] For example, a real estate agent may want a potential buyer to disclose their pay stubs and bank statements to prove they have sufficient income and funds to purchase the house being shown. ZKPs can offer such proof of income. In this instance, ZKPs would use two separate steps: 1) prove the identity of the potential home buyer and 2) link that proven identity to a proven credential, namely income and assets. The *verifier*, in this case a bank that maintains that the individual's checking or savings accounts, can verify that balances and direct deposit pay amounts exceed a certain number for a certain encrypted identity. The *prover*, the individual who wishes to establish proof of financial sufficiency, sends a public key to the *requester*, the real estate agent, who can then verify the prover's identity in a public blockchain containing encrypted identities, without knowing any further information about the prover. Thus, the realtor can obtain assurance of the potential buyer's purchasing power without access to details such as the exact amount of savings available or the actual amount of income earned.

Financial regulators in the United States and across the globe require financial institutions to verify their client's identity—KYC—to facilitate monitoring for money laundering and illegal practices such as financing terrorism and human trafficking. Noncompliance can result in large financial penalties and threaten the financial institution's continuing operations. SSI promotes the creation and sharing of universal verified identity. Once in place, a universal verified identity eliminates the need for repeated identity checks, and it can be used to comply with KYC regulations in a variety of settings. Assured identity in turn can be linked to that individual's or entity's reputation and facilitate direct exchanges of value between identified and reputable parties to a transaction.[3] For example, data analytics applied to an individual's payments record in a blockchain can derive a reputation score based on their payment reliability (not unlike a credit score). The individual, as the prover, can decide to share such a score with requesters, using the ZKP process outlined above.

Trusting Counterparties in a Transaction

How can the firm be certain that the counterparty can be trusted that payment will occur as promised? In the absence of a known counterparty, firms might prefer to rely on central intermediaries, such as a bank, to vouch for counterparties and ensure the transaction is completed and payment assured. Such intermediaries can increase their market power through controlling data accumulated from total transaction flow and setting high fees for such exchanges, particularly when establishing and operating a proprietary platform.

Blockchain Solution: Consensus-Based Transaction Validation Mechanisms
Blockchain protocols employ different consensus algorithms to allow network nodes to authenticate a block of validated transactions.[4] Proof of work (PoW) and proof of stake (PoS) are two commonly used methods for verifying and including new blocks. PoW requires network nodes to expend resources, e.g., address a complex mathematical challenge, solvable through trial and error rather than algorithmically, requiring significant financial investment in computational power. The first node to solve this mathematical challenge can earn rewards for authenticating a new block. In cryptocurrency networks like Bitcoin and Ethereum that use PoW, rewards are granted in those cryptocurrencies, which is the process that results in "mining," for example, creating new Bitcoin or Ether (the currencies used in the Bitcoin and Ethereum networks, respectively). The complexity of the puzzle can increase over time, requiring additional investments in computational power. The significant financial resources needed to become the first node to solve the puzzle are a deterrent against authenticating false blocks. Benefits from such malfeasance would be less than the investment in computer resources needed to control most of the nodes in the network, a necessary condition to furnish the majority validation of transactions and blocks (which the miner knows to be false).

The wasteful energy consumption inherent in performing these PoW calculations, and the delay in finalizing payments (successfully completing computations and authenticating blocks takes time) have inspired alternative approaches, such as PoS. In PoS, potential block validators must post a financial stake to participate ("bonded validators") and can lose their stake for dishonest actions. Most of the validators need to come to a consensus about the authenticity of a transaction before it can be included in a block. Such consensus-based decentralized validation prevents dishonest actors from controlling the validation process or approving transactions that benefit themselves over the best interests of the counterparty and the network. Each node is independent, and all nodes are in a race to be the first to meet the conditions set to earn block rewards. If the node that first met the set conditions subsequently authenticated a false transaction, it would not be in the interest of the other decentralized nodes to authenticate the false transaction. And without a majority of the several decentralized nodes authenticating the transaction, the initial authenticating node would not earn the reward.

Reliable Transactions and Provenance Assurance

How can the firm ensure that activity records for a particular transaction, maintained by the various parties to the transaction, are consistent and accepted as truthful by all concerned parties? If digital transaction records are accessed by unauthorized parties and altered, transaction finalization falls into jeopardy. As the transacting parties struggle to reconcile and correct the errors, the transaction is delayed, which could result in cancellation and negative financial consequences. Inconsistent records between counterparties also make it difficult to trace a chain of transactions back to its initiation, leaving both parties uncertain when and where problems may have originated. For example, in the case of contaminated food in a supply chain, provenance can unambiguously establish when the contamination occurred.

Blockchain Solution: Tamper-Evident Robust Encryption In blockchain encryption, a mathematical function is applied to an input that is to be encrypted. Thus, in a supply chain, inputs could consist of digital data describing the contents of a container, its current owner, other pertinent details such as provenance, and when the container is transferred from a truck to a containership, the change in the container's physical location. This digital data is encrypted, and the resulting output is called a "hash." The hash can be linked and chained to subsequent transactions and further encrypted. The longer the chain, the harder it is for a ill-intentioned agent to decipher the series of hashes back to an initial transaction.[5] Attempts to alter data already included in the blockchain will result in a hash that fails to match the stored hash. The mismatched hash alerts other members of the network to such alteration attempts; the altered data will not be validated and is then ultimately rejected. Blocks of timestamped, ordered data linked with cryptographic hashes to subsequent blocks provide an audit trail of transaction history and helps assert provenance, tracing a chain of transactions to their beginnings. With accurate, updated, timely records concerning current account balances and transaction status distributed to every node, the consensus mechanism blocks *double-spend*. Similar controls can protect data (digital asset) transmission and sharing in blockchain business applications.

Reducing Disputes and Delays Arising from Inconsistent Information

How can a firm quickly reconcile conflicting information with counterparties without redundant work or execution delays? When multiple parties make and keep records of the same transaction, inconsistencies between such duplicate records can arise from errors and misinterpreting events. In such cases, the conflicting records must be reconciled before the transaction can continue, a time-consuming and inefficient process.

Blockchain Solution: Immutable and Tamper-Resistant Audit Trail   Blockchain architecture increases information accuracy, while the tamper-resistant and tamper-evident systems of cryptography-based security increase confidence in blockchain data as a single shared source of truth. Collective validation ensures that all parties have the same verified information, preventing acceptance of erroneous transactions and removing causes for disputes. As data inconsistencies between counterparties disappear, and immutable blocks of data prevent subsequent errors, there is less need to reconcile multiple records of the same transaction held by different parties in different locations. This saves the effort and time otherwise wasted in reconciling inconsistent information between transaction partners.

Integrating Transactions with Payments

Must a firm rely on a trusted intermediary, such as a financial institution, to verify asset ownership and ensure timely payment while bearing the cost of associated intermediary fees? In an e-commerce transaction, customers choose their desired products or services and then separately provide a means of payment, such as a credit card or a bank-to-bank transfer of funds (e.g., Venmo). The credit card firm or bank becomes the trusted intermediary. Because its reputation allows it to be trusted by all parties, it acts as a neutral referee to safeguard the interests of counterparties. As noted above, such intermediary interactions come with intermediary fees, raising transaction costs and slowing down transaction execution. For example, raising capital through initial public offerings (IPOs) and the flotation of bonds can incur investment banking fees of around 5–7 percent.

Blockchain Solution: Tokenization and Automated Execution of Smart Contracts   A distinctive feature of blockchains is the ability to generate tokens of value to facilitate value exchange. Cryptocurrencies, the initial application of blockchain, are tokens—digital representations of money. Tokenization enables instant payment settlement within the blockchain, in which tokens, such as cryptocurrencies can be created and transferred. This obviates the need for a separate payments channel, rendering a payment intermediary superfluous. As intermediary fees disappear, costs come down. Dispensing with an intermediary also removes an additional point of failure and risk, such as the loss of sensitive data. These tokens can be native to the blockchain, or a digital representation of real assets, validated by the specific consensus algorithm adopted.[6]

Smart contracts are contracts that are programmed to be automatically executed when contract conditions are fulfilled. Given automatic execution, accuracy of the APIs and external input used to certify that contract conditions have been met is critical. As such data often comes from outside the blockchain, it is essential to provide secure and tamperproof inputs and computation. Secure oracle networks are one such avenue to trigger smart contract fulfillment, with blockchain utility firms such as Chainlink providing applications to source accurate external data, such as a receipt acknowledging delivery of goods. Such proof can then trigger the smart contract to release funds, thus making value exchange possible within a blockchain, with simultaneous contract fulfillment and corresponding payment. Ethereum, the second-largest cryptocurrency after Bitcoin, differentiated itself by offering smart contract functionality from its very beginning, making it a favorite of financial application developers.

Safeguarding Digital Assets

How can an enterprise, its business partners, and customers control digital assets, such as private data, and prevent such information from being shared, distributed, or sold without explicit permission? Digital assets can be copied and altered, used without the authorization of the rights holders, causing possible economic losses. Encryption to protect such digital data can make the application less user-friendly, interfering with wider distribution and reducing demand.

Blockchain Solution: Programmable Tokens   Digital assets, such as a song or movie, can be tokenized and include information on specific rights to that asset (such as read only or read plus write access) and conditions for the usage, transfer, and disposition of the asset, with blockchain technology guarding against attempts to change such terms of usage.[7] By attaching contractual terms to digital assets via smart contracts, tokens can control how third parties access and use that asset and can authorize changes to that asset's state, such as change of ownership. An organization can then shield its data from unauthorized access and set terms to access such data for each request. Smart contracts thus control the disposition of the digital representation of real assets, expanding the reach of blockchain applications beyond a purely digital arena.

An interesting application is using blockchain to control land title registration and transfer.[8] In many countries, especially emerging markets, land title registries are of recent origin, incomplete, and plagued by fraud and corruption. Bitfury collaborated with the Republic of Georgia's National Agency of Public Registry to create a blockchain-based land registry system to protect property owners' rights and to strengthen data security. The company used its Exonum permissioned blockchain together with a digital property registration process, encrypting the property title with a timestamp and publishing the resulting hash. This allowed for verification of legitimate ownership and audit in real time as well as, retrospectively, enabling tracing of changes in title.[9]

Avoiding Excessive Centralization

How can a firm using a platform avoid platform owner/operator dominance and their control over platform access, fees, and rules of operation? Centralization allows one or a few nodes to exercise control over network access, fees, customer information access, degree of privacy protection, and other sensitive areas. It can also possibly censor transaction flow. For example, as we saw in the introduction, Apple and Google exercise significant control over video game distribution and access on smartphones, allowing them to charge 30 percent commissions. Epic has sued to stop Apple and Google from using their respective iOS App Store and Android monopoly to charge what Epic perceives as excessive 30 percent commission on Fortnite sales. A central controlling entity, as a monopoly, could charge higher prices and prevent the emergence of contestable markets (in the way Facebook acquired WhatsApp and Instagram to reduce challenges to its primacy). Centralization also creates a potential concentrated point of failure. Successful attacks on a central intermediary could result in compromised private information and lost or stolen assets.

Blockchain Solution: Direct Communication between Decentralized P2P Nodes for Greater Transparency   In Epic's case, individual gamers, each as a decentralized P2P node, could access games available for play via Dapps, which could authenticate player identity, and provide tiered access to games, depending on their membership level. As on traditional streaming game platforms such as Twitch or Steam, the Epic game blockchain could make available some or all of their games for free. It could regulate access to the games by setting access conditions based on gamer characteristics, for example, age and maximum time allowed to be spent per period playing the game for minors. An issue, particularly for parents, is uncontrolled in-game purchases by teenagers with parents' credit cards, and access and budget control would alleviate such concerns. It could use the game player's identity to determine permission to conduct in-game purchases, with budget ceilings (determined by parents of minors, for example) set for individual gamers. Blockchain game platforms such as *Axie Infinity* facilitate the creation and sale of in-game creatures—"Axies"—as each Axie is an NFT, they can be bought and sold—all without involving an intermediary platform.[10] More broadly, decentralized nodes can collaborate to jointly create customer solutions, with individual value contributions traceable by establishing provenance. It is important to note that such decentralization does create redundancy by storing the same data at multiple sites, also raising costs.

Achieving Interorganizational Collaboration

How can a firm persuade other independent firms to collaborate in cocreating interorganizational solutions? The complexity of customer solutions continues to grow, demanding the integration of different technologies. While interorganizational collaboration improves the likelihood of success for these integrations, such collaborations can be rife with disagreements about protecting IP, recognizing contributions, distributing rewards fairly, and sharing governance.

Blockchain Solution: Shared Governance and Rule Setting across Decentralized Independent Nodes   Blockchain's independent network of nodes transcends the boundaries of collaborating firms, organically creating an interorganizational framework for cooperation—an ecosystem. The entities governing the blockchain can create tokens that can be used to reward individual contributions for cocreated solutions and to motivate loyalty to the network. They can also be used to elicit desired behaviors, such as those enhancing customer benefit. Thus, in a supply chain, a customs agency that reduces time to clear goods through customs can be rewarded with tokens proportionate to the time reduction relative to a standard. And as a network member accumulates tokens through increased participation in the network's activities, they can be given a greater role in the blockchain network governance, directly proportionate to the size of their token holdings.[11] Taken together, blockchain's technological architecture nurtures ecosystems that facilitate privacy protection at the individual node level while encouraging collaboration at the organization level, with provenance and audit trails delineating individual node contributions and facilitating token-based rewards commensurate with value creation.

In summary, blockchain's unique architecture enables valuable data and asset exchange between entities with unparalleled security, which helps to resolve common problems that plague digital transactions. Table 1.1 outlines these links between blockchain's unique architecture, potential enterprise benefits, and powerful utility in this context.

How Enterprises Can Use Blockchain

Enterprises can use blockchain in a variety of ways. Blockchain pilots and projects within an enterprise can be partitioned into purely intraorganizational applications as well as interorganizational applications. Interorganizational applications require cooperation and joint action with other independent entities, while intraorganizational applications are easier to develop and use, equipping subsidiaries and departments within the enterprise with accurate and widely available data, facilitating efficiency gains. Such lower hanging fruit, applications whose use can be mandated throughout the organization, can lay

Table 1.1
Blockchain architecture, advantages, enterprise benefits, and problem resolution

Blockchain architectural features	Private and public keys; ZKPs	Consensus algorithms: PoW, PoS, etc.	Robust cryptographic encryption	Immutability; timestamped data entries	Tokenization; native tokens; game theory–based incentives; smart contracts	Decentralized P2P independent nodes
Distinctive advantages	Ability to create SSI	Incontrovertible data and decentralized transaction validation	Tamper-resistant and tamper-evident security	Events and transactions can be ordered and linked	Token-based exchange of value; programmable digital assets; secure digitization of real assets	Simultaneous availability of up-to-date transaction information at all nodes; traceability of contributions by nodes; shared governance; cross-border reach
Enterprise benefits	Ease of identity verification; duplication of identity requests is eliminated; protection against illegal access	Trust of counterparties to a transaction; gains from disintermediation—eliminating intermediary control and their fees; malfeasance prevention, reduce fraud	Prevents tampering with and altering transactions; protection from hackers; increased cybersecurity	Creation of a single source of truth; audit trails and ease of establishing provenance; reduction in disputes and delays from inconsistent information	Elimination of the need for a separate payment channel; control over sharing private data; transactions can be linked to contracts; automated contingent contract execution, based on contract conditions fulfillment, proven by external data from oracles;	Avoidance of excessive centralization; greater transparency; elimination of inconsistent counterparty transaction records; value exchange, payments settlement, and finality;

Problems addressed	In digital transactions, how can a merchant be sure of the identity of the party on the other side of a transaction?	How can the firm be certain that a customer's account balance can cover the amount due on a transaction and payment will occur as promised?	How can the firm ensure that activity records for a particular transaction are consistent and accepted as truthful by all concerned parties?	How can a firm reconcile information with counterparties without redundant work or execution delays?	Must a firm rely on a trusted intermediary such as a bank and pay associated fees to verify asset ownership and ensure timely payment? How can an enterprise, its business partners, and customers control private information and prevent it from being shared, distributed, or sold without explicit permission?	tokens as incentives to motivate desired behaviors	How can a firm using a platform avoid platform owner dominance control platform access, fees, and rules of operation? How can a firm persuade other independent firms to collaborate in cocreating interorganizational solutions?	overcoming difficulties in achieving interorganizational cocreation and collaboration; fair attribution of network member contribution and allocation of rewards

the ground for more complex interorganizational applications. The enterprise can learn about blockchain capabilities, develop assessment metrics to evaluate cost–benefit outcomes, and gage the required financial and human resources to develop and implement such applications. In this process, enterprises will also become aware of the complexity of blockchain applications, from learning about appropriate blockchain protocols to education and training needed to obtain the requisite skills.

Interorganizational blockchain applications with goals such as providing collaboratively developed customer solutions superior to currently available alternatives can enhance the firm's and its collaborators' competitive advantage, although they are more complex to design and implement. However, regardless of the type of applications emphasized, the project must be bolstered by a business case that can attract resource commitments, organizational champions, and organizational alignment. I now review a variety of both intraorganizational and interorganizational blockchain applications.

Intraorganizational Blockchain Applications: Improving Efficiency
Stock exchanges across the world use trade clearing and settlement systems to record purchases and sales, change in ownership, and payment approval. CHESS is the Australian Stock Exchange's (ASX) twenty-six-year-old securities trade clearing and settlement system, which also maintains a shareholding register for over 2,200 issuers. As early as 2015, ASX began considering blockchain as a basis for improving their CHESS system.

ASX began designing its CHESS replacement project, which replaces the legacy CHESS system, in 2015, upgrading performance, security and resilience and offering audit trails and analytics capabilities.[12] ASX's David Campbell, chief technology officer, noted that a share sale transferring ownership might involve as many as fifteen people in the chain of transfer, hence the need to move away from a central database to a distributed, shared, real-time single source of truth.

In the CHESS replacement project, all parties to a transaction would have a synchronized, shared replicated ledger cryptographically signed by a legal approver.[13] All parties would have an exact copy of the ledger, updated and timestamped to reflect a transaction's incorporation. Then, as further events occur, later in time, copies of these updated ledgers, duly timestamped, would be replicated across all nodes. Thus, each node would have the latest copy of the ledger, continually updated to reflect new transactions. ASX's DLT-enabled clearing and settlement system offers an immutable, real-time record of trading and change in ownership available to all involved parties, and harmonized data standards obviate the need for data reconciliation between counterparties. Smart contracts would automate updating for corporate actions (i.e., dividend declaration and payout, capital raises), and independent third parties could offer additional microservices (such as shareholder analytics and voting applications) via APIs connected to the CHESS DLT. ASX hopes that encouraging third parties to connect to the DLT will lower barriers to entry, encourage competition, and make available a broad array of improved cost-effective and innovative products.

The new CHESS product design evolved in consultation with customers and regulators, in several stages, with full rollout planned for a single weekend in April 2023. However, ASX clients must opt in to use the new DLT system; those who chose not to use the new system can continue to interact with the system using message-based connectivity with the updated ISO 20022 standard. ASX adopted a measured approach to using DLT, developing, testing, and implementing the new CHESS DLT system over several years. It also worked with external partners to develop the system and will obtain an independent audit to ensure the new system's readiness before industrial-scale rollout.

Intraorganizational Blockchain Applications: New Businesses and Services

Enterprises can use blockchain capabilities to develop new intraorganizational applications, allowing the organization's subsidiaries and departments to share information securely and consistently and track such information flows, with benefits such as improved efficiency, enhanced regulatory compliance, and cost reduction.

BNP Paribas Securities Services and Corporate Events Communication
Corporate events, whether the acquisition of another firm, the declaration of dividends, or the announcement of a key executive's departure, all have implications for a firm's future. In the case of publicly held firms, these events can affect stock prices. The Securities and Exchange Commission (SEC) and other investment regulators also require that corporate events be communicated fairly to all interested parties, and enterprises are understandably aware of the need to protect their reputation and avoid accusations of insider trading by parties favored with early access to such corporate event news.

Philippe Ruault, of BNP Paribas Securities Services, which operates in thirty-four countries, noted that managing and disseminating corporate event information in an accurate and timely fashion had long been a pain point for the custody industry. BNP collaborated with Tata Consultancy Services (TCS) and its Quartz blockchain protocol to secure its corporate event distribution, aiming to avoid missteps and duplication that have occurred along the communication chain of intermediaries in the past. TCS would ensure the simultaneous delivery of secure unique information to all parties worldwide, translating and communicating information initially in seven languages.[14] The value of such blockchain-directed corporate event communication is that it clearly demonstrates the simultaneous provision of market-critical information to all users, enabling firms to defend themselves against any imputation of facilitating insider trading. Regulators can also track the flow of such critical information and ensure that firms have complied with essential corporate event dissemination regulations.

Interorganizational Applications: Improving Efficiency
Blockchain's disruptive abilities naturally lend themselves to improving efficiency by jointly operating with and sometimes replacing legacy systems. I review two such efforts: improving cross-border remittances

services and, in social entrepreneurship, providing midday meals to schoolchildren from underprivileged backgrounds.

Ripple XRP and Cross-Border Remittances   Cross-border remittances are a slow process, incurring high fees, with remittance completion details unavailable for several days. Such remittances are slowed as they transit through a series of banks between the sender and the receiver. Ripple introduced a blockchain-based solution, offering its own cryptocurrency, XRP, along with a proprietary global network, RippleNet, to provide a speedy, lower cost, and secure alternative. Ripple can potentially disrupt the global remittances segment, becoming a major competitor to incumbent global banks. As more firms adopt Ripple's solution, it becomes more viable as a replacement for the traditional remittance services from major banks. XRP's monthly remittance volume approximated $93 billion in October 2021, with a settlement speed of four seconds.[15] I discuss Ripple's blockchain model at greater length in chapter 5, in the context of global supply chains.

Social Entrepreneurship and Akshaya Patra   Akshaya Patra (AP), a charitable organization in India, launched a midday meal program, delivering hot cooked nutritional meals to over 1.8 million children at 19,000 schools scattered across twelve states in India. Children from poverty-stricken homes often come to school hungry, which impairs their ability to concentrate, negatively affecting classroom performance and leading to dropouts. To achieve its goal, AP operates over fifty kitchens—some are centralized and serve over 100,000 meals a day to surrounding schools;[16] in more remote regions, it operates decentralized kitchens run by local women's mutual support groups.

AP must coordinate food and supply purchases, monitor food preparation quality and hygiene, manage food delivery and prevent food waste, and obtain feedback from schools on performance and outcomes. With the help of Accenture,[17] AP introduced a blockchain to manage its midday meal delivery program. Its aim was to increase efficiency, promote sustainability, enhance transparency, and ultimately achieve scalability.

AP, like other NGOs, relies on donor support, and both government grants and private donations are influenced by clearly demonstrated outcomes. The blockchain created trust in those outcomes and offered unparalleled transparency. AP is not unique in using blockchain for social good. Organizations in areas such as land rights, financial inclusion, agriculture, and education have also developed innovative blockchain solutions.[18]

There are several similar applications that extend across an organization's boundaries, involve collaboration with independent entities, and result in ecosystem-wide blockchain use. I discuss a number of these in subsequent chapters, such as national governments piloting blockchain projects to issue national digital currencies (CBDCs) in chapter 3 and the global supply chain solution TradeLens in chapters 5 and 6.

Interorganizational Blockchain and New Businesses and Services

In addition to developing improved legacy solutions and new internal applications, blockchain can help enterprises create new business models and new sources of revenue. It is proficient at enabling collaboration between multiple independent organizations, who can work together to jointly create solutions and be recognized and rewarded for their individual contributions to the overall solution. These initiatives result in developing new business models, obtaining new revenue streams, and, in some cases, developing entirely new industries.

Carbon Credits and Tokenization   As the world's enterprises attempt to alleviate the harmful climate effects of carbon dioxide emissions, awarding carbon credits, in essence an economic incentive to change corporate and individual behavior, has become increasingly common. These incentives promote climate-friendly initiatives, encouraging a move to carbon-neutral and carbon-efficient processes and activities. Carbon credits use a cap-and-trade philosophy, granting carbon credits to firms whose carbon emission are below targets set by regulators. These carbon credits can be sold to firms whose emissions are above regulatory targets, allowing them to use these credits to offset the additional emissions. Carbon credit prices will be determined by the demand for such credits from polluting firms, relative to the supply of such credits from greener firms. Thus, initially, when pollution is high, demand will likely outstrip supply, raising carbon credit prices. Consequently, as the more efficient firms sell their carbon credits to less-efficient firms, the latter group will divert some of their carbon credit purchase funds to investment in emission reduction, thus gradually decreasing global greenhouse gas emissions. Further, as emissions targets are gradually tightened by regulators, carbon credits increase in price, increasing costs for polluters and further stimulating and rewarding climate-friendly behavior.

The process of certifying emissions and creating and managing carbon credit trading markets, however, is costly and opaque. It raises barriers between enterprises, regulators, and consumers. And ESG (environmental, social, and governance) investors would prefer to invest in firms that are actively improving their environmental footprint but may find it difficult to clearly identify such firms. In response to these market problems, IBM has worked with Veridium Labs[19] (based in Hong Kong) to develop carbon credit tokens that can be exchanged and traded within the Stellar blockchain. IBM pointed out that "by integrating the entire process of carbon accounting and offsetting in a token on a public, permissioned blockchain network, ownership rights can be transmitted and traded more easily."[20]

Veridium Lab's solution focuses on pricing and efficiently consuming natural capital (the value of the earth's finite resources). Its blockchain solution includes a tokenized marketplace and a way for firms to track their environmental impacts, with the solution and token making it easier for a firm to calculate the number of carbon credits needed to offset its carbon footprint.[21] Veridium addresses problem areas such as carbon credit illiquidity, tracking, standardization, accounting, and valuation. Its token is derived from a basket of carbon assets independently verified by certification authorities, sourced from companies and NGOs, including its own sister organization, InfiniteEARTH, which earned 130 million tons of carbon credits from creating the Rimba Raya

Biodiversity Reserve in Borneo and developing methodologies for accurately measuring emission offsets from avoided deforestation.

Interior Decoration on a Blockchain: DecorMatters   Homeowners buying new furniture and designing or redesigning rooms are often unsure of how different pieces of furniture will look or fit when actually brought home. Interior designers, particularly aspiring new entrants in the industry, need to market their design skills, find customers, and earn fair remuneration for their services—all while protecting their unique designs from being copied. Furniture retailers need channels to obtain and retain consumers, and partnering with interior decorators and design consultants might be a mutually profitable arrangement. In this context, DecorMatters[22] has launched a business model that consists of its MyDecor app for iPhones as the front end to a site that combines augmented reality (AR), artificial intelligence (AI), and a blockchain. The AR feature allows designers and consumers to visualize and test designs in their home environment before purchase (e.g., ARKit, an app in the Apple Store that offers scene capture and processing, motion tracking and display options, with AR Rule, for the precise measurement of room dimensions within an AR space). AI offers users in-app suggestions and allows designers and retailers to draw on user preferences gleaned from their participation in décor games, where users disclose their preferred choices from alternative options.

The blockchain allows interior designers to offer décor suggestions and plans while protecting their intellectual property and monetizing consumer use of their copyrighted designs. Furniture retailers can offer their furniture lines to consumers through the app, and the designers whose recommendations drive consumer choice of specific lines can earn commission on such sales from the retailers. The retailers can then build longer-term connections with designers and consumers, creating loyalty and repeat purchases, increasing the long-term consumer value. For example, DecorMatters asked users to use the color red and submit bold designs for a variety of rooms, including "entryways, living areas, bedrooms, dining rooms, and even a patio." Users (over four million in May 2021) earn rewards for voting on designs, which allows them to monetize their participation and encourages further use of DecorMatters. This helps designers personalize and market their recommendations and helps retailers plan future product development. DecorMatters underlines how blockchain potential is enhanced when combined with additional technologies, in this case AI and AR. The DecorMatters model can be generalized for use in similar contexts, supporting customer experience and customer relationship management.[23]

Coinbase, a Centralized Trading Exchange Blockchain applications result in an ever-increasing number of tokens and protocol-specific native digital currencies, the best known and used being Bitcoin and Ether. Exchanges where such coins and tokens can be traded are essential to provide liquidity and relatively friction-free acquisition and disposition of such tokens, contributing to underlying business growth. Coinbase, the biggest US digital currency trading exchange listing over a hundred digital assets, is one entity that has been able to take advantage of the need for such core infrastructure needs.[24]

Coinbase's growth and profitability closely follow the growing interest and use of digital assets, by both retail and institutional clients. It went public the same day in April 2021 that Bitcoin reached its then all-time high price of $64,800 (from $7,300 at the beginning of 2020), with its market capitalization briefly exceeding $100 billion. Coinbase serves both institutional and retail clients. However, about two-thirds of its total trading volume of $335 billion, but only about 6 percent of transaction revenue, in the first quarter of 2021 came from institutions, with individual retail investors providing most of its fees. Competition for retail market share will drive down fees charged to retail clients over time, possibly to commission-free trading as with equity trading. Hence, a sustainable business model will move to obtaining a greater share of revenue from offering institutional services, such as custody and payments, and relying less on bitcoin and Ether, which constituted over 70 percent of activity in that same period.

Cryptocurrency trading also carries greater regulatory risk, for example, China's threats to ban cryptocurrencies causing a price drop of over 40 percent. Nevertheless, as blockchain takes hold, the increasing need for infrastructure services linked to digital assets creates long-term market and business opportunities. Early movers such as Coinbase with scale advantages will be more able to withstand volatility and grow revenue and profitability alongside broader market acceptance and use of blockchain technologies.

Monetizing Digital Cards and Video Streams: Gods Unchained Collectible Digital Cards, NBA Top Shot *Magic: The Gathering* is a collectible card game of physical cards. Players purchase an initial deck of three hundred unique cards and then select a given number of these cards to form a deck for playing against opponents. Rules govern the capabilities of each card, and the aim is to outlast the other player's deck. Introduced in 1993, it became immediately popular and *Magic* sold over one billion cards through the end of 1994. *Magic* added expansion sets to the original decks, totaling over twenty thousand unique cards during the product's life cycle, with around twenty billion cards sold by 2016. Imitators such as *Pokémon* soon followed.

Not surprisingly, Immutable, an Australian gaming company, created a blockchain-based digital version of such collectible card games. Immutable introduced its *Gods Unchained* game in 2019, using digital cards based on the ERC-721 standard in Ethereum. Using NFTs, Immutable developed digital versions game cards so that they could be owned by game players and be used in game playing in the same manner as physical cards. They also allow players to trade digital cards, paralleling how physical cards were exchanged, as with the original *Magic* card deck. Along with the game release, Immutable created an Ethereum-based blockchain marketplace where players could buy and trade cards (NFTs in this case), using Ether in digital wallets such as MetaMask. Digital card purchases and trading occurred within the blockchain, while game playing took place off-chain. As a pioneer in using blockchain to move traditional physical card collecting and trading to a digital world, and with ownership and the authenticity of cards no longer in question, Immutable was able to raise over $18 million in two venture capital rounds.

The potential to generate revenue from using NFTs within games led to game developers offering players an option to purchase NFT-based live music streams, available for viewing and listening while playing multiplayer online video games. Many such games are available for free playing online through video game streaming platforms such as Steam or Epic. Since game playing is free, game developers earn income by motivating players to make in-game purchases of game-related items. Players pay for such purchases using standard modes such as credit cards and mobile wallets. The logical next step is to increase the range of items that can be purchased while playing. Digital files of live music video streams by popular musical groups, tokenized as an NFT, are one such purchase option.

For example, when the COVID-19 pandemic forced the cancellation of live music festivals such as Coachella, many of the affected music groups such as 100 Gecs offered live concerts within the popular video game *Minecraft*, which has over 130 million monthly active players. Casual concert fans could drop into these online video games and meet up with friends, wander through the digital 3D game-playing environments "dressed" as their chosen avatars, and then purchase access to the live stream music NFT. A concertgoer summarized the virtual experience by explaining that it "felt like the best parts of going to a concert without the worst parts—being sweaty, being outside, being afraid you're going to lose your keys,"[25] not to mention lower prices, no transportation or parking obstacles, and unimpeded views. Scalability could be an issue in the future because offering large numbers of simultaneous live video streams as NFTs within a game platform can be constrained by server infrastructure availability. In addition, concert fans and video game players do not always overlap as audiences.

NBA Top Shot is another example of blockchain's potential as a revenue generator. In this case, NBA basketball game highlights are sold as NFTs. NBA Top Shot Moments are video highlights from NBA games, officially licensed by the NBA and minted by Dapper Labs as NFTs on a purpose-built Flow blockchain, for sale to collectors. Novice collectors without cryptocurrency experience or knowledge can buy these Top

Shot NFTs using credit cards. This traditional payment mode is used to set up digital wallets containing equivalent amounts of cryptocurrencies, which can be used to pay for the Top Shot Moments. Total Top Shot sales volume exceeded $560 million by May 2021, with nearly half a million owners in total.

Top Shot's value derives from factors such as edition size, rarity, player desirability (i.e., LeBron James versus an up-and-coming rookie), the type of play captured and its significance in a game, and the game's importance. Potential buyers can apply to purchase a pack drop (a common pack contains a set of three moments, serially numbered and packaged together, with a higher priced rare pack including one rare moment and several common moments); demand for these packs is greater than supply, so there is a lower likelihood of being selected to purchase a pack. Fans purchase such packs in the hope that a pack might yield some moments that can be sold individually in future for a significant premium over the price paid to acquire the pack. The alternative is the secondary market, where buyers purchase individual moments in the hope of further appreciation. There are collectors, NBA fans, who like owning the authentic version of a game clip even though it can be seen readily on ESPN; the fact that the NFT certifies both originality and title to the clip is what gives the Top Shot clip value and tradability in the after-market. In a sense, Top Shots are trading cards incorporating short videos rather than static images. Multiple websites display current Top Shot prices; for example, the total value of Top Shots featuring LeBron James exceeded $100 million (as of September 25, 2021).[26]

As the number of Top Shot Moments available for purchase increases with each passing basketball season, it remains to be seen whether collector demand will continue. Other NFTs may become more desirable, and the infrastructure surrounding NFT creation and sale is an important element of this segment. The Flow blockchain, which Dapper Labs uses, is designed specifically to facilitate NFT creation and marketplaces, and it includes a unique multirole architecture that facilitates scalability. Flow deliberately separates roles and splits them between consensus,

Table 1.2
Blockchain application space in enterprises and sample applications

	Intraorganizational application examples	Interorganizational application examples
Improved efficiency	*Blockchain securities clearing and settlement platforms*: ASX's CHESS replacement project—replacing legacy CHESS system; upgrading performance, security, and resilience; offering audit trails and analytics capabilities	*Cross-border payments*: Ripple XRP *Social entrepreneurship*: Akshay Patra
New businesses, new services	*Disseminating corporate events (an SEC requirement for publicly held firms)*: BNP Paribas and TCS; Corporate Event Connect; facilitating secure simultaneous transmission of corporate events; minimizing risks of insider manipulation and trading	*Carbon credits and tokenization*: Veridium Labs *Interior decoration*: DecorMatters *Centralized exchanges*: Coinbase *NFTs*: Gods Unchained, NBA Top Shot

verification, execution, and collection nodes. It uses a newer and easier-to-program smart contract language, Cadence, and is designed to be consumer friendly, making it easy for users to move from fiat currencies to digital currencies when making payments. Dapper Labs's partnership with the NBA to create the NBA Top Shot business enabled it to raise venture capital with a valuation of around $7.5 billion in April 2021.[27] Table 1.2 summarizes the range of enterprise blockchain application possibilities.

All these examples indicate blockchain's wide applicability in enterprises. As table 1.2 suggests, there have been a wide variety of interorganizational applications developed, both in business applications as well as in business to consumer initiatives. Several independent firms collaborate in these endeavors, with each member putting forth their contribution. Each contribution may be relatively small, but together these multiple contributions can result in a major breakthrough, a disruptive solution with considerable potential.

Despite these successes, blockchain adoption has been slow, due to *technological*, *economic*, and *organizational* barriers. In chapter 2, I review technological obstacles to blockchain implementation and then discuss several blockchain start-ups that are tackling and attempting to overcome these impediments to adoption. I also consider start-ups that have developed distinctive business models to gain competitive advantage from using blockchain. However, while blockchain start-ups have had greater success addressing technological impediments, economic and organizational obstacles also require action at the user level, within the firm and its ecosystem. I return to the user's role in resolving economic and organizational obstacles at greater length in chapter 7.

2   Technological Obstacles to Blockchain Adoption and Their Resolution

As with many young, potentially disruptive, technologies, blockchain technology is hobbled by performance drawbacks that create obstacles for adoption at the enterprise level. In consequence, enterprises are reluctant to attempt larger-scale rollouts even with successful proof of concepts in their pilot efforts. Established enterprises have encountered difficulties in advancing blockchain pilot projects to commercial implementation at scale. In 2019, Cathy Bessant, then chief technology officer at Bank of America, commented that the hype associated with blockchain outstripped reality. Wells Fargo's former CEO Tim Sloan was equally skeptical, noting that "blockchain has been way oversold."[1] Indifferent pilot results in many instances have dampened enthusiasm and created organizational hesitance and a "trough of disillusionment," leading Gartner to pronounce that "through 2022, only 10 percent of enterprises will achieve any radical transformation with the use of blockchain technologies." However, continued development could result in business value added from blockchain exceeding $3 trillion by 2030.[2] Therefore, the drawbacks discussed do not negate blockchain's ultimate advantages; instead, they signal its current immaturity as a potential disruptive technology—and that immaturity is not permanent.

The technology involved in blockchain is multilayered. The core layer consisting of the particular blockchain protocol adopted (e.g., Ethereum, Bitcoin, Ripple, or Consensys Quorum) must interact with a second layer that consists of additional blockchain capabilities, which can vary from one protocol to another. This layer can include features such as smart contracts, SSI, and use of ZKP. These in turn interact with a proxy layer of software applications that includes application programming interfaces (APIs) and Dapps, which permit users to access different blockchain platforms. Also necessary are off-chain elements such as off-chain storage, the ability to exchange data with external networks and to communicate with information sources ("oracles") to receive information to trigger automated smart contract execution, and interoperability capabilities. Blockchains must also manage external events such as data supplied by Internet of Things (IoT) microservices (whose provenance and accuracy may be insecure). These technological complexities can delay the move to blockchain as firms with less digital transformation experience face financial, knowledge, and human capital constraints. Incorrect implementation can compromise data accuracy and trust, negating blockchain utility.

To address blockchain technological shortcomings, new blockchain start-ups are presenting myriad innovations aimed at catalyzing continuous improvement. They have developed new blockchain protocols to address security, scalability, decentralization, transaction speeds, interoperability, and ease of development. Blockchain technical development is ongoing, and continuing experimentation has yielded emergent alternative platforms and solutions. Such flurries of advancement are characteristic of disruptive technology environments as pioneering firms seek to stimulate mass adoption by concentrating on performance improvements.

In this chapter, I first review technology impediments. Then I consider blockchain start-ups, examining how they are making blockchain easier to use and removing obstacles that hinder enterprise-level adoption. Several of the firms tackling new or improved solutions to existing problems have partnered with those building industry and vertical market applications. The common goal for these start-ups is use cases for their technology upgrades that highlight the potential of their pioneering efforts for enterprise deployment.

The Blockchain Scalability Trilemma

Blockchain, as originally designed and incorporated into bitcoin, is limited by three seemingly irreconcilable challenges that restrict its commercial potential:[3] it cannot simultaneously maximize security, scalability, and decentralization. Vitalik Buterin, a founder of the Ethereum blockchain, described this as the *scalability trilemma*, stating that blockchain, as constituted, *could only optimize two of the three parameters* of security, scalability, and decentralization. Users want secure networks to ensure that transactions are valid and to protect against double-spend and fraud. And if only a few entities are authorized to guarantee the trustworthiness of a blockchain network (a high degree of centralization), enterprises will have to assess the gains from using centralized networks against the consequences of depending on centralized trust guarantors, who represent potential points of failure. Extensive decentralization strengthens security, as do consensus algorithms, which create immutability through cryptographically assured blockchain validation, and allow reliance on the blockchain as the single source of truth.

However, decentralization leads to transactions recorded at all nodes of the network, making transactions visible to the entire network, reducing privacy, and making blockchain solutions less attractive for some enterprise applications.[4] Privacy can be protected with additional steps such as using new addresses for each transaction; combining transactions from several users; transacting via intermediaries; storing sensitive user information off-chain, possibly in a separate private blockchain; and linking such information via a hash to the specific transaction. Such steps would likely incur additional costs, reducing the incentive to adopt blockchain solutions.

Acting together, decentralization and consensus frameworks as designed in the classic blockchain algorithm can slow down block validation and transaction finality, thus hindering scalability. As the number of transactions increase, settlement takes longer. While it is possible to pay higher fees to give priority to a transaction, this would

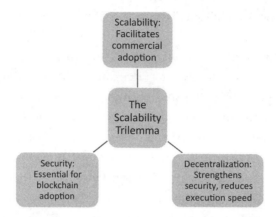

Figure 2.1
Blockchain's scalability

raise transaction processing costs. If consensus methods used to validate transactions and confirm payments are slow, users will seek faster
alternatives. Centralizing authority in the blockchain to speed up transaction time may make the blockchain experience more appealing to
users, but that speed comes at the expense of security. And for enterprises that transact in the billions of dollars in high-volume applications, security is essential.

In an area such as payment processing, blockchain must contend
with well-established alternatives such as the Visa network, which processes an average of 150 million transactions each day (1,700 transactions per second, on average). In comparison, Bitcoin and Ethereum
networks can process a maximum of 7 to 20 transactions per second.[5]
Additional issues arise around using the smart contract capabilities of
blockchain as well as immature technology causing governance issues
around the direction of blockchain evolution, possibly resulting in
backward incompatibility.

Smart Contract Problems
An appealing aspect of blockchain application in enterprises is the
ability to use smart contracts. A major concern is whether contracts,

legally enforceable agreements between contracting parties, have been correctly captured in code, a process that requires close collaboration between legal staff and blockchain programmers. When drafting legal contracts, language may be deliberately ambiguous to grant a range of flexibility to the parties in fulfilling contract performance. There is a risk that coders would incorrectly interpret legal language when developing smart contract code, which creates a need for an additional step to verify that the code correctly reflects its source contract. A second problem arises when incorrect or deliberately false information is supplied by external sources to the smart contract code, triggering execution under false pretenses and causing economic losses.

Unsettled Blockchain Governance, Immature Technology

Governance of blockchain protocols also contributes to their instability and raises doubts about their aptness for large-scale implementation. Gianluca Miscione and his coauthors[6] propose a new mode of blockchain governance that they term "tribal." They note that blockchain governance should be based on consensus rather than rivalry among network participants and tribes develop their own modes of governance, which is not defined by rule of law. This is in contrast with traditional governance regimes, which are characterized principally by market and hierarchy.

Blockchains can change their protocols to speed up transactions, for example, introduce new blockchain innovations such as sharding and side chains. Sharding partitions a blockchain into shards, with each node only needing to update its portion of the blockchain, enabling faster processing speeds and improving scalability.[7] Sidechains are separate blockchains attached to the main blockchain, reducing the processing burden on the main chain and thus increasing its speed and scalability.[8] However, disagreements over the introduction of these newer technologies can cause performance variability and reduce performance. In such cases, previously validated blocks may no longer be compatible with the newer changed protocol—a "hard fork."[9] A hard fork is a significant change to a blockchain protocol, creating a new branch of the blockchain such that once users begin using the new version, transactions validated by the older version are rejected. (However, forks may have value in the sense of incremental improvements, with a 2017 Deloitte report suggesting that forks are more likely to keep blockchain projects alive.)[10]

Such backward incompatibility would be unacceptable to a commercial enterprise, particularly when the members of a multi-enterprise blockchain cannot agree on whether conditions have changed sufficiently to require a change in protocol as well as how the protocol should be changed. Ultimately, disagreements over, and refusal to support, the fork would lead to a schism, a disintegration of blockchain membership, which would affect its utility going forward. In sum, governance disagreements can cause the blockchain to fall apart.

Tackling the Trilemma

Numerous technical solutions have been proposed,[11] and the various proposed solutions make trade-offs between speed, security, and the level of decentralization to best suit their needs.[12] There are several approaches that show promise in resolving these issues:

- *Changing consensus mechanisms used*, from PoW to PoS and other schema. These diverse consensus algorithms all seek to resolve the same problem: how to increase the speed of arriving at a consensus to provide transaction assurance without increasing centralization or making the network less secure.

- *Moving to permissioned networks*, which replace cryptographically derived security with trusted entities to validate transactions. This reduces decentralization and concentrates potential points of failure in a few trusted entities, compromising security. Nevertheless, many enterprise blockchains have opted for permissioned networks to improve on older intermediary-controlled networks, as in banking, without losing processing speed. An example is Ripple's use of its unique node list (UNL), which restricts transaction validation and ledger updating to a few trusted nodes, with most of them initially controlled by Ripple.[13] It is important to note that if an attacker gains control of these trusted entities, they could validate erroneous transactions, enable double-spend, and authorize fraudulent transfers, destroying confidence in the network and reducing its utility. The EOS protocol, from EOSIO, an open-source blockchain platform, has a limited number of block producers, thus reducing the number of nodes participating in validating blocks and increasing processing speed.

- *Creating sidechains outside the main blockchain* as transaction numbers increase to reduce the computational burden of having the blockchain process every transaction. Smaller transactions can be bundled together and validated in sidechains, outside the main blockchain, and then sent back for processing as a single aggregated transaction. This would be analogous to processing credit card transactions, where a total monthly bill for a month's accumulated transactions is presented and can be paid for as one amount. However, as noted earlier, the transfer between a sidechain and the mainchain can be a security weakness, requiring additional steps such as encrypted lockboxes between the sidechain and the mainchain, introducing time lags to verify sidechain transfers before releasing funds in the mainchain (to prevent double-spending), and making sidechains as private permissioned networks, with trusted nodes managing interchain transfers.

- *Vertical scalability* to improve processing speeds at each node, by increasing available computational power. A node with increased computing power can validate transactions faster, improving scalability. However, the overall blockchain network performance will be limited by the computing capability at the weakest node since that node could slow down the time for majority consensus to be formed to validate blocks.

- Other suggested approaches are batching transactions (which can create privacy issues) and using the Lightning network,[14] which proposes a connected off-chain network of two-party payment channels (a multisignature wallet that both parties can access with their respective private keys) so that payment to anyone within the network can be completed through a series of connected two-party transactions (with the network finding the shortest route to complete the transaction). Each channel's total funds are recorded on the blockchain when opening the channel, with another blockchain entry required to add or withdraw funds in that channel.

Learning from Blockchain Start-Ups and First Movers

I now review some significant breakthroughs by blockchain start-ups aiming to maintain blockchain's powerful security protections while improving speed and scalability. The blockchain companies discussed in this chapter have two main objectives. The first objective is overcoming technical drawbacks. Several firms are intent on improving the technical infrastructure of blockchains. They address performance lacunae of blockchain in key areas such as scalability, the extent of decentralization, levels of security, and transaction processing speed. They also address interoperability so that multiple blockchain applications within an enterprise and within an ecosystem can communicate and transact with each other even when using different platforms. Finally, they focus on protecting the privacy of the parties in a transaction and their transaction details.

The second objective concerns industry-specific solutions that generate revenue and increase efficiency. As technical performance improves, new applications spring up, ready to take advantage of these improvements. Several firms are leveraging these technical advances and developing industry-specific customer solutions that they believe are superior to existing approaches.

Improving Blockchain Performance: Algorand
Algorand introduced a new blockchain protocol[15] to resolve the scalability problem in a secure, decentralized, and permissionless fashion. Its approach is built on a new protocol, Pure PoS (adapted to environments known to have untrustworthy network participants), which provides

consensus validation using less computational power compared to the traditional PoW consensus mechanisms used in blockchains, result- ing in speedier processing. Algorand also validates transactions in the order in which they occur rather than waiting to gather transactions into blocks and validate such blocks, thus ensuring immediate trans- action finality. Algorand's approach also guarantees liveness, a fea- ture that facilitates the validation of a correct transaction within a set time limit.

Crucial to its approach is its native token, the Algo. Algorand network members purchase native tokens and eventually earn reward tokens for participating in the network's block validation process. Using its tokens and its Pure PoS consensus method, Algorand guards against malicious users with a two-step method. First, Algorand randomly selects a token owner, a network node, from among all token owners to create a block. That token owner is the only user aware of their block creation role. Next, Algorand randomly selects a set of token owners and provides them with information necessary to validate the new block. Token rewards are granted for participating in this sortition process.

Both the block creation member (a network node) and the validat- ing committee (other network nodes) are randomly and independently selected for each step and each block. Since neither the identity of the block creator nor that of the committee validating the block is known in advance, a malicious user cannot corrupt and thus influence block creation or validation. The validation method is rapid, increasing processing speed. Algorand does not have to sacrifice decentralization because users are also block producers and validators, they are picked randomly, and the user/validator pool is constantly updated.

An Algorand Application: AssetBlock and Commercial Real Estate
These advances have convinced several firms to adopt the Algorand protocol for its blockchain-based solutions: for example, Tether, a US dollar stablecoin provider; Global Carbon Holding, which supports a marketplace in tokenized carbon credit assets; SIAE, a rights man- agement company that had launched four million NFTs representing

creative rights; and AssetBlock, which markets tokenized real estate, discussed next.

As an investment opportunity, commercial real estate is available almost exclusively to large institutional investors. Commercial real estate deals are large, involving several millions of dollars, and that means minimum investments are large. This prevents smaller investors from participating in these investments. In addition, information about potential deals is not centrally located, online or offline, making it difficult for investors without connections to deal sponsors to find timely information and perform due diligence.

Algorand's international accessibility to global investors, its high-speed transactions, and its security and privacy strengths were all factors in AssetBlock's decision to build a commercial real estate investment platform on the Algorand blockchain protocol.[16] AssetBlock finds commercial real estate properties whose sponsors are looking for additional capital. Its platform subdivides a commercial real estate investment in smaller tranches, reducing the minimum size investment. These non-controlling equity investments are then available to accredited investors across the world. These global investors can use digital assets that they own, such as cryptocurrencies converted into US dollars, to invest in the property tranches on the AssetBlock platform. AssetBlock also offers loan funding to acquire the real estate tranche being purchased, accepting cryptocurrencies as collateral along with the tranche of commercial real estate being acquired.

AssetBlock, powered by Algorand, offers solutions to long-standing issues with commercial real estate investment access and security as well as cryptocurrency challenges. Cryptocurrency digital assets held for appreciation do not yield immediate returns, and AssetBlock helps transform such idle assets into new sources of investment capital for commercial real estate. The tokenization of these ownership stakes within a blockchain increases the security of ownership rights and exchange with immediate settlement and payment finality. Accepting digital assets as additional collateral lowers risk for the lender, allowing lenders in turn to charge lower rates of interest on borrowed amounts.

The lower mortgage rate reduces the weighted cost of capital for the borrower and increases the viability of investing in commercial real estate, for example, obtaining higher net present value. Subdividing a large real estate investment into smaller tranches increases the liquidity of commercial real estate investments and allows cryptocurrency owners to diversify their portfolios while retaining the possibility of capturing any appreciation of their digital assets provided as collateral. These innovations help make the commercial real estate market more transparent, efficient, and accessible to a variety of investors from around the globe. Due diligence information—such as senior debt, liens, linked collateral, and changes in ownership—is traceable, immutable, and better protected against fraud, which helps lower loan processing fees.

Converting physical assets into digital assets does bring tokenization risks. The process of creating a digital representation of a physical asset is weaker compared to native digital assets in a blockchain, for example, mining Bitcoin, which are strengthened with validation incentives (PoW and bitcoin rewards to miners). These physical asset conversions are more vulnerable to security threats and fraud, rendering a transition to blockchain less attractive.[17] Algorand's approach to validation does help reduce such vulnerability. Figure 2.2 summarizes AssetBlock's business model.

Blockchain Interoperability: Quant Overledger and Polkadot

Multiple blockchain protocols are available to serve as the core layer in applications, each with their specific advantages and flaws. Protocols can be thought of as distinct operating systems, and a specific protocol may be better suited to a particular specific enterprise use case. Common protocols include IBM Hyperledger Fabric, Ethereum, R3/Corda, Ripple, and Consensys Quorum.[18] Ethereum, with its smart contract functionality built into the protocol, is valuable in business applications where automated transaction execution is desired and contingent on fulfilling contract conditions as coded in the smart contract. Hyperledger Fabric is a private blockchain network that facilitates permissioning and

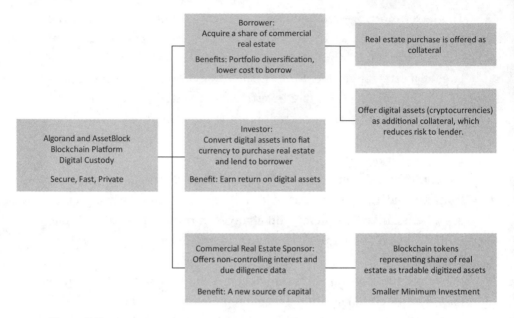

Figure 2.2
Algorand and AssetBlock: Commercial real estate investments

is used in enterprise applications such as digital payments and digital identity, supporting multiple smart contract languages and offering modularity in areas such as consensus schemes and privacy. Fabric is attractive to enterprises as it gives them more control over sharing of private data, allowing them to designate peers within the broader network with whom a certain level of sharing has been agreed upon.

R3/Corda is a private permissioned blockchain developed by a consortium of financial institutions and specializes in applications in banking, finance, and insurance. Consensys Quorum consists of an open-source Ethereum protocol layer with additional product modules available from Consensys to create customized blockchain applications. The protocol chosen influences application quality as well as its suitability for meeting user needs in specific industry contexts. For example, R3/Corda is particularly suited for developing banking applications. Choosing protocols is a foundational choice and is best done in consultation with blockchain technology experts.

Updates to existing protocols and emerging competing protocols offer improved speed and scalability, enhanced privacy, and optimization for specific industry applications. However, the sheer number of protocols and resulting competition create interoperability issues for enterprises. If blockchains are widely adopted, enterprises of all sizes will need different blockchains to communicate with each other, whether they interact internally or across organization boundaries. These blockchains can only be connected one pair at a time, using specialized software developed for each such pair-wise communication. Such a tailored approach is unwieldy, especially as different blockchain protocols are developed into improved versions and gain or lose market share and adherents over time. Without interoperability, it is problematic to migrate data and older applications across different blockchain products or different versions of blockchain protocols.

In addition, transactions cannot be recognized across blockchains because any specific solution is only valid for a single ledger and is only executable within that ledger's blockchain protocol. Transactions validated within a blockchain, with its particular consensus algorithms, provenance, and audit trails are not automatically validated in another ledger either. As stated in a Quant Network whitepaper, "migrations aren't always possible because the transactions only have scope on their blockchain address space . . . i.e., it's not possible to also make them valid in other ledgers."[19] Such transaction data would have to be accepted in the same fashion as data provided to smart contracts by oracles, and the supplying blockchain would need to be trusted, nullifying the disintermediation potential of blockchain. Without interoperability, blockchain use becomes fragmented and utility becomes limited, applications and data are stranded, and firms remain isolated in silos.

Quant Network Overledger

Quant Network's Overledger is one attempt to enable fast and safe communication between multiple different blockchains. Overledger's intent is to permit multiple blockchains, both public and private, permissioned and permissionless, with different consensus mechanisms, to communicate and conduct transactions, transmit data, and interact with nonblockchain legacy systems. Overledger has practical value and is useful even as blockchains are replaced or upgraded. It can be compared to the interoperability capabilities offered by the TCP/IP protocol at the heart of the internet. TCP/IP allows computers to interact as if they are part of a single common network, agnostic to the mode of data transmission (mobile radio, frame relay, asynchronous transfer, etc.). As such, they can transmit standardized data packets without needing to be aware of the contents.[20]

Overledger achieves interoperability by situating applications in an overlayer on top of existing blockchains. Communication, migration, exchange of information, and value occur independent of the blockchain ledgers on which they had been originally deployed. Interoperability allows firms to experiment with different blockchains and to compare relative performance, scalability, and security before settling on a particular platform. Blockchain deployment can happen faster as decision-makers are less constrained by the chosen blockchain protocol. Firms always have a way to migrate to a better solution if one becomes available later, and there is no risk of obsoleting previous investments in blockchain application development. Widely available interoperability creates backward compatibility, allowing firms to rely on a network of blockchains to collectively solve business problems across an ecosystem of firms with shared interests. Overledger also allows developers to build applications that work across multiple blockchains without the need to rewrite or port an existing application for other different blockchains. Applications are likewise stable across blockchains and easily move between different blockchain systems. Overledger has its own app store where new multichain applications can be made available for sale or for free release to potential customers.[21]

Messages in the overlayer trigger actions in the recipient blockchain. As such, the integrity and security of messages that transmit information from one blockchain to another, through the overlayer, is critical to ensuring that Overledger is an acceptable solution for interoperability. Figure 2.3 illustrates the several layers that sit above the blockchain

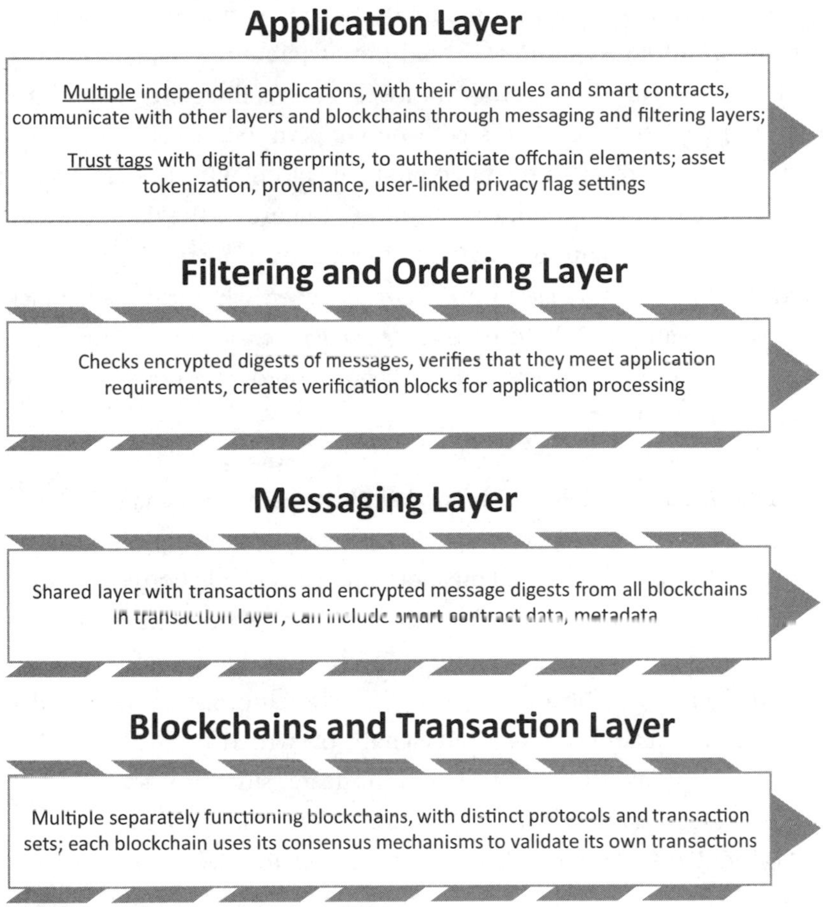

Application Layer

Multiple independent applications, with their own rules and smart contracts, communicate with other layers and blockchains through messaging and filtering layers;

Trust tags with digital fingerprints, to authenticiate offchain elements; asset tokenization, provenance, user-linked privacy flag settings

Filtering and Ordering Layer

Checks encrypted digests of messages, verifies that they meet application requirements, creates verification blocks for application processing

Messaging Layer

Shared layer with transactions and encrypted message digests from all blockchains in transaction layer, can include smart contract data, metadata

Blockchains and Transaction Layer

Multiple separately functioning blockchains, with distinct protocols and transaction sets; each blockchain uses its consensus mechanisms to validate its own transactions

Figure 2.3
The Quant Network Overledger interoperability framework

layer. These layers process messages based on transactions at the blockchain layer and link to multiple independent applications that respond to the messages, allowing communication between multiple blockchains.

While each blockchain that Overledger connects is secure, Overledger employs an additional security measure, TrustTag, to protect its transactions. TrustTag allows data to be signed at the source where it was generated, maintains a hash (encrypted) version of the data stored to assure integrity, and guarantees immutability as well as nonrepudiation (the source cannot later assert that it did not generate the data).[22] TrustTag enables the secure tokenization of assets and facilitates the safe interaction of private blockchains with public permissionless blockchains. The application receives the encrypted data along with the verification block, which, with authentication, allows the use of the data to trigger smart contract execution. Such TrustTag makes it possible for assets to be tracked in a supply chain, for example, even when different blockchains are being used by different actors across the ecosystem. It also permits the use of privacy flags to keep parts of messages private to specific users.

Polkadot Interoperability with Parallel Blockchain "Parachains"

As a competitor to Overledger, Polkadot can link multiple specialized blockchains into a network. Polkadot makes it possible for users to draw on a network of specialized blockchains, each with a distinct set of best-in-class features, thus creating a network of blockchains purposefully united for the business needs of individual organizations. Unlike Overledger, Polkadot offers a relay chain on which multiple independent blockchains can exist and communicate, side by side. Figure 2.4 illustrates how its components coalesce around the relay chain.[23]

Polkadot offers several distinct advantages to enterprise users: heterogeneous sharding, scalability, upgradability, and transparent governance. Heterogenous sharding removes any requirement that various shards (partitions of the main blockchain) have identical specifications; as such, each shard can be designed with distinct features for the business purpose at hand. Cross-chain composability allows multiple data types to be sent between the shards. As Polkadot allows processing transactions in parallel (hence parallelized chains or "parachains"), scalability increases and is enhanced. Nested relay chains, which provide shared security, can increase the number of shards within the network, creating mini-Polkadots and further increasing scalability. (Ethereum plans a similar Ethereum 2.0 version upgrade, moving to proof of stake,

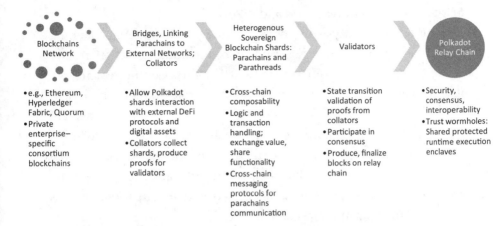

Figure 2.4
The Polkadot blockchain network architecture

to improve its scalability.) Polkadot architecture also ensures secure interoperability since "if one chain has a message reverted, all chains get reverted,"[24] thereby protecting the exchange of data from any corruption or theft.

Polkadot enacts a "fishermen" role for nodes, with collators and certain (full node) parachains allowed to monitor the network and report dishonest behavior, earning DOT (Polkadot's native currency) for their work.[25] These Polkadot terms describe roles that specific nodes play in ensuring security and scalability. Fishermen search for fraud, while collators collect shards and validators approve and seal new blocks to the Polkadot network. Polkadot offers easy upgradability since each blockchain in the connected network can be tailored to any use case, allowing for additional functionality to be added to a blockchain network without having to reengineer existing blockchain. It also emphasizes transparent governance as everyone who owns DOTs can propose a change in the protocol and vote on proposals, forestalling the prospect of contentious hard forks. Finally, Polkadot also allows blockchain to be upgraded and updated without having to fork, enabling such forkless upgrading through the transparent on-chain governance system.

Self-Sovereign Identity: Sovrin and U-Port

Proving one's identity is necessary for many tasks such as obtaining health care, proving university credentials for employment offers, and being declared eligible for government benefits. Centralized, trusted intermediaries traditionally have fulfilled the role of attesting to identity and to the authenticity of documents in return for intermediary fees. The World Bank estimates that about one in seven individuals cannot establish their identities and are thus locked out of essential services such as banking, education, and health care.[26] A lack of provable identity also exposes individuals to dangerous situations such as human trafficking and forced labor.

Essential services have increasingly been provided digitally, and digital identity verification is critical in these transactions. Like physical identification, digital identification is provided only by a few centralized authorities. Centralized identity verification sources can be hacked, compromising security and raising or creating costs, for example, the cost of freezing credit reports due to a data breach, and the consequences of fraudulent use of stolen data or credit information can be financially devastating.[27] John Hagel III and Jeffrey F. Rayport raised alarms about the power of data "infomediaries"[28] and the potentially disastrous results when the individual whose identity is being verified cannot control what information is being disclosed and to whom. In addition, when centralized intermediaries control an individual's information, the individual's identity is not easily portable across different intermediaries for different identity verification purposes. For example, banks are required to know their customers and guard against money laundering, and each bank must separately verify their client's identity with the appropriate documentation.

The challenge is to be able to establish and use digital credentials to prove online identity whenever needed and to use these digital credentials to verify age, address, academic accomplishments, employment status, and proof of asset ownership. Secure digital identities could help reduce identity theft, verify permitted access to networks (and thus improve cyber security), and create trust by authorizing the transfer of an individual's or entity's data between different systems. If individuals could control and prove their identity, and if they had the authority to decide whether to offer the required trusted credentials (and only those credentials), they would command sovereignty over their identity, bypassing centralized intermediaries and the risks inherent in relying on those intermediaries.

The answer to this challenge is self-sovereign identity (SSI), which gives individuals lifetime control of fully portable digital identity. SSI will always be under the control of that individual and cannot be taken away, but control of SSI still requires the owner to build relationships with issuers of verifiable claims to establish trust in their SSI. However, blockchain can facilitate the creation of SSI by providing standard formats for digital credentials and verifying the ownership of public keys. Individuals can sign their digital documents with their private key and concomitantly determine the extent of access to their individualized data. Their public keys would then be registered in a blockchain to be discoverable and used to verify digital signatures. Given a goal of identity for all, the SSI service would need to function as a global public utility, available to all those wanting to establish identity, credentials issuers, and those attempting to verify identity. If SSI is specific to a blockchain and interoperability is not available, the utility of SSI will inevitably be limited.

A broader benefit of SSI supported by blockchain is that customers control their own data and control the sharing of their data for adequate recompense, thereby reducing the power that intermediaries such as Google and Facebook have over individuals. At the same time, SSIs also help lower the security risks associated with centralized repositories of customer data controlled by a few entities. The Sovrin Network is an attempt to provide such an SSI.[29] In addition to verifying digital signatures and establishing ownership, Sovrin offers a standard approach to verifying digital credentials provided by the verified owner. It aims to link credentials owners, trusted issuers of the credentials, and verifiers who seek to establish the truthfulness and provenance of a digital claim. While public key infrastructure (PKI) is widely used in verifying ownership of, say, a website, there are relatively few agents (trusted certificate authorities) who can link public keys with an author's private key and certify ownership. Such services are costly and beyond the reach of most individuals. Sovrin resolves the cost and scarcity of PKIs by creating validator nodes with P2P private agents, who act on behalf of the credential's owner to certify the accuracy of furnished credentials.

The Sovrin SSI model is built using the open-source Hyperledger Indy protocol and includes several key elements:

The *issuer of credentials* follows standard protocol and issues a claim (credentials pertaining to an individual), signs the claim, and makes their public key available through decentralized identifiers (DIDs) on the public blockchain. Thus, a university could issue a claim for certain DIDs, certifying that they are a graduate of the university, and provide details such as field of study, degree earned, and year of graduation.

The *owner of the credentials* countersigns the claim made available by the issuer and presents the claim in standard protocol to the verifier, making the public key available through DIDs on the public blockchain.

The *verifier of a credential* receives a credential (claim) from the owner in standard protocol and looks up the DID to obtain public keys for verifying signatures of both claim owner and claim issuer. The verifier relies on the credential issuer to issue accurate credentials. If the qualifying condition is having graduated from university or having worked at a certain company for a period, the credentials issuer must meet these conditions.

It is important to note that this process requires credentials issuers to establish their reputation for honesty so that they are trusted. If there is no existing trust relationship, an interesting question is, How will new credentials issuers establish trust? Currently, entities such as the Department of Motor Vehicles, universities, and employers are implicitly trusted as verifiers of credentials, and in the initial stages of wider SSI use, they could continue to act as credentials issuers. Newer entities could use algorithms such as PoS or quantities of reputation tokens earned from satisfied users as measures of trust.

DIDs contain the public key for an owner along with any other public credentials the owner is willing to disclose as well as a contact network address. The DID allows issuers and verifiers to look up public keys on the Sovrin Network without having to belong to the same organization or identity federation. Every DID has an associated pair of public and private keys; they are intended to be cheap so that every user can generate as many DIDs as needed to create different subsets of verifiable claims. Claims can be about educational attainment, current employment information, income and whether it meets certain levels, and so forth. This grants the owner control over "who sees what."

Sovrin uses a lightweight consensus protocol or state proof, a cryptographic proof capable of running on a smartphone, to verify that a response to a query is valid. It thus guards against man in the middle attacks where an attacker secretly intervenes in between two parties who believe they are directly communicating with each other, altering or replacing the communication to benefit the attacker. There are yet no widely accepted standards and regulations for protecting identity data, though ZKPs,[30] could become such a standard. ZKPs can provide users in a blockchain with security and assurance that the information has not been changed or tampered with—immutability. ZKPs can share information between counterparties while maintaining privacy and preventing competitors from gaining the information. Interactive ZKPs require the user to convince the verifier that they have certain information, while noninteractive ZKPs provide verification at later stages, as in the case of DIDs and verifiable claims described above.[31] ZKPs are based on mathematical formulas and can be computation intensive, slowing down processing speed.

Sovrin provides privacy assurance, with pseudonymity, through unique DIDs generated for each verifier. Varying government regulations in different jurisdictions, such as the EU's GDPR (General Data Protection Regulation), imply that a global identity utility will need to comply with differing data protection and privacy regulations. No private data is stored on the blockchain; instead, the owner exchanges the actual credentials (verifiable claims) through a private P2P agent (a digital wallet provider) over an encrypted private channel, off-chain. The owner can limit disclosure to a minimum when communicating the credentials by using ZKPs. For example, one could disclose proof that they are eligible to vote, verified with the public key information from DID, without disclosing other details such as residence and actual date of birth, since the only birth detail that matters is whether they were born before a certain date, and perhaps citizenship and residence.

Sovrin tokens are used to create value for verifying credentials, to motivate and reward identity owners and credentials issuers for sharing such data under authorized conditions. As a byproduct, an SSI system can foster a market for digital credential insurance (specifically, insurance against accepting credentials that may be false). Figure 2.5 summarizes the central features of Sovrin Network's approach to securing SSI for all.

Objective Oracles for Smart Contract Execution: Chainlink

One of the distinguishing (and desirable) features of blockchains is their ability to incorporate smart contracts. Many provide ready-to-use templates and development tools to build and implement smart contracts. Smart contracts can be triggered within a blockchain with information that indicates that contract requirements have been met, initiating a subsequent transaction such as a transfer of ownership and exchange of value. The secure and immutable character of data in a blockchain, the ability to track provenance, and the use of tokens native to the blockchain all help automate the execution of smart contracts. Automatically executed smart contracts save time, avoid redundant error checking, and free up capital otherwise tied up during dispute resolution.[32] However, smart contract execution within a blockchain cannot automatically initiate external events, such as payment from a bank account outside the blockchain.

Smart contract execution is often dependent on external data, such as data from IoT sensors (e.g., whether the product has been stored at

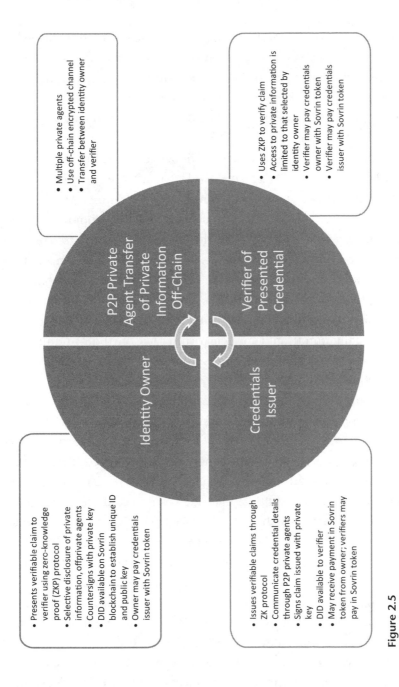

- Multiple private agents
- Use off-chain encrypted channel
- Transfer between identity owner and verifier

- Uses ZKP to verify claim
- Access to private information is limited to that selected by identity owner
- Verifier may pay credentials owner with Sovrin token
- Verifier may pay credentials issuer with Sovrin token

P2P Private Agent Transfer of Private Information Off-Chain

Verifier of Presented Credential

Identity Owner

Credentials Issuer

- Presents verifiable claim to verifier using zero-knowledge proof (ZKP) protocol
- Selective disclosure of private information, off-private agents
- Countersigns with private key
- DID available on Sovrin blockchain to establish unique ID and public key
- Owner may pay credentials issuer with Sovrin token

- Issues verifiable claims through ZK protocol
- Communicate credential details through P2P private agents
- Signs claim issued with private key
- DID available to verifier
- May receive payment in Sovrin token from owner; verifiers may pay in Sovrin token

Figure 2.5

Sovrin SSI and token model: Governance, performance, accessibility, and privacy the right temperature), market data (whether the stock price reached a level to trigger option exercise), or events (such as a tenant vacating a rental property in good condition and activating the return of the security deposit). The blockchain's consensus protocols that help guarantee the security and immutability of data do not extend to data obtained by oracles from external sources.

Oracles are blockchain middleware designed to securely link smart contracts with external data sources and events. More specifically, they link blockchains (and their smart contracts) with distinct APIs for different data sources, with each API being a standard communication channel between its data source and the blockchain. Centralized oracles can help resolve the security weakness inherent in linking with, obtaining, and communicating off-chain data needed by the smart contract. However, this requires that the user or entity trust that the information provided by their transacting partner is accurate and acceptable to activate financially significant contracts within a specified time frame. The central oracle could be hacked or go offline at critical times, becoming a single point of failure and making the contract itself insecure.

Chainlink has developed an alternative, creating a decentralized oracle network[33] capable of fulfilling smart contract data requests while securely obtaining data from external data sources. A key feature is the use of multiple independent oracle nodes within the Chainlink blockchain. These nodes can retrieve the same data point from multiple independent data sources. Multiple data sources reduce dependence on a single source of data, which could be hacked or ethically compromised, and guard against a sole data source being offline. The multiple data points can then be aggregated and reduced to a single reliable datapoint that can trigger the smart contract, using aggregation models such as calculating an average, discarding outliers, and estimating algorithms.

Chainlink establishes external adapters, termed chainlinks, to connect blockchains and APIs; each API has its own chainlink. It uses a reputation system that allows oracles to be graded and receive reputation scores based on factors such as success rate, response time, and continuous availability. This reputation system matches oracle nodes to offer higher quality services and outdo competing oracles. Chainlink allows smart contracts to choose, based on reputation scores and minimum reputation thresholds, which oracles they will call on to obtain data before aggregating them, with reputation scores helpful in making choices. It also allows smart contracts to choose oracles that run TEEs so that the oracle nodes cannot see query details; given a password, a TEE oracle could access a proprietary data source, retrieve data, and enable other actions such as payments.

Chainlink uses a native token, the LINK, to facilitate smart contract payments for oracle services. Oracle nodes are required to deposit a negotiated amount of LINK within Chainlink to respond to a smart contract data query, and the deposit motivates the oracle nodes to provide quality service and high levels of uptime availability. However, an oracle node can lose its deposit if it "feeds outlier data or goes offline."[34] Chainlink can be also used as a plug-and-play oracle solution module within other blockchains that seek to connect their smart contracts to external off chain data and events. Figure 2.6 summarizes Chainlink's architecture.

Oracles can also be linked to AI applications as data sources, such as machine learning algorithms that reach consensus on predictions from an event stream source, before publishing the prediction to a

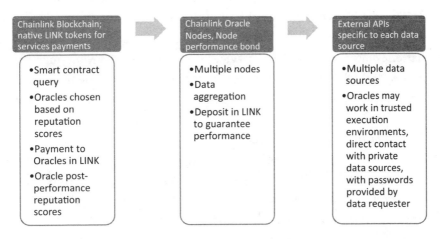

Figure 2.6
The Chainlink distributed oracle

blockchain for further action within a smart contract.[35] For example, a machine learning algorithm could analyze past events to develop indicators about the predicted level of pests and resulting crop damage. The algorithm could then be linked to a decentralized crop insurance smart contract, which would automatically authorize payment if insurance conditions regarding pest occurrence levels are met.

Linking IoT Devices in a Blockchain to Provide Immutable Audit Trails of IoT Sensor Data: Modum

IoT devices are low-power instruments (i.e., sensors) with rudimentary operating systems, limited processing, and storage capabilities. They run on diverse, often incompatible, protocols and standards but are all designed to gather data from several remote locations and feed it back to different kinds of networks, including blockchains. IoT devices are numerous relative to the nodes running the blockchain, making scalability crucial so that large numbers of them can communicate safely and continuously. A centralized server receiving such a large volume of messages can become a bottleneck and a point of failure, but decentralizing IoT communication through blockchain nodes can increase the robustness and continuous availability of data.

Unfortunately, IoT devices and the data they gather and transmit can be a weak security point in an enterprise network. They are more vulnerable to malicious attacks, such as denial of sleep attacks (to drain batteries) as well as denial of service attacks such as the Mirai malware attack,[36] which infected IoT devices to be able to control them remotely and affect performance. IoT devices can be impersonated and are subject to physical tampering, and thus authentication and securing data integrity are critical for them.[37] Blockchain-based consensus for IoT transaction validation, protecting content with private keys, timestamping, and sequencing additions to blocks can reduce IoT security risks while maintaining privacy. However, it is important to note that variations in computing capability may restrict the ability of some IoT devices to process cryptographic encryption, slowing down the network.

Modum links blockchains to IoT devices, capturing and publishing data to the blockchain while ensuring immutable audit trails of data and events. Such integrated IoT blockchain solutions have wide application, for instance, in monitoring supply chain flow in the biopharma industry. Pharmaceutical products are high-value products shipped in high-volume units and are sensitive to damage during shipment. IoT sensors can securely track and transmit data—monitoring temperature, humidity, location (with GPS tracking), package integrity, and so on—to uphold product quality and security as well as compliance with shipping contract terms and regulations. Other applications include monitoring the shipment of medical devices, which can be damaged from shock and tilt during transport. Sensors capable of detecting "shock, tilt, freefall or other acceleration related events" could aggregate and communicate such data at regular time points.

Clinical trials of new drugs under development are another arena where real-time, continuously flowing data from IoT sensors is helpful. Data can be transmitted to clinical trial managers at remote sites, enabling them to monitor quality issues. Such monitoring would also help ensure that trial protocols are followed at the patient's residences over the trial's duration. Life cycle management of assets such as heavy construction equipment can also be aided by sensors. They could track the asset's provenance and history and provide preventive and useful life assessments.[38] Modum solutions have been deployed in several of the scenarios referenced above and includes four major interlinked modules: data gathering, aggregation and communication, data analytics and predictions, and ecosystem-wide secure sharing of supply chain data and predictions while protecting confidential data.

Developing New Business Models with Blockchain

I next turn to blockchain-native start-ups that have developed original business models that exploit the unique characteristics of blockchain. The several examples that follow offer insights into how enterprises can develop new sources of revenue using blockchain and create new businesses.

P2P IoT-Based Low-Power Wide-Area Wireless Networks: Helium

As noted in the discussion of Modum's solution for linking IoT devices securely to blockchains, IoT devices are ubiquitous, with an estimated twenty billion IoT devices in use in 2020.[39] All of these devices must communicate regularly, at specified time intervals, to provide updated sensor information and, when bidirectional links are an integral part of IoT deployment, to receive directions for action. However, IoT devices communicate small amounts of data and do not require the broadband capabilities and the higher cost of WiFi cellular networks. Helium is an innovator attempting to develop a two-sided market for IoT communication rooted in a P2P network, which it has tabbed as the "People's Network."[40]

On the supply side (i.e., creating a network for IoT communication), Helium developed hotspots that could be linked together to create a decentralized wide-area network. Rather than Helium Systems building out a network of Helium Hotspots, entrepreneurs would purchase multiple hotspots from Helium and deploy them in a city, collectively setting up a Helium Network. WHIP, Helium's secure, long-range, low-power, bidirectional wireless network protocol, allows the Helium Network to wirelessly connect to the internet at a significantly lower cost than cell networks. A key requirement is that the Hotspot owners must have a WiFi connection so that they can link up their hotspots to their existing WiFi router and be available to IoT devices for data transfer.

The hotspots form part of the Helium Blockchain, with a new consensus protocol, Proof of Coverage, to ensure that the hotspots actually exist and are providing transmission coverage to IoT devices. Proof of Coverage protects against Sybil attacks and alternate reality attacks— where rogue hotspots simulate WiFi coverage and steal or divert IoT data and use the bidirectional capability to send malicious commands to the IoT devices. The Hotspot owners receive payments (in Helium HNT tokens) for transporting IoT data, transaction validation and inclusion in a block, and for participating in the Proof of Coverage consensus validation. Hotspots validate the IoT geolocation and also store the IoT transaction data along with the transaction's fingerprint and timestamp, providing a tamperproof data and audit trail. All transaction data can be stored on the blockchain.

On the demand side, low-powered IoT devices would use the LoRaWAN[41] protocol to communicate their information over a wide range (around ten miles) to any Hotspot in the network. The IoT devices are mapped to the company ID on the blockchain, becoming trusted devices and using private/public keys to encrypt data transmissions and be validated at the receiving end. IoT device owners do not pay a fee to join the Helium Network; they only pay for actual data transferred, a-pay-as-you-go system based on microtransactions for transferring small data packets. IoT users pay in Data Credits, which can be obtained by converting HNT tokens. The low-power consumption of the IoT devices extends battery life and hence their dependability. Other user advantages include easy connectivity to Helium Hotspots, the ability to pool data from multiple IoT devices, and an immutable record of secure, timestamped IoT location-verified transactions. Helium estimated that it would cost about $35 monthly for 2,500 IoT devices to transmit a data packet every thirty minutes. A sample application might be a company selling fresh, perishable pet food stored in IoT-equipped refrigerators, using the Helium Network to obtain temperature updates, stock status, and freshness levels.

Tracking assets of almost any kind would be a good fit with the Helium IoT communication solution. Interesting industry-specific applications include the following:

- Conserv, which uses IoT and Helium Network to monitor relative humidity, temperature, vibration, and light levels to ensure optimal environmental conditions for the display and storage of valuable art and archival materials.
- Clean Water AI, which combines IoT data transmitted through Helium, from the edge to the cloud, where it is linked with AI pattern

recognition and machine learning to detect bacterial presence and contamination in drinking water.

- Agulus, which uses IoT and Helium to automate irrigation infrastructure on farms. IoT sensors collect field data (soil moisture content, depth, nutrients) and relay data to a cloud control center. After analysis, Agulus can activate irrigation systems, pumps, and sprayers.

A major issue is that Helium is dependent on existing WiFi signals. WiFi providers could interpret this reuse of the WiFi connection they provide as free riding. They could demand payment, set conditions for Helium Network access, and raise the cost of Helium services to the IoT community. A second issue is geographic coverage as the Hotspot Network must be matched to the geographical distribution of IoT devices. By essentially crowdsourcing the buildup of hotspots across the US and, later, other parts of the world, Helium Systems is expecting market forces to balance demand for IoT data transfer and the supply of hotspots to conduct such data transfer, without necessarily seeding the market. If this matching process is slow to occur, IoT users, for whom sensor data transfer is essential for their business purposes, might resort to alternative communication channels, and Helium's innovation advantage might dissipate. Helium Network's architecture is displayed in figure 2.7.

Insuring Blockchain Projects and Digital Assets: ConsenSys Diligence

Blockchain applications will become more numerous as users become more comfortable and confident using blockchain. This will increase awareness of the risks attendant to the growing use of blockchain and create demand for insurance against theft by hackers, erroneous smart contract execution, or blockchain front-running.[42] (Front-running occurs when market makers and traders take advantage of their knowledge of incoming large orders, which are likely to influence prices, by taking a position before the execution of the large order, thus benefiting from the expected price change.) Professional blockchain software development firms and individuals might want professional liability

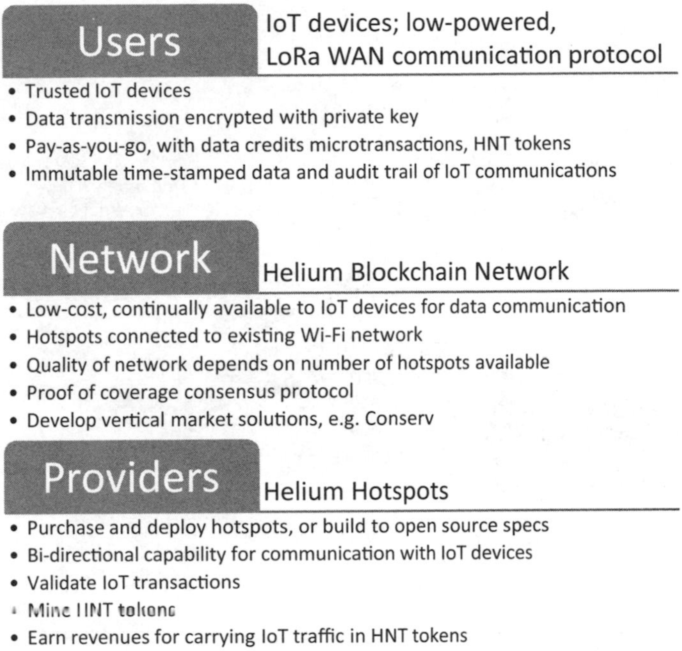

| Users | IoT devices; low-powered, LoRa WAN communication protocol |

- Trusted IoT devices
- Data transmission encrypted with private key
- Pay-as-you-go, with data credits microtransactions, HNT tokens
- Immutable time-stamped data and audit trail of IoT communications

| Network | Helium Blockchain Network |

- Low-cost, continually available to IoT devices for data communication
- Hotspots connected to existing Wi-Fi network
- Quality of network depends on number of hotspots available
- Proof of coverage consensus protocol
- Develop vertical market solutions, e.g. Conserv

| Providers | Helium Hotspots |

- Purchase and deploy hotspots, or build to open source specs
- Bi-directional capability for communication with IoT devices
- Validate IoT transactions
- Mine HNT tokens
- Earn revenues for carrying IoT traffic in HNT tokens

Figure 2.7
Helium IoT communications network

coverage; large clients might seek surety bonds from their blockchain providers, particularly when usage is ongoing, as with TradeLens or decentralized finance applications.

Each source of risk must be addressed individually to reduce total blockchain application risk. Consensys Diligence[43] is an application designed to audit smart contracts. It detects bugs and security vulnerabilities in blockchain project code during smart contracts development (i.e., coded flaws in permission structure) and departures from intended permissions. Fixing code during development is preferable as code errors that remain after commercial operations launch can have larger-scale consequences. EY (formerly Ernst & Young) offers a similar set of blockchain analyzer tools, which includes a test studio, as part of its Smart Contract & Token Review software suite. Users such as SolidBlock, an asset tokenization firm, have used this facility to customize smart

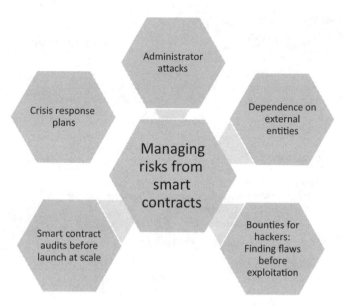

Figure 2.8

Reducing smart contract risks. Source: Based on Mardlin, questions decentralized finance users should be asking decentralized finance developers.

contract tests against commonly experienced attacks and to simulate transactions and decentralized finance contracts on the public Ethereum blockchain, before public release.[44] In 2021, EY announced an incremental $100 million investment in such tools and to fund broad blockchain and crypto asset research.[45]

Figure 2.8 summarizes the various risks underlying blockchains and their smart contracts. Enterprise blockchains are likely to be permissioned, and governance is likely to include an administrator or administrative team with some level of centralized control. That person or team could have powers that include interrupting system functioning, upgrading a part or the entire system, and delaying actions. In such a situation, the administrator could become a point of vulnerability—hackers could gain access to administrator's passwords and private keys, compromising the system.[46] Applying measures such as time delays before administrative changes are implemented or subjecting administrator actions to a decentralized team approval could attenuate risk.

Blockchains and smart contracts also depend on external parties such as oracles for data to activate smart contracts, external tokens, third-party modules (such as special purpose smart contracts), and external exchanges. All such interactions need to be secured against hidden bugs. One interesting approach to this challenge is to offer bounties to capable hackers, who detect and disclose security holes and flaws to administrators before such deficiencies are exploited by attackers. Such bounty programs can be coupled with a variety of additional measures for added protection, for example, smart contract audits, structured methodology to detect flaws before deployment at scale, specialized security analysis, and checking against the Smart Contract Weakness Classification database registry of smart contract vulnerabilities.[47] Scenario planning and incidence response strategies should accompany any other mitigation measures to control damage from flaws and attacks.

Blockchain-Based Organizations: Aragon

Decentralization is an intrinsic aspect of blockchain, and tokens are commonly used to create market incentives for decentralized blockchain nodes. If tokens can be conceived of as votes, with individual nodes using tokens to voice their choice or opinion, then blockchains with native tokens can be used to create new decentralized forms of organization—a decentralized autonomous organization or DAO. Adding smart contracts allows blockchain-driven platforms to create new, borderless organizations that are sovereign and censor resistant, with participative decision-making and dispute resolution mechanisms all based on smart contracts. However, organizations must contend with difficulties such as voter apathy, bribery attacks, and plutocratic domination. Against this backdrop, DAO projects have attempted to ameliorate these flaws in member representation, seeking to "align the organization with stakeholders' interests and improve cooperation and participation through game theoretic monetary incentives"[48] and to create "cooperatives in cyberspace."

Aragon is one example of using blockchain to create such decentralized democratic organizations.[49] Each Aragon-based organization has a set of smart contracts that describe the organization's stakeholders and their rights and privileges. If minority interests are to be protected, that is, if they can veto what might otherwise be a majority vote, smart contract rules must contain provisions outlining when a majority vote is insufficient. These steps can be structured as a series of smart contracts within the Aragon Network, which provides the infrastructure and services for Aragon platform members to assign roles, raise funds, adopt accounting practices, and vote on different proposed actions using tokens as votes.

The Aragon organization structure can help avoid disputes. As an example, consider the finance function within an organization, which has sole access to the organization's resources and can make payments to entities outside the organization but only if proposed by a member of the organization. Such payments must be within an established budget, and payment can only be made if authorized by a majority of members—voters. A vote request would be sent to the organization's token manager, who would solicit all token holders, that is, the voters, and forward the results of the token holders' actions. The action approved by most of the token holders would prevail.

This DAO model creates a degree of transparency for financial flows, permitting larger numbers of the DAO members to influence such flows. However, if some voters held more tokens, they would have greater influence over the vote outcomes—not unlike the situation in the United States, where mutual funds, exchange-traded funds (ETFs), and index funds collectively control most voting shares in US corporations—and effectively control the voting outcomes on major proposals put forth by these firms. Hence, if organizations wish to move to a DAO model, they must decide how to address the consequences of having dominant members with greater weight in voting rights. As with blockchain as a whole, DAO with token-based voting rights is in its early stages and will evolve gradually as it experiments with different token-granting incentive schemes, before gaining broader acceptance.

IP/Content Management: Open Music Initiative

The music industry has long been criticized as unfair to musicians, with disagreement over fair sharing of revenue among the several parties involved in creating and selling music, including the multiple revenue streams from distribution, publishing, streaming, sales, and licensing.[50] It also suffers from the unauthorized copying and distribution of these copies. In an attempt to address this issue, the Berklee College of Music, with MIT Connection Science, has spearheaded the Open Music Initiative.[51] Together, they have developed a multilayered open blockchain protocol for identifying music creators—the music metadata layer—and then linked this data to the licensing and royalties management layer—connecting music rights with licensing and payments due—and to the music virtual assets layer.

The blockchain can also link the music assets to tokens, facilitating the exchange of assets, decentralized music rights trading, and usage tracking.[52] Deploying these layers to cover the music ecosystem can pave the way for tracking usage and state changes, transfers, and eventual micropayments for access to such music assets distributed among the various rights holders. One such application from the Open Music Initiative is the RAIDAR licensing platform on blockchain, which allows rights holders, for example, music students at Berklee, to license their music to others such as to filmmakers, virtual reality apps, and video games.[53]

The goal of the music metadata layer is to link a musical work, song, or track to one authoritative metafile containing music creation data for that musical work. This metadata would include a cryptographic hash of the music digital file, and each metadata file would have a unique file identifier similar to the DOI (digital object identifier) used for text documents. Multiple versions of a musical work would have multiple different DOI numbers. Copies of the creation metadata registry would be stored in multiple unmodified open access searchable repositories and made available to the public, through APIs.

The creation metadata would be linked to a separate blockchain registry and be digitally signed by the music creator or authorized entity, using private-public key pairs, thus validating the metadata for inclusion in the blockchain. A shorter version of the metadata would be stored on the blockchain; timestamped, including a cryptographic hash of the full metadata file; and would have the same DOI. Such blockchain-based metadata could enable the identification of music creators, support their copyright claims, and provide "a relatively immutable and nonrepudiable timestamped public evidence of the existence of the musical work."[54]

Such metadata would not include the actual musical content (the sound files) that would be stored in protected access locations or the legal and copyrights rights ownership data as well as other confidential information. The musical content files and corresponding ownership rights information would reside in other layers but be linked to the creation metadata. Smart contracts could unambiguously link to the metadata of a song or track, facilitating licensing of the exact version in case multiple versions exist. Legacy systems could also rely on the blockchain registry data in referring to music content and ownership.

Conclusion

The various examples discussed in this chapter reveal blockchain technology in ferment, with a host of blockchain initiatives tackling current disadvantages that have held back enterprise efforts in this arena. Many of these efforts emphasize open-source architecture, which points to the ethos underlying public blockchain development. Others focus on vertical market, industry-specific solutions, and collaborative partnerships are common as these firms search for breakthroughs. These efforts are in a nascent stage, with adherents and supporters launching pilots and providing feedback to continue improving the proposed innovative solutions.

Enterprises are likely to opt for permissioned consortium blockchains for the foreseeable future, with a few trusted nodes, rendering unnecessary slow and computation-intensive consensus schemes. However, such limited decentralization creates concentrated points of failure; though with only a few members given permission to access the blockchain network, fear of ill-intentioned actors is reduced. Enterprises must balance learning and building on start-up initiatives with the pressures from operating within ecosystems with legacy systems and traditionally accepted best practices. This need for balance influences paths to commercial-scale blockchain implementation, discussed in the concluding chapter.

I now move on to blockchain application in specific industries. In chapter 3, I consider cryptocurrency applications and their evolution into newer forms of digital money, in the guise of stablecoins and national government–supported CBDCs. The world of payment is rapidly embracing digital currency payments with important consequences for the global financial system, national monetary policy, and enterprises and individuals.

3 Digital Currencies, Payment Systems, and Their Enterprise Implications

In this chapter, I look at the evolution and significance of digital currencies and private stablecoins and their influence on payment systems. I examine the government response to digital currencies in the form of CBDCs and the ensuing competition with private stablecoins and cryptocurrencies. I also look at the policy implications of digital currencies, and regulatory concerns, before turning to the impact of digital currency on the global financial system, monetary policy, enterprises, and consumers in both the B2B and B2C context. Because of their reliance on blockchains, we can interpret the ubiquity, importance, and growing number of use cases of digital currencies as an indication of blockchain's increasingly essential role in the financial sector. As digital currencies continue to gain in popularity and usage, blockchain will enter the mainstream.

Cryptocurrencies, Stablecoins, and CBDCs

Bitcoin, the first major application of blockchain, emerged out of the financial turmoil that brought the world's financial system to the edge of collapse in 2008. Part of the fallout of "the Great Recession" was strong mistrust in financial institutions and governments. Libertarians in particular sought a financial system beyond the control of governmental authorities. The idea was to create a currency independent of any nation-state that could be held and transferred without banks as intermediaries, thereby allowing individuals and firms to transact directly with one another. The result was Bitcoin.

Money is a social construct, with a group of people—typically a nation-state—agreeing to accept an item as payment in exchange for goods or services that have value. Payments, be it shells, blocks of salt, bars of gold, or banknotes, are necessary to finalize an economic transaction. Money has several functions: to serve as a unit of account, a store of value, and a means of exchange. But it needs to be stable to be used to measure the value of a good or service. People are willing to accept money because its stability means it retains its value, in turn allowing it to become a means of exchange. Money and payments have evolved significantly over time. Money, in the form of coins and paper currency backed by a government, was a significant innovation in the means of payment (China in the eleventh century, late 1600s in England to finance King William's war with France) and radically transformed commerce.[1]

In the past millennium, new forms of payments such as bank money (money created by banks through loans and fractional banking), credit and debit cards, mobile wallets, and cryptocurrencies (like Bitcoin) have transformed the economic landscape. In a relatively short time, customers have become accustomed to a wide variety of digital payment forms, such as paying with their smartphones, using contactless cards, and signing up for buy now, pay later plans at the point of sale. China's experience with AliPay (Ant Financial/Ali Baba) and WeChat Pay (Tencent) suggests that consumers and merchants are eager to use digital forms of payment in their online transactions. In China, nearly 80 percent of smartphone users used proximity (NFC) mobile payments in 2019, with AliPay and WeChat Pay together accounting for 95 percent of the volume.[2] All these apps, however, still link back to fiat money sources such as bank deposits and verified credit limits. The move to encourage the use of blockchain-based digital currencies as a means of payment has broad implications, further explored in this chapter.

Bitcoin: The Starting Point

Bitcoin was an early cryptocurrency and was followed by other cryptocurrencies, notably Ether, used in the Ethereum blockchain network with links to smart contracts ("programmable money"), and XRP in the Ripple network. However, it has had difficulty gaining widespread use as a payment system due to its significant volatility and transaction costs. This makes it difficult and costly to use as a unit of account and a means of exchange. Most Bitcoin is held as an investment vehicle rather than used in day-to-day transactions. Bitcoin total market capitalization approximated $1.15 trillion on October 24, 2021, with 18.85 million Bitcoin in circulation (90 percent of the maximum Bitcoin issuable), with one Bitcoin priced at $61,000, and then declining dramatically, in January 2022, to around $35,000, reducing market capitalization to about $750 billion. In comparison, daily transactions in forex trading in US$ approximated $6.6 trillion per day in April 2019.[3]

That said, cryptocurrencies have been used as a means of payment in high-value, high profile transactions. For example, Tesla announced in late 2020 that it would accept Bitcoin payments[4] (a decision reversed by May 2021, with reasons adduced being high volatility and energy wastefulness inherent in Bitcoin mining), and in another example, an auction of digital art that sold for around $69 million was paid for with Ether.[5] However, these are exceptions, and bitcoin use remains relatively scarce in routine commercial purchases. Nonetheless, whether or not bitcoin fits the traditional characteristics of money, it has continued to grow—as a store of value and as a vehicle for speculation and investment. Major payment systems such as Square have started accepting bitcoin as an option in addition to more traditional means of payment such as credit and debit cards. What is needed is a way to combine the digital ease of handling bitcoin with the stability of major fiat currencies such as the US dollar.

The Emergence of Stablecoins

Cryptocurrency volatility, with Bitcoin ranging from under $4,000 to $60,000 during 2019 and 2021, led to the rise of stablecoins. Stablecoins are linked to a stable asset such as the US dollar and are backed by significant collateral, such as DAI, which is pegged at a 1:1 ratio to the US dollar (DAI is issued by MakerDAO, which uses DAO as part of its name to indicate its use of decentralized governance). Other stablecoin are backed by reserves of equivalent amounts of fiat currencies, e.g., USDT (Tether) and USDC (US Dollar Coin), which hold US dollar reserves in amounts matching the number of USDT and USDC minted. Demand for stablecoins has been significant enough that major banks such as JPMorgan responded with its own digital currency, JPM Coin,[6] which has a value equal to one US dollar. JPM Coin can be used for transfer and payment between institutions within the JPMorgan Quorum blockchain, allowing for instantaneous settlement and transfer of value.

Digital currencies as a means of payment are growing in importance. Stablecoins remove the volatility inherent in cryptocurrencies and meet the consumer's desire for convenient, easy-to-use, speedy, and cheap payment mechanisms that work domestically as well as internationally. At the same time, digital currencies raise the specter of competition between private and public money and between state-based and stateless decentralized cryptocurrencies that are unregulated (and possibly unregulatable), such as Bitcoin.

Watching the rise of digital currencies (stable and unstable), central banks around the world have become concerned about the potential negative effects that digital currencies launched by private firms could have on state-based monetary systems. In response, many central banks have launched pilots to test CBDCs. During Congressional testimony in February 2020, US Federal Reserve Chairman Powell responded to Facebook's announcement about Libra (now Diem) by saying it was "a wakeup call that this is coming fast and could come in a way that is quite widespread and systemically important fairly quickly."[7] CBDCs could become yet another form of blockchain-based money, joining a continuum of cash, bank money (checks, loans backed by central bank reserves), private cryptocurrencies, and stablecoins.

Digital currencies—all of which run on blockchains—impact firms, the overall economy, and consumers. Consumers might enjoy the convenience of paying with digital currencies even as they become aware of its volatility, limited liquidity and redemption risk, and the consequences of losing their private keys. At the macroeconomy level, governments worry that a loss of confidence in private digital currencies, resulting in panicked withdrawals, could pose systemic risk, affect financial stability, and affect monetary policy transmission. A US concern is how sovereign CBDCs from countries such as China might affect the US dollar as a global reserve currency.

The Consequences of Digital Currencies

The rise of digital currencies has brought to the fore several consequences for enterprises, summarized in figure 3.1 and discussed in the following sections.

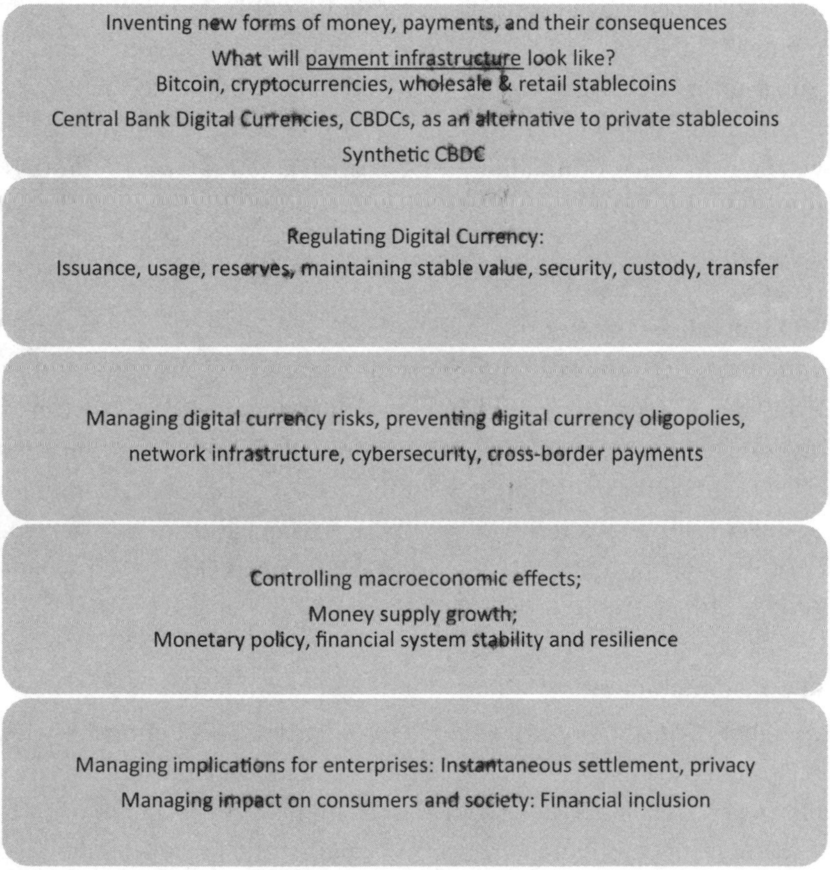

Inventing new forms of money, payments, and their consequences
What will payment infrastructure look like?
Bitcoin, cryptocurrencies, wholesale & retail stablecoins
Central Bank Digital Currencies, CBDCs, as an alternative to private stablecoins
Synthetic CBDC

Regulating Digital Currency:
Issuance, usage, reserves, maintaining stable value, security, custody, transfer

Managing digital currency risks, preventing digital currency oligopolies,
network infrastructure, cybersecurity, cross-border payments

Controlling macroeconomic effects;
Money supply growth;
Monetary policy, financial system stability and resilience

Managing implications for enterprises: Instantaneous settlement, privacy
Managing impact on consumers and society: Financial inclusion

Figure 3.1
Digital currencies: Key consequences

Inventing New Forms of Money: Digital Currencies, Private Stablecoins, and Payment Systems

As discussed earlier, cryptocurrencies are volatile. Stablecoins are intended to provide the benefits of using digital currencies while reducing their volatility, by holding currency reserves (i.e., US dollars). Stablecoin value can also be maintained using algorithmic processes to adjust supply in relation to demand. By removing the concern over volatility, a stablecoin becomes more viable as a means of payment, particularly when designed to enhance ease of use for consumers. Stablecoins can offer low-cost, convenient, and instantaneous settlement. As stablecoin providers compete with other stablecoin operators for customers, they attempt to gain competitive advantage by providing pleasing user interfaces, superior app design, better integration with e-commerce transactions, and cost advantages (i.e., no processing fees).

Global stablecoins, when acceptable in and adopted as a means of payment in multiple countries, become even more attractive to firms and individuals transferring payments across borders. They offer speed and lower cost, factors of particular importance to individuals sending overseas remittances to their families in emerging markets. They can be also more efficient, less costly, and near instantaneous, when compared to current bank-based transfers or the use of specialized remittance agencies such as Western Union. These advantages can help achieve high-volume consumer adoption and potentially lead to their greater systemic financial importance.

Stablecoins and Risk

For all of their stability as compared to other types of cryptocurrencies, stablecoins do carry risks. Stablecoin value can be volatile due to uncertainty about whether stablecoin issuers are holding adequate reserves underpinning stablecoin issuance and whether the reserves are holding their value. Stablecoins, such as Tether, have varied in value, though they are expected to hold US dollar reserves equivalent to the amount of Tether created. Tether accidentally created Tether coins to more than double the amount in circulation, dropping prices by about 12 percent, though the mistake was quickly rectified.[8]

One set of risks stem primarily from the greater influence that private financial entities might obtain over the payments system. In addition, there is liquidity risk, when redemption requests may not be instantly settled due to lack of funds; default or credit risk, when stablecoin issuers cannot satisfy redemption requests; market risk from losses in underlying assets held to back stablecoin value; and possible foreign exchange risk when a portion of assets are held in foreign currencies.[9] In all, stablecoin's vulnerabilities[10] arise from

- rules and governance of a specific stablecoin arrangement;
- processes for creating and removing stablecoins from circulation;
- management of the reserves supporting the stable value and custody of these assets;
- operation and robustness of the infrastructure supporting stable coin use;
- transaction validation, exchange, trading, and price setting of stablecoins; and
- private key storage and access to digital wallets containing stablecoins.

Private stablecoins can be managed through centralized management as in the case of Circle's USDC, or through decentralized governance as at MakerDAO, where MKR tokens are issued and enable MKR token owners to participate in governance, that is, setting reserve requirements and making changes to the Maker DAI protocol (and its underlying algorithm). As the use of a particular stablecoin becomes increasingly widespread, it can exert greater influence over commerce and money supply, and flawed governance can increase the risks from such influence. Since stablecoins seek to maintain one-to-one stability with a chosen fiat currency, changes in reserves must be accompanied by a concomitant increase or decrease in the number of stablecoins in circulation. Independent custody of such reserves backing stablecoin is essential to guarantee that reserves are segregated and adequate and are not used for funding operations.

Stablecoin managers must also be capable of maintaining liquidity so that the demand and supply of the stablecoin are continuously matched in the marketplace; otherwise, stablecoin volatility ensues. This could involve the stablecoin operator obtaining listings of the stablecoin on multiple digital currency exchanges and maintaining an internal inventory of stablecoin to deploy in purchase or sale operations to maintain stablecoin price stability. Moreover, stablecoin holders (clients) need to use their private keys to access their stablecoin holdings, and stablecoin operators can offer to store their clients' stablecoin holdings or interact with private digital wallets where each owner holds and controls their private key. While the former centralized holding of clients' holdings is akin to bank account operations, it increases vulnerability to hackers. However, enabling individual client control of their private keys and storage of holding in private wallets requires clients to be educated to safeguard their private keys and access control to their wallets since losing the private key would prevent them from accessing their holdings.

Different stablecoins may also vary in their operational resiliency, that is, their ability to quickly recover from cyberattacks and security breaches and to maintain robustness in the face of "black swan" events, such as the COVID-19 pandemic. In 2020, for example, the sudden need for increased liquidity and a boost of confidence in the face of the COVID-19 pandemic-related unforeseen global recession prompted significant intervention by the Federal Reserve, the European Central Bank, and other central banks. Although panic was contained, a question did arise: how might stablecoins function in the face of such catastrophes? Depending on the scale and rapidity of stablecoin adoption, they do have the potential to affect financial system stability. Stablecoin operators therefore must address consumer trust, possibly asking whether trust would be higher if stablecoins were regulated and their asset stability backstopped by stablecoin operators' access to central bank reserves.

One approach is to set regulations requiring adequate equity capital to be available and that underlying reserves be invested in safe liquid assets, such as central bank reserves. These assets would need to be safeguarded and unencumbered. Regulations requiring stablecoin operators to issue a total volume of stablecoins less than client funds on deposit plus the issuing entity's equity capital would help cement that trust. Interestingly, if funds migrate to stablecoin providers from banks, thereby reducing bank deposits, this could affect total funding available at banks to make loans, as the fractional banking model relies on leveraging customer funds on deposit. The rise of stablecoins could therefore reduce the money supply.

Sovereign nations may wish to prevent the usage of stablecoins issued in foreign jurisdictions within their domestic markets, even if such regulations are difficult to enforce. A globally accessible stablecoin could be procured online in any country, and local authorities may find it problematic to locate the stablecoin provider and enforce overseas entity compliance with local regulations. Hence, to the extent that a global stablecoin is decentralized and global, stablecoin regulations transcending borders would require a mutually agreed upon cross-border cooperative regulatory regime. Nations would have to agree on the specific provisions and then cooperate to monitor, share information, and enforce compliance or else financial entities would seek opportunities for cross-border regulatory arbitrage.[11]

In a sign of what is to come, the G20 Financial Stability Board report offered ten "high-level" regulatory recommendations, primarily to delineate scope of regulation, keep consistent with existing regulations, develop new approaches to facilitate cross-border regulation, and match regulatory sweep to the specific regulatory needs of emerging GSCs.[12] In the future, regulatory criteria could include preserving stability, ensuring liquidity, preventing runs, reducing costs and friction of cross-border transactions, protecting consumer assets and their privacy, guarding against illegal activities and fraud, enhancing cybersecurity to prevent hacking, encouraging user-friendly interfaces, and allowing pilot testing. There would need to be different regulations for wholesale and retail stablecoins, and governments would need to balance domestic and multilateral regulation while not stifling innovation. A US report on stablecoins pointed to market integrity risks, need for investor protection, controlling use in illicit finance, systemic risk, and market concentration as reasons to regulate stablecoins, asking for Congressional legislation, requiring depositary insurance for stablecoin issuers and building on work by international forums such as the Financial Stability Oversight Council.[13]

Private Stablecoins from Financial Incumbents: JPM Coin

Given the growing impact of stablecoins on banks, on the level of their banking deposits, and on the overall customer relationship, banks have responded by creating stablecoins of their own. JPM Coin, created in 2019, is one such pilot project. Maintaining a stable value equal to $1, it is intended to facilitate transfers between JPM institutional clients. Client funds in specified accounts are converted into JPM Coins, which are transferred to the named recipient and are then converted instantly to US dollars. JPM Coin can help in settling bonds and commodities transactions since instantaneous settlement can permit instant delivery. JPM notes that the technology is "currency agnostic" and could be used to transfer other currencies. It is also intended to be compliant with existing regulations while "reducing clients' counterparty and settlement risk, decreasing capital requirements and enabling instant value transfer."[14] The collateral for JPM Coins is the US dollar, held by JPMorgan in a 1:1 ratio. The underlying assumption is that JPMorgan can adequately hold US dollar reserves, backing its JPM Coin unencumbered. And because JPMorgan is regulated as a systemically important financial institution, JPM Coin can command high trust.

The blockchain underlying JPM Coin is JPMorgan's proprietary Quorum variant of the Ethereum blockchain. It is permissioned and access is restricted to JPMorgan global institutional clients. Client identities are verified with KYC protocols, and the blockchain can mask the identity of the sender as well as the amount of money being transferred.

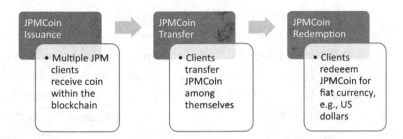

Figure 3.2
JPM Coin's issuance, transfer, and usage process

JPMorgan's technical expertise in blockchain provides assurance of high levels of cybersecurity and AML compliance. Quorum, which allows transfer of value, is complemented by JPMorgan's Interbank Information Network, another blockchain intended to transfer information between correspondent banks. JPM Coin is a competitive entry in the world of private stablecoins and cryptocurrencies.[15] Figure 3.2 illustrates the JPM Coin issuance, transfer, and usage process.

Other major, systemically important banks have developed their own strategic responses to the expanding digital currency field. Among them is the group of banks working in a consortium with Fnality.[16] They are aiming to create and share a blockchain financial market infrastructure, Fnality Global Payment, which could offer payment and instantaneous settlement within their wholesale banking market for several currencies, including the US dollar, the Canadian dollar, the British pound, the yen, and the euro. Making it easier for banks to settle financial transactions with one another despite being in different currency areas permits their business clients to opt out of having bank accounts in multiple countries.

JPMorgan and the Fnality Consortium are two of a multitude of competitors that range from banks to private cryptocurrency start-ups, all jostling to create digital currencies embedded in viable blockchain payments systems. The breadth and intensity of the competition indicate that digital currencies will take on increasing importance within the financial system in the near future.

Facebook's Diem Project (Formerly Known as Libra)

The world of cryptocurrencies and stablecoins expanded again when Facebook introduced Libra, a stablecoin linked to a basket of stable currencies, including the US dollar. In its original form as introduced in 2019, Libra's value would also be linked to the value of a basket of multiple currencies.[17] The Libra blockchain would assure transaction and data storage security, validate transactions using consensus algorithms, and seek to eventually become a permissionless network. Libra's salience would depend on several factors, including whether or not customers could earn interest on their Libra deposits and the level of risk inherent in having uninsured holdings.

Libra also intended to foster a decentralized SSI for each user, reducing their dependence on third parties to verify their credentials. Its goal was to provide such identity to the unbanked across the world's emerging markets, thus advancing financial inclusion—not that Facebook and Libra were the sole entities seeking to create such SSI mechanisms. If the digital identity's reach were limited to within the Libra network, it could further tie individuals to the network, promoting network effects and increasing switching costs for users.

A letter from the US House Committee on Financial Services to Facebook founder and CEO Mark Zuckerberg noted that Libra could become systemically important but would operate as an unregulated "shadow bank" and a parallel financial system.[18] From its initial announcement, Libra triggered alarm from governments and competing cryptocurrencies alike. It received considerable pushback from governments and monetary institutions including the US government, the EU, the Bank of England, and the Bank for International Settlements. (Since many of the critical studies and reports refer to Libra, for continuity, I retain both the Libra name and the subsequent name change to Diem in its newer iteration.)

Given Facebook's large member base—over two billion—an immediate concern was the company's domination of payments, which would offer it, a for-profit shareholder-owned company, significant influence over monetary policy, particularly over the monetary policies of smaller nations and emerging markets. Although Facebook created the independent nonprofit Libra Association to manage the open-source Libra blockchain and the Libra currency, this did not allay fears. And although Facebook is "one member among many," members were handpicked by Facebook to be sure.[19] An oligopoly like Facebook's would restrict the range of digital currencies tradable on the network and favor Libra; banks would lose customers to the Libra network. Governments would prefer to have multiple private stablecoins operating on a payment rail whose core layer is controlled by the government, a topic explored further in the following section on CBDCs.

Libra's potential puts governmental control over money supply and monetary policy at risk. It could jeopardize confidence in monetary systems when security breakdowns occur, whether that failure stems from hacked digital wallets, Libra value instability, private sector locus of ownership and control of data from financial flows, loss of privacy of personal financial transactions, fears about unequal competitor access to the Libra payments network, and lack of interoperability between the various emergent private stablecoin networks. There were also concerns over the use of cryptocurrencies for illegal activities, such as money laundering and terrorism financing. These concerns had already led the United States to require US cryptocurrency trading exchanges to follow KYC and AML provisions, which help US authorities identify individuals and entities carrying out nefarious cryptocurrency activities. Central banks were concerned that such objectives could be compromised by Libra.

The opposition to Libra led several Libra Association members to exit, including some of the largest payments companies such as Visa, Mastercard, PayPal, and eBay.[20] In response, Facebook introduced Libra 2.0 in April 2020, later renamed Diem, with significant modifications. In this iteration, Facebook offered single-currency stablecoins (in addition to the multiple currency reserve basket approach), introduced measures to comply with US and international AML, KYC, and Combating the Financing of Terrorism (CFT) regulations, dropped the goal of an eventual permissionless network, and augmented the robustness of reserves by underpinning Libra stablecoin value with a 1:1 reserve (i.e., a stablecoin associated with the US dollar would hold equivalent of dollars and dollar-denominated securities).

The social network would also hold "assets with very short-term maturity, low credit risk, and high liquidity" and "maintain a capital buffer,"[21] and suggested that when a central bank develops a CBDC, Libra "could replace the applicable single-currency stablecoin with the CBDC." Libra would also accept oversight of the basket composition by regulators, central banks, and organizations such as the International Monetary Fund. In addition, it would consider implementing redemption stays and early redemption haircuts as measures to deal with stress scenarios such as a run on Libra reserves. With these changes, Libra hoped to obtain approval from sovereign nation-states and become a key player in the global cross-border payments environment. However, continued government questioning eventually led Facebook to announce the discontinuance of their Libra effort.[22]

CBDCs

Governments want to be able to monitor and prevent systemic risk in their financial systems. As such, they aim to preserve domestic autonomy over their currency and maintain control over the money supply, interest rates, and changes to monetary policy through central bank actions. The rise of private stablecoins have led central banks to consider the launch of their own CBDCs, such as digital US dollars or Chinese yuan. CBDCs are a government attempt to control private stablecoin growth and configuration, possibly replacing cash while retaining the primacy of government-controlled and issued monies. CBDCs could have secondary objectives such as greater government visibility into economic transactions and activities of individuals and firms.

While not CBDCs, the US Federal Reserve and the European Central Bank have already launched payment systems that attempt to recreate a key and desirable feature of a digital currency: instant payment settlement. The US Federal Reserve introduced FedNow, a new interbank real-time gross settlement (RTGS) service that allows customers to send and receive payments "any time, any day, anywhere, and have full access to those funds within seconds,"[23] with pilots launched in 2020. Europe and the European Central Bank have a similar fast payment system, TIPS (Target Instant Payment Settlement). Neither of these require blockchain and are alternatives to a CBDC regime. CBDCs, if and when available, could offer similar instant payment settlement, significantly increasing liquidity while decreasing the amount of working capital allocated by enterprises. Access to the RTGS system is restricted to a few large banks, and such banks must maintain deposits to cover risks of default during the settlement process, thus increasing their working capital investment.

CBDC Features

Central banks, as CBDC operators, would be "responsible for many of the following steps: performing customer due diligence, offering or vetting wallets, developing or selecting the underlying technology, offering a settlement platform, managing customer data, monitoring transactions, and interacting with customer requests, complaints, and questions."[24] A CBDC would function as a stable store of value similar to cash, focusing on safety and trust, but could reduce functionality, allowing banks and other nonfinancial institutions to add functionality to a CBDC instead. Banks could offer additional services through APIs— such as enabling the earmarking funds for specific purposes, for example, ensuring that government transfer payments are used for intended purposes such as rent or childcare-related expenses. This would help CBDC creators to differentiate themselves from private stablecoins, "facilitating the unbundling of its payments processing function from that of credit creation and risk analysis."[25] In effect, this would increase CBDC robustness and reduce its vulnerability to security attacks.

CBDC accounts at the Fed could make direct and immediate transfer payments such as one-time unemployment subsidies granted during the COVID-19 pandemic to recipients, and these accounts could also earn interest. While creating CBDC would incur high fixed costs and be more suitable for major economies with stable currencies, once created, operating costs would be low—lower than those associated with operating a cash-based regime, with expenses associated with printing money with anti-counterfeiting features, storage, and distribution. Costs would drop lower still if CBDC were implemented in a tiered system, with banks offering and managing CBDC accounts for their customers while maintaining central bank reserves since they already have retail clients and vast experience with being user-friendly when catering to retail customers. In comparison, governments are not emulated for customer friendliness.

CBDC availability, with their lower risk and greater trust, would make private stablecoins less attractive as a replacement for fiat currency. In turn, central banks could earn seigniorage (the surplus a government earns when it issues currency, being the difference between the currency's value and its production costs) by issuing CBDCs. In addition, central banks could offset any interest offered on CBDC deposits[26] through reduced operational costs relative to cash and by substituting for financial assets such as money market funds (though this would be less important as interest rates near zero[27]). CBDC deposits that earn interest would become an alternative to money market funds, which are used to hold and earn interest on temporary cash surpluses.

From the consumer perspective, governments of major developed nations, as sponsors of CBDCs, may be seen as more trustworthy than for-profit private entities in managing a nation's currency and money supply, thus reducing systemic risk. Compared to private stablecoins from for-profit entities, using CBDCs could be nearly costless since customers can avoid intermediary fees. CBDC use would reduce costs and increase efficiency of asset exchanges by introducing tokenization of stocks and bonds. Simultaneous, almost-instantaneous sale, and settlement of equities and financial instruments would also be possible, making back-office clearing and settlement unnecessary. Another useful feature of CBDCs (as well as stablecoins and cryptocurrencies linked to smart contracts in a blockchain) is the ability to have money perform specific functions, for example, deduct and send variable percentages of sales tax directly to a treasury on a given purchase.[28] Such features would need to accommodate privacy protection, with the Digital Monetary Institute (DMI) suggesting privacy by design, to obtain political and legislative support and consumer acceptance. The DMI also emphasizes the ability to work offline, handling peer-to-peer transfers.[29]

In creating CBDCs, governments can choose between creating wholesale markets only or both wholesale and retail CBDCs. If wholesale only, the central bank could restrict CBDCs to banks and selected financial institutions. In this arrangement, central banks could authorize narrow banks (those that only take deposits and do not make loans) to offer and facilitate CBDC transfers to their retail clients. The Federal Reserve recommended such as intermediated approach, noting that US legislation does not authorize direct Federal Reserve accounts for individuals and would significantly expand the Federal Reserve's role in the US economy.[30] There is political opposition to such an expanded Federal Reserve; for example, Congressman Tom Emmer introduced a bill to preempt the Federal Reserve from issuing CBDC directly to individuals.[31] In this wholesale case, the national CBDC controls the payment infrastructure while commercial banks and financial entities provide customer-facing services. Thus, a broader range of institutions can manage and distribute government-backed CBDCs. Such an approach can preserve contestability and prevent the rise of oligopolies. If CBDCs were marketed directly to the public, the government would be the sole source of stablecoin for the financial system. In a retail CBDC scenario, CBDCs would be available through individual digital wallets. In the case of the United States, users might need to maintain individual accounts with the Federal Reserve, which would require the Federal Reserve to manage and operate millions of individual accounts, a customer service task that may overtax its capabilities.[32]

CBDCs, if exchangeable across borders, can have a favorable impact on cross-border payments, making them faster and cheaper. As in the domestic market, the CBDC issuer would need a complementary network of local entities to convert and facilitate local currency redemption. To thrive, the cross-border aspects of CBDC design would need to focus on functionality, reducing risk, and providing advantage over private decentralized cryptocurrencies. However, CBDCs could have a negative impact on commercial banks. If individuals are allowed to have accounts with central banks, they might reduce funds on deposit with commercial banks, lowering the bank's ability to make loans to small business, affecting their growth. Commercial banks might have to lower fees and offer better interest rates for depositors to compete, ultimately reducing their profitability.

Synthetic CBDCs

Given that a CBDC could negatively affect banks and their role as financial intermediaries,[33] an alternative might be synthetic CBDCs (sCBDCs).[34] An sCBDC is a public–private partnership wherein stablecoin providers are backed with and have access to central bank reserves. They are required to meet predetermined equity levels and function as narrow banks without lending functions, thereby fitting into existing bank regulatory frameworks. An sCBDC would make central bank reserves available to digital currency providers while all other functions would be carried out by these digital currency providers. Governments could also regulate private stablecoin issuers as they currently regulate banks to protect consumers and the public interest (e.g., enforce AML, KYC, CFT) and maintain control over monetary policy.

Synthetic CBDCs would not increase or decrease the total amount of CBDC in circulation, thus avoiding the risks of new forms of private money creation while allowing the separation of the payments platform on which CBDC functions from the reserve settlement system used in support of bank lending. Synthetic CBDCs address the "design (of) a central bank–issued monetary instrument that can flow across different payments platforms, while preserving the independence and integrity of the reserve settlement system for those engaged in the subjective and risky process of bank lending."[35] Regulations underlying sCBDC could require open standards and interoperability across different stablecoins (with central bank reserves transferred from one stablecoin account to another) as opposed to requiring consumers to seek cryptocurrency exchanges to exchange one digital currency for another. An sCBDC backed by a sovereign nation, by full faith and credit of the state, would also be seen as less risky because access to central bank reserves would reduce liquidity and market and default risk. Further, paying interest on sCBDC reserves could also extend monetary policy to such digital currencies.

Thus, CBDC can take on three configurations. A retail CBDC, in which the central bank offers accounts and issues CBDC to all users, including individuals, firms, and other organizations, possibly encompassing millions of users. A second wholesale model issues CBDC to a limited number of banks and nonbank organizations, which are regulated and hold reserves with the central bank in proportion to their CBDC issuance and transaction volumes. The third model, the synthetic sCBDC, allows multiple private, competing stablecoin issuers to issue their own stablecoins, and prospect for users, but requires all stablecoin providers to hold reserves with the central bank and follow regulations such as KYC and AML compliance. Figure 3.3 outlines these three alternative CBDC models.

Since sCBDCs require access to central bank reserves, governments could limit such access to domestic stablecoins, depriving global oligopolies such as Diem (Libra) of sCBDC privileges in that country. This could create greater contestability in the domestic market, at a cost. If regulations underlying granting sCBDC status endow such status only to domestic providers, they may be unable to compete in cross-border digital transactions, reducing the value of the digital currency as a payment mechanism.

Issues in Implementing CBDCs

If CBDCs are successfully launched, and in timely fashion, their national government imprimatur will significantly influence corporate and consumer acceptance of digital currencies and accelerate their use. Firms and consumers will expect that CBDCs or their retail equivalent to be widely accepted in financial transactions, requiring that enterprises

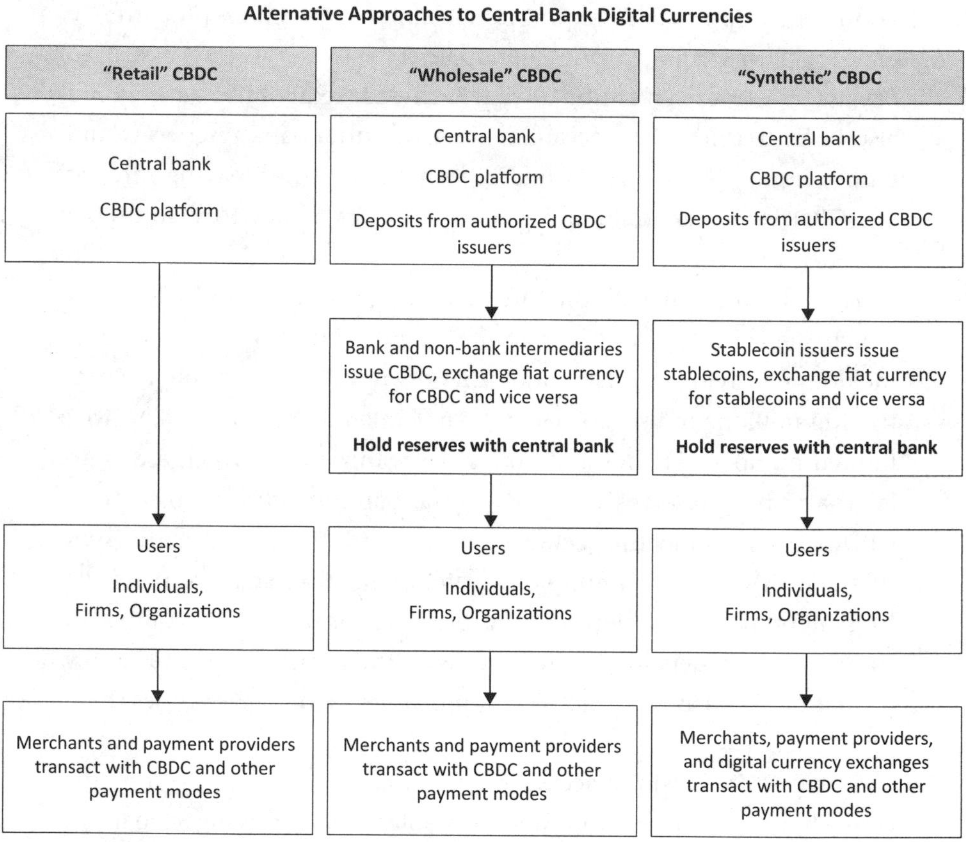

Alternative Approaches to Central Bank Digital Currencies

"Retail" CBDC	"Wholesale" CBDC	"Synthetic" CBDC
Central bank CBDC platform	Central bank CBDC platform Deposits from authorized CBDC issuers	Central bank CBDC platform Deposits from authorized CBDC issuers
	Bank and non-bank intermediaries issue CBDC, exchange fiat currency for CBDC and vice versa **Hold reserves with central bank**	Stablecoin issuers issue stablecoins, exchange fiat currency for stablecoins and vice versa **Hold reserves with central bank**
Users Individuals, Firms, Organizations	Users Individuals, Firms, Organizations	Users Individuals, Firms, Organizations
Merchants and payment providers transact with CBDC and other payment modes	Merchants and payment providers transact with CBDC and other payment modes	Merchants, payment providers, and digital currency exchanges transact with CBDC and other payment modes

Figure 3.3
Alternative approaches to CBDCs

begin preparing for this eventuality. As part of such preparation, enterprises will benefit from understanding issues affecting the launch and use of CBDCs in financial transactions and payments. Aside from providing customer service, there are several implementation issues related to launching a CBDC.

Security: Protecting the CBDC against hackers is paramount as any CBDC will be attacked constantly from the moment it goes live. Therefore, the CBDC needs to be resilient against attackers. Bitcoin and Ethereum provide examples for developing secure networks, using decentralized nodes and PoW-based validation approaches.

Safety: Customers may also want safety assurances, akin to depositor insurance. Consumers and businesses will need to be insulated from the liquidity and solvency risks of digital currencies. This raises the question of whether CBDCs will need deposit insurance if they are federally issued and managed.

Privacy: Because digital currency provides the ability to track every financial transaction, consumers may have privacy concerns. CBDC designs that offer the same or similar bearer instrument anonymity as cash would be better received, but this conflicts with the need to protect against illegal use, that is, money laundering. CBDCs also must contend with existing regulations, such as Europe's GDPR privacy framework. Individual transaction and aggregate data could be stored in a decentralized fashion, and for limited periods, to alleviate privacy concerns.

Customer relationships: As noted earlier, a central bank such as the US Federal Reserve would need to get involved in the payment chain of the entire economy, operate, and maintain a single global network. This means the Fed would need expertise in technology choices, customer interaction, app development, and brand management—areas in which they have limited capabilities, especially compared to private firms such as Facebook. For example, customers may want to link payments to social media so that users can broadcast their financial transaction across their social media network and allow friends to "like" and comment on their spending and purchasing patterns (as one can with Venmo). Compared to private for-profit entities, would government agencies such as the Federal Reserve be capable of managing a consumer payment app for millions of customers?

Innovation: Continuous innovation from the likes of AliPay, PayPal, and Paytm suggests that introducing basic CBDCs and fiat cryptocurrencies (with deliberately limited functionality) would foster innovation, with private sector firms competing to add APIs to increase functionality. And if CBDCs coexist with private stablecoins, interoperability with private stablecoins would be necessary to offer a smoothly functioning payments system.

Regulation: As noted earlier, preventing illegal transactions with digital currencies is a major concern. In response, the US government has already extended its "travel rule"[36] requirement to digital currency transactions above certain amounts. Information about both the sender and the receiver of a digital currency transfer must be made available to monitor possible money laundering, terrorism financing, and other illegal usage. A centralized global registry of virtual asset service providers (VASP), with each VASP having an identifier akin to IBAN or BIC (in SWIFT) along with a standardized interoperable message layer pinning the required information to the blockchain transaction, would be one way to comply with the US requirement. One such solution is OpenVASP[37] from Switzerland, which uses Ethereum's Whisper off-chain messaging system. Whisper obscures the identity of the two interacting VASPs as well as the message contents from outside observers. Unless such regulations are commonly implemented across countries, some customers will seek countries where regulations are less onerous (as perceived by the entity issuing the stablecoin) and where implementation and enforcement are weak.

Financial inclusion: Wide access to smartphones could allow more unbanked individuals to have access to a CBDC, leapfrogging legacy banking systems. However, CBDCs would also have to avoid marginalizing people who use cash, though this is likely to be a temporary problem as the convenience and ease of use should help migrate recalcitrant cash users to a digital payment world. Promoting inclusion would also need to overcome barriers such as access to a reliable internet connection, affordability constraints limiting device ownership, and lack of reliable access to energy for charging devices.

CBDC Pilots

In this emerging world of digital currency, central banks have stressed collaboration, cooperating with other central banks to study the consequences of implementing a CBDC. Several central banks jointly announced their intent to share experiences in developing and implementing a CBDC pilot—the Bank of England, Riksbank, Bank of Canada,

Bank of Japan, ECB, Swiss National Bank, and the Bank of International Settlements.[38] Riksbank, the Swedish central bank, began a year-long pilot with Accenture to test how a digital krona, the e-krona, could be stored by the general public in a digital wallet and used to make deposits, withdrawals, and payments using multiple devices including wearables, smartwatches, and cash cards. The pilot is considering ease of use, simplicity, security, and performance in assessing the value of moving to an e-krona.[39] In another collaboration, the Monetary Authority of Singapore (MAS) launched Project Ubin;[40] it will collaborate with the Bank of England and the Bank of Canada to pilot cross-border currency payments, simultaneously using different national digital currencies and linking to private stablecoin networks, in several phases. This pilot seeks RTGS-using blockchain protocols such as Hyperledger Fabric and Quorum, deployed on Microsoft's Azure cloud.

China has also been developing plans to launch a digital yuan, no doubt motivated by the ascendance of mobile money payments in that country. Mobile money payments accounted for nearly 80 percent of all payments and totaled $49 trillion in 2019.[41] China is also eager to escape the hegemony of the US dollar as a global reserve currency. President Xi announced in October 2019 that "China must seize the opportunity of blockchain."[42] The Chinese office of State Cryptographic Administration has spearheaded a new cryptography law, effective in January 2020, that sets out rules for governing a digital yuan, giving control to the People's Bank of China. This in effect reduces the importance of Alipay and WeChat, which currently dominate payments in China.

If Chinese consumers wanted to switch to cash in a crisis, the availability of a Chinese CBDC would let individuals store digital yuan in central bank–authorized wallets. *The Economist* suggests that this digital yuan would be the "anti-bitcoin," as a state-controlled digital currency would give China complete surveillance of all payment flows in the economy and, in turn, even greater power to prevent money laundering and tax evasion. A programmable digital yuan would also allow the Chinese government to ensure, for example, that stimuli aimed at providing loans to small businesses were indeed disbursed along these guidelines. This might reduce Chinese privacy, though perhaps that is a lesser priority, considering the generalized governmental control of citizens' activities through social credits and censorship of the Chinese internet. Mobile app trials of the digital yuan were conducted in April 2020. In January 2022, China made its digital yuan available to Chinese citizens, with 260 million domestic downloads to access the Chinese digital currency by the end of the month, with about $15 billion transacted that month using China's new digital currency.[43] China's introduction represents the largest launch of a CBDC at a national scale and is a harbinger of significant changes to the global monetary system.

Policy Implications of Digital Currency

What is the future of money and how will it affect firms? Cash is a mutually agreed upon store of value and an anonymous means of payment, with no further exchange of information necessary to complete a transaction. Money created by banks, such as checks (based on bank deposits and thus a claim on a store of value) and loans issued by banks to firms (through fractional banking, with loan volume based on deposits, bank equity, and their access to federal reserves in the overnight markets, aka, their ability to borrow) are traditional means of payment. Bank money claims depend on verified ownership of and sufficiency of funds backing the claim. Transfers satisfying the claim that affect bank balances are recorded by the relevant parties (to prevent double-spend). Verifying claims also slows down payment, which is one of several ways in which newer stablecoins and blockchain-based cryptocurrencies such as Bitcoin have an edge over cash and bank monies.

Stablecoins provide consumer benefits such as ease of use, convenience, instantaneous payment and settlement, and ubiquitous mobile availability, all at low costs. Cross-border acceptability further advantages stablecoins, enhancing their attractiveness as a means of payment and substitute for cash, bank accounts, credit cards, and mobile wallets linked to verified claims such as bank accounts. Safety concerns and limited trust in stablecoin issuers are negatives, but as I have discussed,

CBDCs can become an acceptable stablecoin alternative to traditional money by offering safety and trust in addition to other stablecoin features. CBDC availability would reduce the attractiveness of private digital currencies since the CBDC would be seen as safer; hence, it would allow governments to better control the total digital currency in circulation. Taken together, it is easy to see how stablecoins, cryptocurrencies, and CBDCs could displace cash and bank monies.

Broader use of digital currencies, whether cryptocurrencies, private stablecoins, or official CBDCs, would affect the entire global economy, influencing payments and the financial system, the competitive structure of the financial industry, money supply, and monetary policy, all of which would culminate in systemic financial effects. These impacts would then also affect enterprises, consumers, and individuals across society. Central banks and government authorities must consider the policy implications as they consider creating CBDCs, partnering with banks and other nonfinancial institutions in a tiered digital currency system and promulgating new digital currency regulations.

The policy ramifications include impacts on the financial system and systemic risk as the functions of money, both new and old, change, affecting payment infrastructure and cross-border payments. Such changes can increase systemic risk as private entities begin to have a greater influence on the financial system. As some of these newer financial entrants gain market power, they can affect financial stability and competitiveness in the financial sector. This in turn brings macroeconomic policy consequences, such as the impact on monetary policy transmission, monetary independence, and the relative importance of major currencies such as the US dollar and the euro in global finance. Such macroeconomic and cross-border changes will then affect enterprises, consumers, and society, impinging on privacy protection, promoting financial inclusion, and upholding financial integrity.

Impact on the Global Financial System and Systemic Risk
Government agencies such as the US Federal Reserve and the US Treasury, and their foreign counterparts, have a collective responsibility in

maintaining smooth ongoing operations and confidence in the global financial system. Digital currencies are a disruptive force that requires concerted collective action to prevent negative consequences from emerging.

Maintaining Financial Stability and Financial System Integrity The G20 Financial Stability Board notes that stablecoins can enhance efficiency but also pose risks to financial stability. The board highlights the potential volatility of stablecoins, the inadequacies in underlying exchange infrastructure, and possible stablecoin failure that could ultimately reduce confidence in financial institutions.[44] However, in the rare instances when there is a loss of confidence in private money and a panic, such as in the 2008 financial crisis or the 2020 rush to liquidity caused by a collapse of demand during the COVID-19 pandemic, a sovereign nation-backed CBDC becomes a sought-after refuge. A CBDC can help stabilize the financial system, insulating it from systemic risk. A run to safety in the form of CBDCs or bank deposits also helps lower systemic risk in general by creating a reduced reliance on private digital currencies as well as a lower likelihood of panicked attempts at a redemption of digital currencies.

Upholding financial system integrity by monitoring and preventing illegal activities is a high priority. The current payments system has such safeguards in place, and digital currencies would not receive official recognition and permission unless such compliance was in place. Digital currency issuers can prevent illegal activities if they ensure that their users comply with KYC, AML, and CFT principles. The US requires that cryptocurrency transactions above certain amounts comply with the "Travel Rule," which requires sender, receiver, and transaction amounts to be identified. Safeguarding cross-border digital currency transactions against money laundering, tax evasion, corruption, and terrorism financing would require consensus and cooperation across countries to harmonize financial integrity regulations.

Cash and bank deposits are backed by full faith and trust in governments and federal reserves (e.g., bank regulation, depositor insurance).

Such trust in the newer forms of money would depend on the support provided by the private entities issuing stablecoins (e.g., JPMorgan or Facebook) and on the decentralized (permissionless) entities governing a cryptocurrency blockchain (i.e., not asset backed, as stablecoins are). Regulations setting minimum reserve levels for stablecoin issuance and monitoring trading exchanges for such digital currencies can reduce their destabilizing potential.

Enhancing Cross-Border Payments   Cross-border payments are complex, with uncertainty over exchange rates used to finalize transactions, high fees, and lengthy transaction completion times. Governments have begun collaborating on pilot programs to investigate efficiency gains from using digital currencies. Such a move requires sovereign national governments to collaborate and accept the use of CBDCs in foreign exchange transactions, leading to hesitation due to the implied reduction in national economic sovereignty. For example, the growing use of another country's CBDC can lead to unintended changes to the money supply, affecting the ability to implement monetary policy. Experiments such as Project Jasper and Project Ubin, a collaboration between the Bank of Canada and the MAS, are attempts to have central banks take on a role as clearing agents, replacing networks of cross-border intermediary banks, and using CBDCs as a means of rapid low-cost exchange and settlement. These issues are discussed in further detail in chapter 5.

Preserving Financial Sector Competitiveness   Network effects suggest that over time, digital currency providers deemed most trustworthy would emerge and these few would dominate the payments landscape, forming oligopolies and making enterprises and individuals more dependent on these providers. In choosing specific stablecoins as the preferred means of payment, firms and individuals are deciding which stablecoin provider to trust. Users would prefer to choose from several competing stablecoin providers, as alternative payment rails, rather than become dependent on a monopoly or oligopoly. An oligopoly would reduce enterprise choices as well as their bargaining ability to negotiate terms on issues such as preserving their primacy in customer relationships, controlling customer data, and charging fees associated with a specific payment choice. Such network effects may have motivated the launch of Libra, with Facebook hoping to dominate the world of digital currencies in the same way that it and its apps have dominated social media and messaging. Such a monopoly could give the stablecoin provider broad insights into customer behavior and enable an extension of their monopoly into adjacent markets, for example, credit ratings and offering debt financing.

It is in the context of preserving competitiveness and preventing payments oligopolies that CBDCs can play an essential role. They can provide narrow payments functionality, offer a payments platform, and adopt a tiered structure,[45] partnering with banks and nonbank financial institutions, as "distributors" of CBDCs, and interfacing with retail accounts for businesses and individuals.

Macroeconomic Policy Consequences

As digital currencies become more widely accepted as a form of money, they have implications for monetary policy transmission and a nation's monetary sovereignty. They also cast a geopolitical shadow—affecting the role of major fiat currencies as global reserve currencies (e.g., will the US dollar continue to enjoy global prominence?), leading to regionally dominant islands of fiat digital currencies.

Monetary Policy Transmission One concern is that digital currency (especially private stablecoins) could prejudice governmental control over money supply and its ability to conduct monetary policy. If governments implement CBDCs and choose to offer interest on CBDC accounts, varying this interest rate would make it easier to transmit monetary policy.[46] This is because CBDCs would be a substitute for money market instruments, and banks would need to match CBDC interest rates to prevent customers from switching out of their bank deposits for CBDCs. Interest-bearing CBDCs would make negative interest rates possible (assuming that the option to switch into cash to avoid negative interest for CBDC account holders is circumscribed). That is, cash would be replaced with digital currencies, in particular, CBDCs, and as digital currencies are programmable and can have conditions attached to them, CBDC issuers wishing to use negative rates could attach a smart contract to a CBDC deposit, charging a fee to hold the deposit and returning an amount smaller than the initially deposited principal, effectively charging a negative interest rate. Furthermore, any CBDC impact on reducing reserves in the system could be offset with open market operations to inject liquidity, leading the Bank of International Settlements to suggest that the "presence of CBDC would have limited impact on monetary policy implementation."[47]

However, CBDCs could lead to some level of bank disintermediation if banks lose deposits to CBDCs and to private stablecoins. Customers might move their bank deposits to a CBDC account or tokens to have access to digital currency to use in their online transactions. They may prefer the relative greater safety of a CBDC account, particularly if it is interest bearing. If this disintermediation occurs, enterprises will have a harder time borrowing from banks whose supply of loanable funds from bank deposits would be reduced. Banks might have to offer higher interest rates to retain deposits, driving up lending rates. There would be a differential impact on smaller borrowers, who are more reliant on bank lending and are generally unable to float bonds. Consequently, borrowers might seek new relationships with digital money providers with access to loanable funds. They may resort to borrowing from the shadow banking sector and P2P borrowing channels through stablecoin providers. However, such digital currency entities may charge higher rates as it may be costlier for them to assess credit and price risk. Overall, there may be fewer sources for small businesses to borrow from, driving up borrowing costs.

Thus, introducing CBDCs, through impact on the banking sector, could affect monetary policy, as interest rates may diverge from the desired target rates, requiring further intervention. As Jack Meaning and his coauthors suggest,[48] "it is difficult to draw definitive or quantitatively-robust conclusions about the impact of CBDCs on the monetary transmission mechanism" as it would depend on the design of the particular CBDC in question, the economic environment into which it is introduced, and the structural changes that might follow, such as possible bank disintermediation.

Monetary Independence Globally transacted stablecoins would enable citizens of countries with weak currencies and volatile economies to switch to global stablecoins. While improving individual welfare, this transition could negate the ability of their home countries to exercise monetary policy, forcing leaders to peg their weak currency to a stronger one. Thus, stablecoins could reduce monetary sovereignty and increase currency substitution in countries with weak currencies, high inflation, poor governance, endemic corruption, and limited enforcement of rule of law. In times of stress, significant volumes of domestic currency that has been converted into global stablecoins could lead to significant capital outflows, negatively affecting exchange rates and the domestic financial sector. Such cross-border impact on national economic sovereignty will increase national resistance to accept a switch to wider use of digital currencies. However, such disruption might be inevitable and may enhance consumers' welfare in the long run as they are less exposed to currency volatility in less well-governed economies.

Geopolitical Consequences: Role of the US Dollar The successful launch of a foreign digital currency would also have geopolitical implications. The US dollar functions as the world's reserve currency, with much of the world's trade and cross-border debt denominated in US dollars. A CBDC with cross-border acceptance from a strong stable economy would impact the role of the US dollar, affecting its strength and the US's ability to impose sanctions and to borrow from the world at reduced rates.

China and Russia are two countries that would prefer a diminished role for the United States in the world's financial structure and are keen to reduce the US dollar's role as the world's reserve currency.[49] China would favor the yuan as a replacement for the US dollar in trade and borrowing, particularly in nations for whom China is a major trading partner and source of lending. The Chinese government bond market has been stable and offers a significant premium over US government securities (around 1.9 percent premium in April 2020), increasing demand for Chinese yuan.[50] Given Chinese proficiency with digital payments through Alipay and WeChatpay mobile wallets, and learning acquired from Chinese pilot programs, the launch of a Chinese CBDC (e-CNY) in January 2022 via Android and Apple apps is unsurprising. The e-CNY is issued by the People's Bank of China and is disseminated through six large state-owned banks and the internet banks WeBank and MYBank, who can open e-CNY digital wallets for users, conduct KYC diligence, and invest in infrastructure for e-CNY use. Users can obscure their identity from counterparties, but law enforcement could obtain access to investigate illegal transactions.[51] However, limited Chinese government interest in protecting individual privacy might limit a digital yuan's viability in cross-border transactions and its impact as a first mover.[52]

There are reasons to oppose the creation of a US national digital currency: concerns about loss of privacy, US government bureaucratic inefficiency in providing customer service, and the negative impact on commercial banks. Private sector innovation (e.g., PayPal, Venmo, Tether) is currently available to address consumer desires for digital payments. Finally, there is the belief that "the dollar will reign so long as the Fed keeps the dollar inflation rate low."[53] The Federal Reserve notes that a potential US CBDC should be "privacy-protected, intermediated, widely transferable, and identity-verified," but does not take a position on the ultimate desirability of a US CBDC.[54] The Fed emphasized that to proceed with a CBDC, Congress would need to pass a law and the executive branch would have to provide support as well. A key point is that the Fed backs an intermediated mode of a US CBDC, with the private sector interacting with users to offer digital wallets and manage CBDC holding and payments.

Without coordinated development across major economies, the launch of multiple CBDCs could lead to islands of digital currencies, with incompatible regulations and a lack of interoperability. This would negatively impact cross-border payments, trade, and exchange of digital fiat currencies, increasing friction in global payments and trade, in which case allowing private stablecoins to flourish might be the preferred alternative to promoting CBDC development for use across borders.

Impact on Enterprises

The growing popularity of digital money has strategic implications for enterprises. Digital money affects enterprise control of their payments, from the cost and efficiency of payments systems to the depth and quality of their customer interactions. Control of customer and payment data, enterprise liquidity and working capital, and the extent of dependence on payments intermediaries could also be affected. How might a move to adopt digital currencies affect corporations? How should they react?

Impact on Liquidity and Working Capital   To the extent that stablecoins and cryptocurrencies coexist with CBDCs, firms must decide whether to accept and conduct transactions in these newer forms of money while also accepting traditional payment forms such as credit cards, stored value, and intermediary solutions such as PayPal and Venmo and point-of-sale applications such as Square. Near-instantaneous settlement of receivables due (as well as instantaneous payment on their payables) would be attractive to customers and suppliers, reducing overall working capital needs and the amount needed to be invested in their business.

Moving to digital currencies will affect working capital since instantaneous settlement will affect float in both receivables and payables. Their access to loans, terms, and loan amounts will be affected by their current banking relationships and by the ties they build with emerging new financial institutions underlying digital currencies and their linked P2P loan networks. Access to an improved payment infrastructure with lower costs will be a benefit, while they may face new risks from instability in the value of digital currencies.[55] Their position in the payment ecosystem might affect their level of control over their customer relationships and their ability to control transaction security and to protect privacy. As firms develop financial relationships with stablecoin providers, they will also seek to balance such new relationships with existing banking relationships.

Controlling Cost and Efficiency of Payments Systems, Use of Payments Intermediaries As enterprises move to a digital currency environment, they may decide to be agnostic in accepting and transacting in multiple digital currencies, letting customers dictate their choices. Their clients' perception of the relative convenience of transacting with different forms of money will shape the balance that enterprises will develop between traditional money and its newer forms. In countries such as Kenya, M-Pesa has evolved to offering bank and savings accounts, advancing financial inclusion, and offering firms partnering with M-Pesa access to potential customers who may have been formerly out of reach. It is likely that as a response, banks would offer digital currencies from their networks, such as the JPM Coin.

Some constraints affecting enterprises include the costs of transacting in multiple digital currencies, the availability of seamless exchange between the several digital currencies, and safety and liquidity considerations that affect where and in which currencies enterprises hold their excess funds. Firms must take into account the costs of network operations and cryptographic security costs, offset by the rapid accessibility to funds due from instantaneous settlement. Enterprises could pass lower transaction costs and lower fees on cross-border payments on to consumers, reducing prices and aiding revenue growth. They could also increase their activity in cross-border trade to the extent that the digital currencies are designed as efficient payment vehicles for both domestic and international operations.

Enterprises may need to affiliate with multiple payments ecosystems and manage these network roles, choosing which payments alternatives to emphasize in their operations and what role to play in shaping and managing these emergent ecosystems. Network externalities will determine which stablecoins, whether private or CBDC, will dominate since individuals will be more likely to patronize digital money that is already extensively used by others as a means of payment. A CBDC may have an advantage over private stablecoins as the paper money that the government issues is widely used and trusted.[56] The payments choices individuals and consumers make can influence the enterprise's global reach in innovation, manufacturing, and customer fulfillment.

Protecting and Controlling Customer Interactions and Payment Data
Firms may lose some of the closeness of customer relationships as digital money providers gain access to money flows wherever their digital currency is used. If regulations governing a digital currency regime enhance contestability, enterprises could retain control by negotiating data access conditions and setting restrictions on currency provider visibility into their data as a condition for favoring one of several competing digital currencies. Enterprises may also want to work with and encourage industry and business associations to lobby for regulations restricting data access and protecting user privacy within digital currency networks.

Experimenting with Digital Currency Pilots   Given the accelerating interest in digital currencies, and the variety of impacts on firms, firms need to begin preparing for this disruption. One approach is to launch digital currency pilots that would allow the firm to assess the impact of digital currencies on their operations and performance. Assessing pilot results can help firms develop a strategy for adapting to a digital currency environment. As an immediate step, they should aim to learn about digital currency technology and benefits, scalability barriers, implementation issues, and assurance of customer satisfaction. Pilots can deliver proof of concept and key findings to support outcomes, such as revenue enhancement and working capital reduction from instant settlement and fast low-cost payment alternatives for customers.

Firms can gain experience with negotiated agreements and procedures with digital currency platforms and exchanges to protect and firewall proprietary consumer data, granting data access, sharing, and other data-related privileges while protecting customer privacy through opt-in permissions. They can assess their competitive advantage enhancement from granular customer transaction data available from digital currency platform usage. They can also better understand how to manage the proliferation of competing digital currency providers such as Tether, USDC, and Monerium (digital currencies linked to multiple national fiat currencies) and digital currency exchanges, such as Coinbase. They can also experiment with choosing between blockchain protocol partners with experience supporting digital currencies, such as Algorand or Consensys Quorum, to support digital currency options for customers. Selection criteria should include interoperability with digital currency protocols and platforms of B2C customers and supply chain partners.

In summary, digital currency usage offers many benefits for enterprises:

- Digital currencies allow for instant settlement and offer low-cost payment alternatives for customers, leading to revenue enhancement and working capital reduction possibilities.

- Due to network effects, firms accepting digital currencies could become dependent on dominant digital currency providers, enabling them to mediate customer interactions and capture valuable transaction data, thus attenuating their customer relationships. Firms might then consider working with their industry peers and regulators to wall off the payments function as a utility, reducing digital currency providers access to proprietary customer knowledge.

- Using digital currencies enhances access to global customers due to improved speed and transparency and reduced complexity and cost of cross-border payments.

- Digital currencies use could affect consumer privacy as regulations protecting financial integrity require firms to maintain customer transaction records and allow governmental access under specified conditions. Salient considerations to address include customer data storage, duration, location, and balancing regulatory compliance with preserving customer anonymity.

- Digital currencies require enterprises to enhance their technological readiness and human capital capabilities, ensure network robustness, support cryptographic encryption, and offer user-friendly digital currency applications as well as risk mitigation measures.

Revenue enhancement and impact on capital invested in the firm

- Instant settlement; fast, low-cost payment alternatives for customers, possibly reducing working capital needs
- Access to larger pool of formerly unbanked customers
- Reduced availability of bank loans due to bank disintermediation

Linking DC with smart contracts

- Allows earmarking funds for specific purposes, e.g., release of funds against specified invoice presentation and linked bill of lading clearance
- Helps reduce fraud and counterfeiting

Enhanced access to global customers

- Improved speed and transparency and reduced complexity and cost of cross-border payments

Upgraded technological readiness and human capital capabilities

- Ensure network robustness, cryptographic encryption, offer user-friendly DC applications, and comprehend technological risk with corresponding mitigation measures
- Higher costs of network operations and cryptographic security costs

Network effects

- Dependence on dominant DC providers, who could mediate customer interactions and capture valuable transaction data, attenuating the firm's customer relationships
- Work with industry associations and regulators to wall off the payments function as a utility, reducing DC providers, access to proprietary customer knowledge

Maintaining consumer privacy

- Regulations protecting financial integrity—know your customer and anti-money laundering provisions, require maintaining customer transaction records and allowing governmental access under specified conditions
- Ameliorate with decentralized customer data storage, reduced duration, restricted access location, and balancing regulatory compliance with preserving customer anonymity

Figure 3.4
Digital currency benefits for enterprises

These digital currency benefits for enterprises are summarized in figure 3.4.

Impact on Consumers and Society

The shift to digital currencies also affects consumers and society. Using digital currency can make economic transactions visible across the nodes in a blockchain. It may also shut out portions of the population who lack access to financial system infrastructures and devices.

Protecting Consumer Privacy and Security There is a general expectation of the privacy of economic transactions. While governmental tax and treasury authorities might require the disclosure of economic activity, the privacy of such information is preserved by limiting disclosure only to relevant parties. Individuals and corporations have a right to expect anonymity when using digital currencies, which are subject to governmental visibility to curb illegal transactions and maintain financial system integrity. Given the possible use of digital currencies in illegal transactions, for example, in demanding and collecting ransomware, balancing privacy while giving governmental authorities access to digital currency transactions to is a high priority. Digital currency could be designed to offer some anonymity using serial numbers for CBDC tokens. These serial numbers would be used in addition to the CBDC token, with the serial number offering anonymity even though the underlying digital currency is a CBDC. Serial numbers would need to be changed each time a CBDC is exchanged. Central banks could prevent double-spend through having a serial number lookup in a centralized registry (not on a blockchain) and perhaps restricting access to the serial number registry to only the issuing central government

A related matter is the potential loss of consumer privacy in payment transactions. Depending on the payment infrastructure design and regulatory financial integrity requirements, identities of parties to a transaction, the transaction amount, location, timestamp, and other related transaction information might be included along with the transaction itself. Such data removes privacy surrounding consumer transactions and can be used to monitor and analyze consumer behavior at a granular level. Enterprises can be proactive on behalf of their customers by limiting collection and access to such data, and consumer lobbies may also press for greater privacy as a condition of moving to digital currency payment infrastructure. Competing digital currency providers can also offer greater privacy as a means of differentiation and source of competitive advantage.

User friendliness, convenience, and ease of use will matter as consumers will be more likely to adapt digital currencies if it is well integrated with other services such as credit scoring and other payment apps such as Venmo. Equity considerations suggest that consumer protection rules should insulate digital currencies in widespread use from the impact of fluctuations in value. Such consumer protection should include processes for securing digital wallets and maintaining access to private keys. Regulations governing private stablecoins must ensure customer service provision from its providers and clear procedures for dispute resolution and asset recovery.

Advancing Financial Inclusion, Improving Access to Financial Infrastructure
An individual's access to digital currencies depends on their access to the internet, whether wired or wireless, and access to devices such as smartphones. Since internet connectivity and smartphone signals can be erratic, providing offline access until connectivity is restored would be an essential technological complement to any digital currency system. Innovations such as accessing stored value via Bluetooth, enabling P2P smartphone communication and transfer with PoS devices, and exchanging encrypted transaction information and balance updates are encouraging steps to overcome connectivity obstacles among the unbanked. Cheap, affordable smartphones are widely available across emerging markets, improving access to financial applications, with M-Pesa being a stellar example.[57] Women are a particular segment of interest, as 1 billion women are among the unbanked[58] (out of 1.7 billion unbanked in total, nearly one-quarter of the world's population).

A critical issue is whether the unbanked will have access to new payment forms such as stablecoins and CBDCs. Will financial inclusion improve or deteriorate? Private stablecoins, operated by entities that may have profit goals, are likely to value financial inclusion and develop apps and innovations to reach as many individuals as possible[59] and thus more of the unbanked, who represent significant market potential. And governments, as CBDC issuers, are also likely to offer access to as much of their citizenry as possible, facilitate transfer payments, lower payment and remittance costs for the poor, and move the informal sector into the formal economy.

Services such as M-Pesa have gradually augmented their services to motivate citizens to use them, adding savings accounts, insurance, and loans to the basic payment functionality. Newer competitors are likely to follow similar paths,[60] and governments can play a role by

Table 3.1 Policy implications of digital currency

Impact on the global financial system and systemic risk	Macroeconomic policy consequences
• Maintaining financial stability and financial system integrity • Preserving financial sector competitiveness • Enhancing cross-border payments	• Monetary policy transmission • Monetary independence • Geopolitical consequences: role of the US dollar in the world economy; islands of digital currencies
Impact on enterprises	**Impact on consumers and society**
• Controlling cost and efficiency of payments system, use of payments intermediaries • Protecting and controlling customer interactions and payment data • Affecting liquidity and working capital • Experimenting with digital currency pilots	• Protecting customer privacy and security • Advancing financial inclusion, improves access to financial infrastructure

developing regulations that include advancing financial inclusion (and metrics to measure progress) as a condition of licensing and access to banking networks. Digital currencies, by substituting for cash, would shelter the unbanked from vulnerability to theft of their cash while also offering interest on positive balances, augmented services, protection from fraud (through cryptographic requirements for transaction validation), and instant settlement—a particular boon for the constrained budgets of the poor. However, the loss of private digital keys is a negative as it would lock out owners from accessing their digital currencies. Given limited financial literacy among the unbanked, arrangements to retrieve lost private keys is essential, and innovations such as relying on circles of trust[61] to backstop the loss of a private key would be essential in advancing financial inclusion. The several policy issues that arise are summarized in table 3.1.

Conclusion

In summary, the rise of digital currencies, of stablecoins and CBDCs, rooted in blockchain technologies, has significant potential to change the payments world. These changes will affect the macroeconomy and the structure of the financial industry and will impact enterprises and individuals. Enterprises would benefit from understanding the implications of digital currencies for their operations and proactively taking steps to manage this transition. They must decide how to accommodate growing customer demands for digital payments operations, consider the consequences of adopting digital currency payment systems, and participate in the emerging digital currency ecosystem to maintain their competitive position relative to their customers and suppliers. I next consider, in chapter 4, the proliferating applications of digital currencies, and the challenge they pose to financial incumbents, in the emerging world of blockchain-based decentralized finance: DeFi. DeFi start-ups present a significant disruptive challenge to traditional financial services incumbents as its initiatives range across a variety of segments, from deposit and savings accounts to collateralized loans, financial derivatives, insurance services, and raising capital through bonds and equity offerings.

4 Decentralized Finance

Capital is an essential element of economic activity. Entrepreneurs must marshal risk capital from sources such as personal funds, angel investors, venture capitalists, institutional investors, and equity markets. Loan capital, with interest payable at fixed or varying rates, and secured to some extent with collateral, can flow to entrepreneurs from multiple sources too. Convincing sources of risk capital to invest in or lend to an entrepreneur's ventures is not always easy, and for investors with capital to deploy, finding and qualifying worthy recipients is challenging. At the heart of these difficulties is the matter of trust. Can investors trust entrepreneurs and borrowers to use their capital as agreed upon and to use it prudently? Will interest and principal repayment be fulfilled on the agreed upon terms? This trust gap brings about the need for intermediaries who can conduct due diligence on behalf of investors and lenders and bring such aggregated information to their clients for review and decision.

For both risk and loan capital, financial intermediaries bring investors and lenders together with entrepreneurs and firms seeking capital. Beyond providing access to sources of capital (in some cases, helping raise risk capital and credit) and facilitating lending and repayment, financial intermediaries can offer several other ancillary and related services. These complementary services include banking and custody, payments processing, remittances, savings accounts, exchanges for trading and settling financial assets and derivatives, investment advice and management, international trade financing, letters of credit (LCs), and personal finance. Financial intermediaries also serve evolving needs such as requests for insurance products, estate planning, and financial advising.

In addition to matching providers and customers, financial intermediaries manage counterparty risk by helping clients comply with regulations and detecting, preventing, and protecting against fraud. They can exercise control over assets (on behalf of customers), furnish customers with access to subsets of transaction data, and assume systemic risk. In essence, financial services incumbents offer a trusted means to reduce client risk in return for intermediary fees, which can amount to a significant portion of transaction amounts. Additional costs can include service fees, long lead times to finalize a transaction, limited transparency, a lack of user control over personal data, and unilaterally determined terms of service and pricing.

Several fintech mobile-first firms have emerged in recent years, aiming to provide these intermediary services at a lower cost by transacting via smartphone. Some of these fintech challengers include Revolut and N26 in Europe; Robinhood and SoFi in the United States; and Paytm, Ant Financial, AliPay, and WeChat Pay in Asia. Many of these firms have diversified to launch integrated service offerings, spreading into adjacent markets. These fintech firms are attempting to gain competitive advantage over incumbents with AI-linked software, user-friendly interfaces, smartphone access, cloud services, social media, and data analytics. In this context, blockchain offers an additional means of disrupting traditional financial intermediaries and their privileged position with clients.

What is Decentralized Finance?

Blockchain can provide many of the core requirements of financial services offerings, such as meeting the need for trust, providing fast and cheap liquidity, furnishing accurate immutable timely data, establishing provenance and thus auditability, and ensuring high security. It can do all this while also significantly reducing intermediary fees though disintermediation and enabling direct interaction between counter-parties. Blockchain makes possible decentralized P2P financial services and can lower the cost of developing, launching, and trading financial instruments. Not surprisingly, many emergent firms have used block-chain to offer financial services on a blockchain, emerging as competition for incumbents. Decentralized finance, or DeFi, describes this trend of leveraging technologies, blockchain among them, to disrupt the financial sector.

In addition to serving end users such as investors and banking customers, DeFi provides services for issuers, financial asset portfolio managers, and regulators.[1] Issuers can raise capital by issuing digital securities with embedded smart contracts that contain terms and conditions and incorporate required KYC and AML information updated in real time. Digital assets can be subdivided, increasing liquidity and small investor access to a greater variety of financial assets. DeFi can also help issuers by incorporating asset life cycle events including auto mated interest and principal payments. Portfolio managers can benefit by accessing decentralized exchanges (DEXs) and new classes of investments with smart contract-enabled programmable features. And regulators can benefit from the immutable and transparent nature of blockchain transactions, with automated audit and examination of compliance, freeing them for deeper analysis and risk prediction.

DeFi protocols tend to be open source, offering interoperability and a common software infrastructure to encourage use across several asset classes. They are designed with an eye toward wider use to encourage developers to build apps and provide new services built on top of the DeFi protocol. Smart contracts and automated execution play a central role in DeFi operation with, for example, smart-contract-controlled automated market makers to grow the DeFi market. (Automated market makers use liquidity pools to trade digital assets rather than match buy and sell orders as in a traditional exchange, thus automating orderly exchanges, which is critical to making and maintaining a market.)

DeFi growth is closely linked to the Ethereum protocol. DeFi mostly operates on Ethereum and uses Ether and other ERC-20 tokens; the ubiquity of Ethereum and the large volume of value committed to Ether made it attractive for DeFi applications to build on Ethereum. The total value locked in Ethereum DeFi applications in October 2021 was near $160 billion, compared to just around $1 billion at the beginning of June 2020 (though this may be an overestimate due to the double counting of funds locked and then borrowed against when used as collateral). Maker and Compound, discussed later in this chapter, are two of the dominant DeFi applications, along with Aave and Curve, with about 35 percent of total Ether committed to these protocols.[2]

DeFi expects to increase disintermediation with a flood of new P2P money applications, which can facilitate lending, borrowing, trading including on margin, swapping stablecoins, investing in futures markets in digital currencies such as Bitcoin, creating and exchanging tokens based on digital currencies, and using options and derivatives for commodities and foreign exchange, through newly created DeFi firms such as Balancer.[3] Balancer is a multitoken automated market maker and exchange that functions as a self-balancing weighted portfolio.

Figure 4.1 shows the growing range of DeFi applications. I discuss several such examples of DeFi across various financial segments in the following sections to illustrate the growing range of blockchain in financial applications.

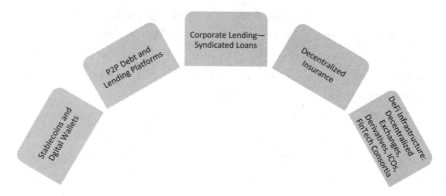

Figure 4.1
The growing range of DeFi

As discussed in chapter 3, blockchain-based cryptocurrencies like Bitcoin and Ethereum have many advantages, but their volatility reduces their attractiveness as a store of value or means of exchange. Stablecoins are necessary for digital currencies to gain wide acceptance and to "cross the chasm" into mass market adoption. Stablecoins can be created by linking the stablecoin with fiat currency reserves on a one-to-one basis; stablecoins such as USDC (US Dollar Coin) or USDT (Tether) are created in this fashion, with USDC or Tether created in an amount equivalent to the total of US dollars held in reserves. An alternative approach is to use cryptocurrency reserves as the basis for issuing stablecoins, with continual algorithmic adjustment of the ratio of cryptocurrency reserves to stablecoins issued to adapt to the price volatility of the underlying cryptocurrency reserves. MakerDAO and its DAI stablecoin is one example of this approach.

MakerDAO and Its DAI Stablecoin

MakerDAO and its DAI stablecoin is one of the many available stablecoins that has been met with significant adoption. As cryptocurrencies have limited use as a means of exchange in commercial transactions (due to volatility and high transaction costs for small deal amounts), investment and speculation became the dominant motive for purchasing cryptocurrencies, with the hope that these currencies—Bitcoin, Ether—would appreciate, furnishing capital gains to their holders. Thus, Bitcoin and other digital currencies would be idle assets while awaiting appreciation. A December 2020 estimate suggested that "60 percent of all Bitcoin in the circulating supply has not moved in the last 12 months"[4].

In response, Maker and its competitors developed a business model built around creating stablecoins to motivate cryptocurrency "hodlers" (HODL is a term in the cryptocurrency world for long-term holders of bitcoin and other digital currencies), to deploy their idle capital. Lending idle cryptocurrency creates liquidity and income for digital currency holders. The stablecoin model at Maker combines converting volatile cryptocurrency into stable digital currency, with a provision for lending the stablecoins created. This is analogous to banking and fractional reserve-based lending at commercial banks, in which banks hold reserves that are a fraction of total deposits on hand but can make loans that are many multiples of what is on hand because they are backed by a central authority such as the US Federal Reserve. This arrangement adds to the money supply.

Once Maker's protocol creates DAI from cryptocurrency, deposited by its customers, DAI, being stable, can be used as a means of payment for transactions. It can also be exchanged or held as savings. The Maker protocol complements DAI creation with interest rate setting on loans—Maker's stability rate, which is similar to the Fed's target rate.

Maker, as well as most other DeFi applications, use the Ethereum protocol. Ethereum's smart contract facility is a feature particularly useful in structuring financial applications. Maker and its DeFi competitors use ERC-20-compatible tokens, such as Ether. ERC-20 is the standard for how tokens are created within Ethereum, and it defines the necessary basic functions that all smart contracts and ERC-20-compatible tokens are expected to fulfill.[5] These include information about the total supply of a given token, an account owner's balance, and the ability to transfer a specific number of tokens as directed to or from a specific customer address. These features permit a spender to withdraw or return a specified number of tokens from or to a specified address and activate an approval module to carry out an instruction, such as transferring or withdrawing digital currency. Maker includes additional functions specific to its stablecoin DAI, such as the ability to mint and burn (cancel) tokens within Maker; this function applies to DAI as well to the separate MKR token used within Maker to give MKR owners a say in governance.

To counteract cryptocurrency instability, Maker pegged and maintains its DAI to the US dollar at a 1:1 ratio. Each DAI created is backed by the Ethereum token, Ether, and is deposited with Maker. The stablecoin creation process begins when a customer deposits Ether with Maker and agrees to lock up the deposited ETHER in a vault. Once the Ether has been deposited and secured, Maker's collateral rules kick in with an internally set collateral-to-DAI ratio, initially established at, say, 150 percent. The collateral ratio is set by Maker governance members and is partly dependent on the volatility of the cryptocurrency underlying the collateral; the more volatile collateral would bear a higher collateral ratio. As the value of Ether fluctuates, some degree of overcollateralization is necessary—Maker's intent is to boost confidence in DAI through overcollateralization, increasing the safety of the DAI stablecoin. At a 150 percent collateral ratio, depositing 1 Ether (worth, say, $300 on cryptocurrency exchanges at the time of deposit) would allow the creation of 200 DAI, which the depositor of Ether could borrow (the collateralized debt position).

This model, which creates DAI via a "permissionless credit factory on Ethereum,"[6] is similar to margin loans provided by stockbrokers. Margin loans allow an investor to avoid liquidating positions while still maintaining access to a portion of invested capital at a cost of the margin interest rate. When the borrower pays back the DAI, the Ether deposited in the vault can be retrieved, less a stability fee charge (akin to interest; the annual borrowing rate varies with the specific cryptocurrency deposited and the collateral ratio. When Ether was deposited at a 150 percent collateral ratio, the stability fee was around 3.5 percent in June 2021).

DAI can also be locked in a Maker's DSR (DAI Savings Rate) contract to earn a variable interest rate in additional DAI, generated from the stability fee (the rate is determined by Maker governors). In effect, Maker offers a savings account for Ether, with interest paid in DAI. Total DAI supply grows in relation to the demand for collateralized lending. Smart contracts automate Maker transactions, including issuing DAI loans, managing loan repayment, collecting interest rates, liquidating bad loans, and managing vaults.

DAI is tradable on cryptocurrency exchanges, and Maker relies on arbitrage and the link to deposited collateral to maintain the DAI-to-dollar parity. Raising or lowering the stability fee results in reduced debt or increased borrowing, changing the demand for and supply of DAI. If DAI drops to $0.99, the debtor can purchase 200 DAI for $198 and

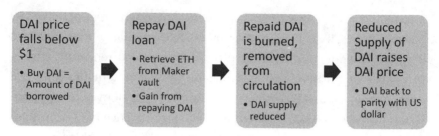

Figure 4.2
How Maker DAI maintains stability with the US dollar

repay the original 200 DAI debt, making a small gain. When the DAI is repaid, it is removed from circulation, reducing the total supply of DAI and raising its price, bringing it back into parity with the US dollar. If the DAI repaid were not canceled, the total amount of DAI would exceed the amount of collateral, causing DAI value to drop below the desired 1:1 parity with the dollar. This process is illustrated in figure 4.2.

A similar process, in reverse, would occur if the DAI price was greater than $1, with the borrower selling DAI on a cryptocurrency exchange for a gain. This would motivate other ETH holders to create DAI on Maker and sell it for a gain. This process would then raise DAI supply, lowering its price and bringing it back to parity with the US dollar.

The Maker system includes automated bots, Keepers, that participate in this parity-preserving feature (among other things). In March 2020, at the height of the COVID-19 pandemic crisis, a rush to liquidity led the DAI peg to break, and the DAI price reached 1.37 DAI to the dollar, before settling to between 1.01 and 1.03 through July 2020. However, Ether is volatile, as its value fluctuates. If Ether's value falls to the point where it is worth less than $300, the borrower would need to contribute more Ether to the vault to avoid breaching the 150 percent collateral requirement or return the borrowed DAI. As noted above, the borrower would have to pay the stability fee to retrieve the Ether. (The Ether values used above are for illustrative purposes. Ether's price fluctuated between $1,416 and $4,620 from February 2021 to February 2022, and was valued at $2,790 on February 19, 2022).

To protect the overcollateralization and safety of DAI, and to prevent bad debts from increasing and overwhelming the Maker system, the system's stabilizer rules allow for automatic liquidation of a vault if the loan becomes risky (i.e., if the collateral ratio is breached and falls below the set ratio of 150 percent). Off-chain DAI prices are collected from trusted oracle feeds chosen by MKR voters, and a median DAI price is fed on-chain via an Oracle Security Module to the Maker protocol (with a time delay for security protection if an oracle is compromised). To avoid having their loans being liquidated automatically for breaching collateral floors and being forced to pay a penalty fee, DAI borrowers are motivated to collateralize at greater than the minimum 150 percent.

Maker rules allow external third parties—that is, traders operating in the market, referred to as Keepers, who often use automated bots—to liquidate the debt and move the system back to safer levels, earning a profit in the process. Keepers also bid DAI in amounts that are just sufficient to purchase enough of the collateralized Ether in the associated vault to pay off the debt and associated fees.[7] Any leftover collateral (typically due to overcollateralization and the automatic liquidation when a high collateral ratio is breached) would be returned to the vault owner, who continues to own the DAI acquired by borrowing against the Ether originally provided as collateral.

Maker's governance structure is an essential element of Maker's stablecoin strategy. Maker token ownership allows participation in governance through voting, and voting rights are attached to Maker MKR tokens with one vote per MKR. MKR token holders, acting as a DAO, adjudicate issues such as debt ceilings for different types of collateral, the risk premium built into interest rates on borrowing, procedures for capping bad debts. They also ensure Maker system stability by balancing total Maker system collateral locked up with total system debt. MKR tokens can rise in value as Maker becomes more successful in establishing its DAI stablecoin, with more DAI issued, borrowed, and repaid. The rise in the value of MKR governance tokens would be similar to owning shares in a growing company. This creates incentives for users to manage the Maker protocol prudently and maintain DAI stability.

Maker governance includes a Maker Buffer, which holds the DAI earned from a vault liquidation collateral auction as the stability fee. If the Maker Buffer exceeds a set ceiling, a surplus auction is held, with the excess DAI sold for MKR tokens, which are then burned, reducing the supply of MKR and raising its value. Burned tokens are sent to a wallet without a private key so that no one can access this wallet, and the DAI or MKR coins sent to this wallet are irretrievably lost. Conversely, if a collateral liquidation along with DAI in the Maker Buffer is insufficient to fully pay off a debt position, MKR is minted and sold for DAI to fully liquidate the debt, lowering the MKR token price as a result. (Note that MKR is not mined like Bitcoin and is instead created by the Maker governance body. Maker was initially launched with a supply of one million MKR.)

Initially, Maker accepted Ether as the sole basis for conversion into stablecoins. Later, it moved to a multicollateral lending model, accepting additional cryptocurrencies, such as the USDC (originally created by Circle, a private digital currency company, and later managed by a consortium including Circle, Coinbase, and Bitmain). Maker plans to accept additional digital assets as collateral, with the possible inclusion of real assets as collateral in the future.

Stablecoins and the Money Supply

In the US banking system, the interest rate spread between the effective Fed funds rate and the repurchase (repo) rate determines financial system liquidity (see figure 4.3). The daily turnover in the repo market exceeds $1 trillion, and the repo rate allows institutions to earn interest on temporary excess cash by lending it overnight to other institutions that need it to fund short-term liquidity needs. The Federal Open Markets Committee adjusts the Interest on Excess Reserves (IOER) rate to move the Fed funds rate to its desired target range. If the overnight interbank lending rate is greater than IOER, then banks will loan or expand credit and vice versa. Similarly, Maker can adjust the collateral

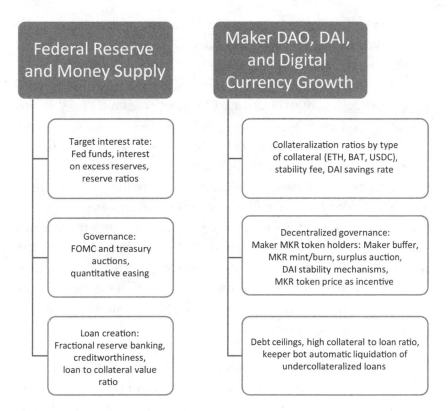

Figure 4.3
Traditional money supply and digital currency systems

level, the liquidation of undercollateralized debt, and the stability fee to influence the creation of DAI loans, subject to its self-imposed debt ceiling. It is important to note that this debt ceiling has been raised as the market and acceptance of DAI grows, thus influencing the growth of a parallel digital currency money supply.[8]

The money supply implications of DeFi applications like Maker become increasingly salient in the context of US dollar importance, whether considering the dollar as a reserve currency, its liquidity, or as a high-quality asset purchased by banks to meet reserve requirements. As the US deficits grow ($3 trillion for the year ending June 2020, 14 percent of GDP) and as the money supply increases (it has grown from about $14 trillion in 2012 to near $23 trillion at the end of 2019 because of quantitative easing), a digital currency–based financial system might gain traction in the face of perceived US financial system fragility.

In addition, as the ownership of digital currencies increases and prospects for wider use of stablecoins are brighter, consumers need secure, accessible, and easy-to-use storage, with ease of cross-wallet transfer. Storage and retrieval alternatives for digital assets include online custodial digital wallets from various sources such as digital currency exchanges (e.g., Coinbase), physical hardware wallets such as Trezor and Ledger, purely mobile wallets (a virtual wallet app on smartphones that points to a location on a blockchain to store and retrieve digital currencies) such as Edge, and desktop wallets (similar to mobile wallets but installed on desktop and laptop computers) such as Exodus, integrated with Trezor. Physical hardware wallets are secure physical devices, similar to flash drives, that can hold private keys and thus secure access to digital currencies.

Challenging Maker: The Compound Protocol and Yield Farming

As a first mover in introducing stablecoins, Maker obtained significant market share of the total value invested in Ethereum ERC-20 Ether tokens, with the total value locked in Maker vaults reaching $16 billion in February 2022.[9] Compound challenged Maker with innovative differences in its business model. Founded in 2017, Compound launched a competing money market protocol within Ethereum and, with the introduction of its COMP token in June 2020, grew rapidly. By February 2022, $ 6.7 billion in total value was locked in Compound, compared to around $16 billion in Maker.[10] The distinctive differentiating features of Compound are summarized below.[11]

Compound accepts a broad range of Ethereum assets (e.g., Ether, DAI, Tether), though not every Ethereum-compatible token asset is supported. Ethereum token owners can deposit their Ethereum-compatible token assets in Compound and lend them via the Compound protocol, earning interest on what would otherwise be an idle asset. The interest rate on borrowing is algorithmically determined and varies by asset, depending on the demand/supply interaction for that Ethereum asset; smart contracts match supply with demand and compute a continuously varying interest rate. The Compound protocol permits lenders to borrow from the pool of a specific asset (e.g., the Ether pool). Pools are created by combining the Ether deposited by all of Compound's clients. Thus, lenders do not directly lend to borrowers; instead, the Compound protocol provides a loan from the pool of a specific asset to borrowers seeking to borrow that particular asset.

By aggregating assets supplied by all the users, and lending from this pool, Compound increases liquidity for each lender. Lenders can also withdraw assets without waiting for a specific loan to mature. In doing so, Compound creates frictionless borrowing of Ethereum tokens, without P2P negotiation of debt maturity, the interest rate, or collateral. Borrowers must deposit their own Ethereum-compatible tokens on Compound as collateral, with the total amount they could borrow being a portion of the amount of collateral deposited. The value of each asset provided as collateral is determined by a price oracle, which pools prices for that asset from the top ten cryptocurrency exchanges. The amount that a borrower can borrow depends on the riskiness of the assets furnished as collateral. These assets vary in their collateral strength, varying from zero to one for riskier to less risky assets. The riskier the collateral, the smaller the amount that can be borrowed against that collateral. If a user exceeds their borrowing capacity because of a decline in the value of collateral, a portion of the borrowing is repaid with collateral discounted at a certain rate. This is also known as the liquidation discount, and it creates an incentive for arbitragers in the Compound community to step in and pay off portions of the debt with their assets of the same type, in turn taking ownership of the portion of the borrower's collateral that would have been liquidated.

Compound governance was initially centralized, with administrators choosing parameters such as the interest rate algorithm for each type of asset and determining which Ethereum assets would be accepted on Compound for deposit and borrowing. To decentralize governance, Compound launched the COMP token, passing governance into the hands of COMP token owners. New COMP tokens were issued every day and divided proportionately across asset classes and then equally between borrowers and lenders in each asset class;[12] thus, every Compound user now has a voice in governance.

Some typical use cases on the Compound protocol include borrowing tokens to use in the Ethereum ecosystem, borrowing Ether or other Ethereum assets using existing ownership assets as collateral (margin loans), and shorting a token to pay off the original debt and realize a profit. Specialized Dapps such as InstaDapp offer a Maximize COMP Mining feature[13] to aid users in achieving greater returns through "yield farming," which helps Ethereum asset owners put their idle assets to work. In yield farming, digital currency owners—liquidity providers— lock up their assets in a liquidity pool, which uses smart contracts to lend from the pool. The liquidity providers who have contributed their assets to the pool earn transaction fees, interest on the loan, and, sometimes, governance tokens, which could appreciate the underlying entity; for example, Compound grows and increases its total amount of lending.

The growth in Maker and Compound, and newer competitors such as Aave, Curve Finance, and Uniswap, underlines the increasing attractiveness of DeFi protocols and business models. Their growth also stimulated the rise of several complementary DeFi opportunities, including DEXs and decentralized derivatives markets.

DEXs and Trading Systems

Financial instruments need exchanges where financial assets can be priced and traded. In the United States, the Depository Trust and Clearing Corporation (DTCC), owned by a consortium of financial institutions, handles the settlement and clearing of securities trades, with settlement times of around two days. The country averaged around $1.3 trillion in securities trades daily in 2019, and DTCC registries update trades to reflect changes in ownership and payment for the securities traded. To protect against counterpart risk of nonpayment, financial institutions set aside capital to cover the risks before actual settlement.

In addition, they maintain their own records of delivery and settlement. Reconciling conflicting information consumes resources and takes time, and thus improving these back-office functions (which are often mainframe-based batch processes) could reduce settlement times and save on costs. Centralized exchanges such as Coinbase have emerged to facilitate digital asset trading and custody, and they improve on the drawbacks inherent in the DTCC system—slower settlement times, the need to set aside capital to cover nonpayment risk, and back-office reconciliation of counterparty transaction records.

Blockchain-based trading systems can offer secure instantaneous trading, settlement, and payment. Paxos, a blockchain start-up, was authorized by the SEC to launch a limited pilot using blockchain to settle stock trades.[14] The twenty-four-month pilot, on a private, permissioned Ethereum protocol, was limited to the most actively traded and least volatile stocks, with a cap of 1 percent of total daily trading volume of those stocks. A limited number of financial institutions were allowed to participate as trading partners, including Credit Suisse, Nomura, and Société Générale.

The blockchain enables the smart contract–based exchange of digital representations of securities, and by creating a single unified record of the trade, reconciliation becomes unnecessary. Thus Paxos's blockchain-based trading could facilitate delivery versus payment and same-day settlement and could even allow settlement multiple times a day, increasing intraday liquidity. This would free up capital currently devoted to protecting against counterparty risk. While the automated stock transfer would occur on the Paxos blockchain rather than inside the DTCC system, with cash held as a stablecoin in Paxos custody accounts, DTCC would still maintain the updated stock registry, insulating the trading system against glitches during the pilot trials. While initial participation was restricted to counterparties where both sides are part of the Paxos Settlement Service network, Paxos could seek SEC authorization to offer its blockchain solution to all broker-dealers in the United States to settle their securities transactions as trials proceed successfully.

As cryptocurrencies gain popularity, especially digital currencies such as Bitcoin, Ether, and DAI, there is an increasing need for liquidity so that cryptocurrency owners can easily change one cryptocurrency into another or into fiat currencies, earn interest on their holdings thorough lending or savings deposits, and leverage their holdings. Likewise, the rise of DeFi has led to a corollary rise in DEXs, among them Uniswap, Kyber, Balancer, Curve Finance, and Bakkt, all of which dispense with centralized market makers, like in Coinbase (as discussed in chapter 1), and instead offer different versions of fast and secure decentralized P2P trading. With DEXs trading digital currencies, it is only a short step to trade digital representations of fiat currencies and commodities, and of real assets such as equity securities, as shown by Paxos. Thus, any asset that can be securely and immutably represented digitally has the potential to be traded on DEXs, disrupting traditional centralized exchanges.

Balancer: DEXs and ETF Provision

Balancer Exchange is one such protocol that allows users to trade a variety of ERC20-compatible tokens while also creating "programmable liquidity." Balancer offers liquidity pools featuring portfolios containing several different ERC20 token assets with underlying tokens of different weights in each distinct portfolio. This means Balancer can provide access to ETF-type cryptocurrency portfolios. In a shared liquidity pool, the creator of that pool decides which tokens will be accepted in the pool, with a maximum of eight different tokens, and sets weights for each token within the portfolio. Once the tokens and their weights are chosen for that shared liquidity pool, they cannot be changed.

A Balancer user then reviews the different portfolios available and decides which portfolio they would like to invest in, choosing a portfolio where the weighted averages of the currencies in that specific portfolio match their investor preferences. To invest in that portfolio, users swap some of their cryptocurrency holdings with other users, on cryptocurrency exchanges, to generate specific amounts of each of the currency components in that portfolio, which they then contribute to

Balancer to gain a share of the portfolio. Furthermore, once an investor is part of a liquidity pool, that investor can earn fees in exchange for providing liquidity and facilitating trading of cryptocurrencies in their pool. So instead of paying an ETF money manager, ETF investors in Balancer earn income by virtue of making an investment, independent of any other income generated by the portfolio such as interest or appreciation.

Balancer also offers services for traders who wish to swap a set amount of a specific cryptocurrency for another. Once a trader places a swap order, an algorithm executes this swap across some subset of the liquidity portfolios so that the portfolio composition weights are preserved even as the prices of the underlying tokens change. Different portfolios will offer different prices depending on their need to swap currencies to maintain the desired portfolio composition, perhaps lowering prices for tokens that they have an excess of and need to sell to bring the portfolio back into balance.

One consequence of such automatic market making and automatic balancing is that larger orders are likely to cause prices to vary more since the larger order will have a greater effect on a portfolio's balance across the desired portfolio composition weights.[15] This price change, termed "slippage," is broadcasted to traders at the time of placing an order so that they can set limits on how much slippage is acceptable for the order to be executed. Such traders pay swap fees as set by each portfolio, and the algorithm favors trades with portfolios that have lower swap fees (as a percentage of the trade amount), provided they have the specific tokens being sought by the user. Taken together, the portfolios earn swap fees for providing liquidity in specific currencies, while the algorithm drives portfolios to lower their swap fees, thus lowering trading costs across the Balancer system.

Balancer also offers BAL tokens, which allow the BAL token owner to participate in Balancer governance, with the amount of BAL tokens increasing with the portfolio's size. As such, larger portfolios provide greater liquidity to the Balancer system and earn more BAL. This gives them a greater voice in governance, meaning an increased voice in deciding the level of swap fees, rulesetting to decide which ERC20 tokens will be accepted, setting the algorithm features that allocate a trade across different liquidity pools, and so on.

Balancer adds additional nuances to its liquidity pools, allowing single-owner private pools, with that owner announcing tokens accepted for the portfolio, setting portfolio composition weights and swap fee percentages, and having full control over these parameters. Private pools are attractive to large investors and professional money managers who wish to offer cryptocurrency ETF services with transparency about portfolio composition and weights. Such private pools offer creative opportunities for new blockchain utilities that wish to create a market for their native tokens and increase their token liquidity. For example, new blockchain start-ups can launch bootstrapping liquidity pools[16] with a portfolio composed of their tokens and other well-established tokens, such as Bitcoin or DAI, and over time can diffuse ownership of their tokens. Thus, Algorand, discussed in chapter 2, could use Balancer to popularize its ALGO tokens and increase interest in using and participating in Algorand as a blockchain protocol.

Digital Asset Derivative Markets: Synthetix
Derivatives are another essential cog in the trading system. They allow investors to trade on the expected performance of underlying assets without having to own the asset itself (e.g., stock call and put options). Synthetix, a blockchain start-up, created a decentralized synthetic asset issuance protocol built on Ethereum that also functions as a trading platform for synthetic forms of fiat currencies (e.g., DAI as a synthetic form of the US dollar), cryptocurrencies, and commodities. It offers decentralized derivatives trading, generating native tokens called SNX that are tied to the value of collateral deposited with the Synthetix protocol. In this case, the ERC20 tokens deposited are digital representations of various assets such as fiat currencies (US dollar, euro, etc.), cryptocurrencies, and commodities (gold, silver). These could be extended in the future to other real assets such as equities.

After generating SNX in the system, users can lock the SNX and mint a second token, Synths, with a high collateralization ratio of 800 percent or greater. Thus eight hundred SNX could generate one hundred Synths, which can be exchanged for derivatives of fiat and cryptocurrencies and commodities. Price changes of the chosen asset and the derivative's value are tracked by an oracle; in the case of cryptocurrencies, Synths can also be used to short them, thus tracking declines in the price of Ether, Bitcoin, and more.

Each trade of a Synth generates a fee, around 0.3 percent, on average, which goes to SNX holders as a reward for staking collateral. SNX holders can also earn an additional reward from a weekly increase in the number of SNX at 1.25 percent a week through 2023. Synths are the users' debt and must be repaid for the SNX collateral to be unlocked. The user debt changes continuously as a proportion of an individual user's debt to the total debt of the Synthetix system as a whole, with total debt value changing as the price of the underlying assets change. As Synthetix explains, "in this way, SNX stakers act as a pooled counterparty to all Synth exchanges; stakers take on the risk of the overall debt in the system."[17]

Synthetix is also experimenting with Ether alone as collateral, which would require a lower collateral ratio of 150 percent and allow users to generate Synths directly against Ether rather than first exchange them for SNX. The user debt is then denominated in Ether, and the user does not participate in the pooled debt aspect of the system nor do they receive fees or rewards (because they do not assume debt pool risks). Because risk hedging of a larger volume is possible, trader access to digital asset derivatives markets increases trading volume, which improves market efficiency. As blockchain firms gain experience with decentralized stablecoins, P2P lending, DEXs, and derivatives markets, the same principles and mechanisms can be used to develop decentralized marketplaces. Over time, the swarm of competing protocols delivering similar functionality will thin out, and a few robust and full-featured protocols could become dominant. This process is being hastened with the rise of industry-wide consortia such as R3/Corda and Ripple, which are becoming widely adopted, allowing third-party apps to be built on top of these standard protocols, increasing their utility and helping them become industry standards.

Initial Coin Offerings

Blockchain platforms made it possible for firms to raise capital directly from investors through initial coin offerings (ICOs) and, in a newer evolution, initial exchange offerings (IEOs). ICOs are an alternative to IPOs and can democratize access to capital. They can also help decentralize innovation through shared governance within the emerging organizations.[18] However, ICOs and IEOs have been affected by limited oversight and poor performance.

The central issue for ICOs concerns the rights and interests that a token or coin provides. How should investors value the token received in return for their ICO investment? Cryptocurrency exchanges and DEXs listing ICO tokens set token prices, offer resale possibilities, and provide liquidity to ICO investors. The concern is whether price setting on a particular exchange for the tokens is fair or manipulated, with thin volume and sporadic trades reducing the efficiency of price discovery.

Related questions include whether additional token issuance is linked to the growth in demand for services of the ICO firm and whether there is a ceiling on the total number of tokens issuable. It matters whether the ICO launch document offers a detailed business plan, whether budgets for the use of ICO funds raised are spelled out, whether funds raised might pay off early initial investors, and whether legal provisions protect investor interests.[19] Vitaly Buterin and others have proposed a decentralized autonomous ICO (DAICO), with ICO investors releasing funds from ICO proceeds as development efforts meet milestones or else funds would be returned to ICO buyers after a set period.[20]

ICOs have attempted to avoid being classified as securities since such a classification increases compliance requirements. The SEC has long used the Howey test (i.e., investing money or valuable goods and services in a common enterprise, with reasonable expectation of earning a profit, derived from the efforts of others) to determine whether an issue is a security with an investment contract and hence subject to securities regulations. Using these criteria, the SEC considers some ICO tokens as meeting the Howey test and therefore needing to be regulated as securities, which token issuers prefer to avoid.

To the extent that there is less investor protection, ICO investors are more susceptible to fraud and price manipulation. ICOs as a fundraising vehicle reached their zenith with $7.8 billion raised in 2017 and 2018, before falling to $1.2 billion in 2019. ICO buyers expected the tokens to gain value as the underlying service grew and increased its customer base and usage. However, the proposed services were often at a conceptual stage with little clear prospect for being converted into functioning utilities capable of attracting significant numbers of paying customers.[21] Initial equity investors in a firm that subsequently launched an ICO could still retain control of the firm while using ICO funds to return capital to themselves. As many newly issued ICOs faltered, regulators began to increase regulatory requirements to protect investors from fraudulent ICO launches. One response has been the dynamic coin offering, offering investors a refund between nine and sixteen months after issuance if the company failed to meet its planned milestones, for example, Orion Protocol, which raised around $3.5 million in this manner.[22]

Clearer regulations can clarify and strengthen the role of ICOs in raising capital. For example, Switzerland has classified ICOs into different categories—payment ICOs, such as cryptocurrencies, which are used as a means of payment; utility ICOs, which access an existing functioning application or service through a blockchain-based infrastructure; and asset ICOs, which enable physical assets to be traded on a blockchain and are closer to securities investments, with debt or equity claims on the issuer.[23]

IEOs and Initial DEX Offerings

By 2019, IEOs had supplanted ICOs as the preferred vehicle for launching new blockchain firms, accounting for about 80 percent of all new digital firm launch funding. While ICOs are direct sales between the company and its investors, cryptocurrency exchanges supervise IEOs, hosting the sale of the new tokens on the issuer's behalf. Launching the sale of tokens on an exchange is akin to floating new offerings through a lead underwriter. The exchange selects which token sales to host and subsequently list on its exchange. Selection is determined by parameters such as the issuing company's potential, the issue quality, and maintaining the exchange's reputation as a place to trade quality tokens. Potential token buyers become members of the exchange to bid for tokens, with exchanges often requiring that buyers hold that exchange's tokens and pay for the issuing company's new tokens with the exchange's tokens. Thus, a company like Bitfinex could require potential buyers of an IEO to own and pay for the new IEO with Bitfinex's own Leo tokens.

IEOs have evolved into initial DEX offerings (IDOs), where the coin or token is launched on a DEX, with lower fees, community approval of the offering (akin to crowdfunding), better immediate liquidity, and token holdings secured in the owner's wallet with private keys. Major IDOs include Universal Market Access, which is a protocol to build synthetic assets on Ethereum, and Ethereum-based decentralized crypto exchanges such as SushiSwap and Uniswap.[24] The rise of NFTs is likely to lead to similar investor risks, as NFTs are easy to create and supply can expand well in excess of fluctuating demand.

Blockchain and Commercial Syndicated Loans
Except for large borrowers whose scale and creditworthiness allows them to directly offer loan instruments, small- and medium-sized borrowers must find banks willing to arrange and syndicate loans on their behalf or must work with other commercial and investment banks to find lenders willing to buy a portion of their syndicated loan. The lead bank underwriter negotiates the loan amount, duration, terms, collateral, loan covenants and interest rate, and pricing, resulting in a legal document signed by all parties. The loan syndicate launches the loan

when lenders for the bulk of the total loan are in place and market conditions are propitious.

Managing the loan registry, collateral management, and secondary markets and trading; recording changes of ownership; and arranging interest payments are subsequent tasks that are time-consuming and often paper based, require reconciliation, and are subject to regulatory filing and assurance of compliance. If the loan must be modified, lender consent must be obtained and a revised loan must be registered with the updated conditions. This cycle ends with principal repayment, loan retirement, and cancellation of loan documents. The entire process is subject to legal review and approval by legal counsel representing all of the parties to the loan agreement, a slow and costly process.

Introducing blockchain as a platform for syndicated loans can streamline the process, increasing efficiency, speeding up the process, and reducing costs. Programmable smart contracts underlying the debt instrument bring flexibility, easing the insertion of changed loan terms and automating interest payments. The immutable nature of transactions creates a single authenticated source of the loan registry, loan terms, ownership changes, and related material; unauthorized changes are immediately evident, with all parties having access to and sharing the updated state of the loan. In addition, the on-chain record can include governance features such as voting rights and exercise as well as speedy settlement facilitation. Costs are also reduced, particularly intermediary fees and ongoing transaction costs, though additional costs may arise from coding and debugging associated smart contracts. Taken together, these features make syndicated loans more accessible to a wider pool of potential borrowers. In summary, blockchain-based digital assets are programmable, immutable and transparent, and efficient and liquid and can comply with regulatory standards.[25] Figure 4.4 illustrates the transformation that blockchain can bring to the syndicated loan process. In the following two sections, I examine two applications of blockchain for the bond life cycle.

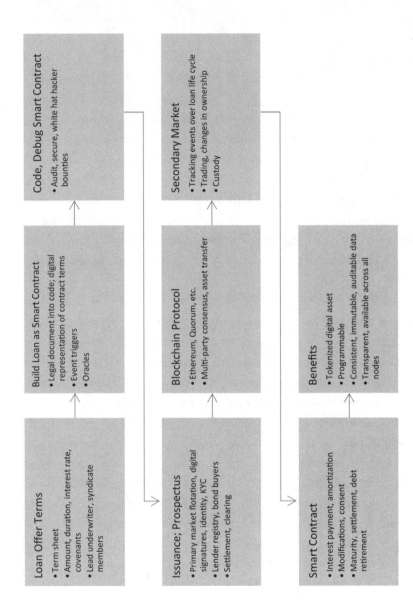

Figure 4.4
Blockchain platform for the syndicated loan process

The Deutsche Bank Smart Bond Pilot   An example of using blockchain to manage the syndicated loan process is a pilot project at Deutsche Bank (DB).[26] DB was interested in developing a proof of concept: can we model and execute a bond life cycle on blockchain—from clearing securities and finalizing settlement to triggering interest payments—and thus implement bond amortization and retirement? The first step was to convince decision-makers that blockchain could bring competitive benefits, and a pilot project to develop and implement a prototype could help inform future decisions about deploying blockchain in this space. The project initiators had to become evangelists and bring together a community of enthusiasts from diverse areas—legal, data analytics, IT, finance, client relations, and partner relations—to form a coalition that would help seek organizational support. To get budget approval, the project needed high-level champions with budget oversight authority and influence over strategic direction. Initial funding approval came once such champions were convinced to support a pilot.

Implementing the pilot meant collaborating with third parties outside of DB: blockchain specialists. DB chose to work with multiple blockchain protocols/platforms to provide future flexibility and to gain experience with a range of platforms. This would also help it choose a platform for managing loan syndication and to collaborate with cross-industry partners. And if partners were willing to work with the same blockchain protocol, collaboration would be easier. To simplify matters, the pilot was not conducted with live data; instead, the blockchain platform, once designed, was tested in a simulation with historic data. The pilot ultimately proved that blockchain could create a tokenized version of the loan and manage its life cycle.

DB's next step was to involve external parties—legal advisors, potential buyers, market makers, and custody agents—in an interorganizational test of the concept. The importance of interorganizational collaboration in successfully using blockchain for a syndicated loan led DB to become a founding member of the R3 financial consortium, which sought to validate blockchain use in the financial sector; set and agree on common standards; and contribute to interoperability between blockchain protocols at different member financial institutions. R3 established a common open-source blockchain protocol—Corda—for consortium members to experiment with blockchain and to make rapid and error-free settlement possible.

A critical element to moving beyond a pilot requires measuring project achievements to justify continuing with the blockchain experiment. Metrics developed to measure project achievements included an increase in back-office efficiency, cost reduction, reduction in settlement times, improvement in clearing and payments, reduction in errors and need for reconciliation, and utility of access to detailed, accurate, and timestamped transaction data. As the pilot moves to implementation at scale, issues to address include the following:

- Can financial digital assets be transferred without an intermediary?
- Can smart code execution prove rightful ownership without the need for an intermediary?
- Can the smart contract correctly record future state changes, such as interest payment as agreed, changes in ownership, maturity, and retirement of the bond?
- Can transactions executed on the blockchain platform satisfy regulatory requirements and achieve compliance?
- Can the new platform integrate with legacy systems, such as SWIFT message matching?
- Given that several banks had to be persuaded to cross organizational boundaries to test the pilot applications,[27] would current and future consortium members agree to collaborate, contribute funding, and share intellectual property in a full-scale implementation?

The World Bank's Blockchain Bond-I An example of blockchain-based bond implementation is the World Bank's bond-I. The Commonwealth Bank of Australia (CBA) is the sole arranger of this blockchain bond issued in 2018 in Australian dollars for $110 million AUD. CBA's Blockchain Centre of Excellence had piloted a prototype blockchain bond with the Queensland Treasury Corporation earlier. It was created, allocated, distributed, and managed on a blockchain platform operated by the World Bank in Washington, DC, and CBA in Sydney.[28] The World Bank and CBA expected the bond issue to demonstrate the role of block-chain as a "facilitating platform for different participants."[29] They developed the blockchain bond over a one-year period on a private Ethereum blockchain permissioned network of authorized participants with the participation of early adopting blockchain bond investors. It was the first blockchain bond issued by a government entity, and the pilot served as an opportunity to resolve both technical and legal considerations.

A few months after initial issuance, secondary trading on the bond-I was enabled with the support from market maker TD Securities, underlining the blockchain's ability to raise capital, coordinate trades, and deliver "a verified, permanent record and instant reconciliation."[30] The bond-I platform capabilities included automated bond auction, bookbuild and allocation, electronic bid capture, real-time updates, enhanced visibility subject to participants' permissions, and an auditable and immutable transaction record for "probity and operational risk management."

The FinTech Insurance Market: Leveraging Blockchain with AI, IoT, and Analytics

Insurance offers an essential service. To help individuals and firms avoid catastrophic risk that could bankrupt firms and irreparably harm individuals, insurance companies pool risks and offer indemnification against extreme outcomes in return for a known smaller, immediate payment—an insurance premium. Insurance companies succeed to the extent that they can create a large enough pool of clients so that risk is diversified across this pool. Premiums are set based on actuarial analysis of historic data so that, on average, the total premium, together with income from investing the collected premiums, exceeds the payouts for realized losses among some subset of the pool members. This ultimately provides a profit or dividend for the insurance company and its insured members.

Succeeding in the insurance business depends on accomplishing several key interrelated steps: using analysis of historic data on insured losses to price premiums correctly and competitively; selling directly to customers and through broker networks with significant market coverage to obtain customers; retaining customers so that annual policy renewal provides a steady stream of premium income; and reducing risk through judicious reinsurance of a portion of total risk assumed. This last task allows firms to set a floor on their losses (as well as a ceiling on their income), thus circumscribing risk assumed and smoothing it over longer periods of time. Assuming that premiums are competitively priced, customer retention is primarily affected by the quality of customer service, principally in claims processing. Distraught customers seeking compensation for what they believe are covered losses are unlikely to renew if they perceive that their claims are reduced or unjustly denied. However, insurance companies may have difficulty balancing customer claims with policy conditions that protect the interests of the company, particularly through detecting and rejecting fraudulent claims.

Blockchain allied with AI and analytics can help insurance companies with the challenges described above. Blockchain, with its immutable data and provenance trail, can track the changing pool of insured assets, their ownership, and values. AI-based chatbots can automate the process of tailoring insurance coverage and offer premium quotes derived from customer data. Other AI chatbots can speed up claims processing by linking to oracles that channel weather data, police reports, and other sources, while other AI chatbots can enhance customer engagement and the customer experience.

At one such blockchain insurance company called Lemonade, the playful AI chatbots Maya and Jim[31] are examples of AI deployment supporting customer satisfaction. The automation enabled by chatbots and smart contracts can lower costs, providing a structural cost advantage through automating key processes in a scale-dominated industry. Cumulative customer data can enable dynamic premium pricing, particularly at renewal points, and such cumulative data can serve as the basis of forensic analysis to deter, detect, and guard against fraud. In this context, tokens generated within the blockchain can be used to incentivize desired behaviors; at Lemonade, for example, policyholders can designate a favorite charity to receive donations resulting from funds remaining in the claim pool, which in essence rewards customers for lower loss ratios and claims to premium income. Table 4.1 summarizes some of the benefits of blockchain deployment in insurance applications.

Blockchain benefits the entire insurance cycle, from customer acquisition to premium quotes, from customer servicing and claims processing to customer retention, and from improving insurance marketing to lowering costs and raising customers' perceptions of fairness.[32] Secure blockchain data can help verify customer identity at the initial customer acquisition stage and later during customer service interactions. Blockchain also ensures privacy and data protection while updating records with newly verified transactions such as premium payments or revised policy terms. Similar data linkages can help verify group benefits for specific groups as the package of benefits available under insurance can vary from group to group. Immutable validated data provide a permanent record and help build trust between the insurance company and its insured clients and can be used in reducing fraud and detecting tampering and counterfeiting.[33]

Another platform, Insurwave,[34] offers a blockchain and IoT marine hull insurance solution, allowing companies such as Maersk to manage insurance for over 350 containerships operating around the world. Each insured ship is registered on the blockchain, with an algorithm calculating premiums and policies made available to ship owners. Using IoT devices, each ship's voyages and collateral data such as location, weather, and environmental risk conditions are recorded. Accumulated data is used in premium calculation at policy renewal and in claims assessment and disposition. An ancillary benefit is a complete immutable record of ship life cycle events, which is useful for regulators, owners, and potential buyers on a ship resale. Such data in standardized formats can be securely exchanged with reinsurers, transparently reconciling transactions, and with third parties, for claims subrogation, eliminating information silos.

Table 4.1 FinTech insurance: Leveraging blockchain with AI, IoT, and analytics

Basis of differentiation	Goal	Problems	Solution: Benefits from blockchain and complements
Customer experience	Delight the customer	Policy centric, questioning claims, and slow-to-approve claims, leading to reduced customer retention	Foster of trust between insured and insurer; AI bot helps get coverage; pleasing U/X; app based; appeals to younger client segment demographic
Affordable	Great prices		Transparency while preserving competitive privacy
Claims processing	Fair, rapid	Balancing fraudulent claims against fairness, preventing fraud.	AI bot using analytics to assess claims; processing data provided by IoT devices. rapid resolution, quick settlement; payment authorization and funds transfer leading to policy renewal and customer satisfaction
Cost control	Lower cost advantage and cost competitiveness	Lack of scale and people-intensive processing	Bots and smart contracts reduce cost and errors
Fraud control	Fraud reduction and prevention	False claims and forged or inaccurate documents	Insured asset losses and subrogation rights
Regulatory compliance	Efficient and timely compliance with changing multiple jurisdictional demands	Incomplete and slow compliance	Regulator access to secure immutable, accurate data allow compliance verification and analytics
Privacy and data security	Accurate, exchangeable, and permanent records	Beneficiaries unaware of insurance benefits, esp. life insurance; unclaimed payouts	Immutable permanent registry facilitating beneficiary contacting and payment
Customer retention	Reduce policy complexity and denied claims which lead to customer exit	Differentiating commodity services where price differential is limited	Improved customer experience; clearer claims verification and disposition
Industry partnering	Increase use of reinsurance partners	Sharing data with reinsurers and obtaining acceptance; incompatible IT systems; data standards	Improved reinsurance placement; clear contract terms; easier renewal and claims allocation and settlement

The Blockchain Insurance Industry Initiative (B3i) was formed to develop smart contract–based reinsurance (what is described as "frictionless risk transfer") to protect against excess losses in property insurance, or the "catastrophe excess of loss" application. B3i brings together real-time information sharing, which enables the reconciliation of accounts between the insurance company and its reinsurers and allows for automatic payouts.[35] Insurance blockchains like B3i can also smooth out the regulatory processes, enhancing auditability for regulatory bodies that can use smart contracts to query secured data and evaluate it for compliance with regulatory standards. For example, Amica Insurance[36] was able to smooth its claims processing once claims adjusters could draw on the blockchain to get timely accurate claims data, such as policyholder information, cause of claim, policy coverage and terms, policy claims history, and other essential documents. The claims adjuster could record customer statements, access maps, and submit documents, photos, and claims assessment reports available to others involved in claims adjustment, all through secure and timestamped audit trails.

Linking blockchain with IoT and AI (e.g., IBM's Watson IoT) is another avenue for improving insurance business efficiency. IoT devices can automatically detect insurance-triggering events, such as car accidents, further triggering repairs, authentication of repairs, completion at approved facilities, and ultimately linking to claims processing and payments. If policyholders agree to opt in and permit deployment, Groupama Insurance, for example, places IoT smart sensors on insured cars to track location, speed, acceleration, and related variables, enabling it to offer and deploy AI-aided insurance. Its policyholders are offered a discount on premiums in return for using the IoT sensors. One benefit of using them is real-time communication of collisions; if deemed serious, emergency services can be dispatched immediately, possibly saving lives.

Groupama has experienced a reduction in fraudulent claims, lower theft, and reduced reckless driving. This is because the IoT devices facilitate the transmission of precise car movements, which can be analyzed with algorithms derived from big data collision records and, together with traditional claims inspector reports, can validate and speed up claims processing and settlement. The accumulating dynamic data complements historic actuarial tables in improved risk prediction and risk prevention.[37] It also enables concierge-style insurance: with knowledge of individual driver habits, Groupama can coach drivers and warn them about dangerous conditions, whether that is impending adverse weather or road hazards. This leads to improved customer experiences and reduced claims, driving higher policy renewal rates. This kind of IoT-based data-driven insurance must comply with privacy regulations, and as such, Groupama requires customer consent to collect data and promises its customers it will never share customer data with third parties.

The potential for blockchain deployment in insurance has led to the launch of blockchain protocols specific to insurance, such as the Etherisc pilot. This P2P flight insurance pilot, built with the Etherisc protocol, pays the insured for flight cancellations or delays. It works by a smart contract first issuing the insurance in response to a request initiated by a client; payment is authorized when oracles verify a flight delay. This automates both issuance and claim processing in a transparent decentralized fashion. Another interesting pilot of the Etherisc application is crop microinsurance to small paddy rice farmers in Sri Lanka[38] through a collaboration between Aon, Sanasa, and Oxfam. Oxfam coupled its deep experience working with farmer communities in emerging markets to Etherisc's blockchain protocol and decentralized risk pool expertise. Aon brought its expertise in reinsurance and innovative policy design to the project, while Sanasa added its local insurance industry and cultural knowledge. Many farmers in Sri Lanka's remote areas are unbanked, with limited incomes and liquidity; bureaucracy and banking infrastructure is physically and financially out of reach for this population too. The proof-of-concept goal is to use blockchain to lower costs and increase efficiency while facilitating a farmer's access to affordable microinsurance with fair and transparent payout upon occurrence of extreme weather (which could cause crop losses).

The longer-term goal is to offer an open-source generic insurance framework underpinning the Decentralized Insurance Protocol from Etherisc, enabling an "ecosystem of product builders, risk pools, oracles, claim adjusters, distributors, and underwriters to create insurance applications on the Ethereum blockchain." An example of this is Raincoat, a collaboration with HurricaneGuard in Puerto Rico to develop cost-effective insurance against storms. It uses public data from the National Oceanic and Atmospheric Administration to detect hurricane windspeeds within a certain radius of the insured's area and deliver automatic payouts.[39]

Blockchain growth will also create demand for cyber insurance to protect against loss of access to digital wallets, from misplaced private keys to theft, and professional liability insurance for blockchain development teams and firms, with policies to guard against project completion issues. In summary, combining blockchain protocols with insurance offerings can lead to improved efficiency gains, lower costs, more transparency, real-time data sharing with business partners and regulators, better claims processing, and fraud reduction. With accurate accessible data improving risk assessment and risk pricing, new products such as parametric insurance and automated marketing and claims adjustment are on the horizon.

Enterprise Response to DeFi Disruption

DeFi on blockchains can be cheaper and more secure and can give users control over their financial operations and personal data. Blockchains can offer a secure and lower-cost environment in which to conduct financial asset transactions, provide record keeping and regulatory compliance, and engineer cryptocurrency/digital currency stability. These environments are ideal for organizing exchanges in which to trade digital assets as well as financial instruments that are linked to the performance of those digital assets (i.e., derivatives). Each major category of DeFi innovation has built on previous advances. In response, incumbents have launched blockchain pilots and projects of their own, one of the better-known examples being JPMorgan's Quorum, a private version of Ethereum. The Quorum blockchain was a response to the challenge from emerging DeFi entrants. It aims to prevent the erosion of JPMorgan's market position and to allow it to compete in the emerging DeFi world. Quorum has attracted over three hundred banks to its Interbank Information Network, which is integrated with the Microsoft Azure cloud platform.

JPMorgan's Quorum team adapted the original open-source Ethereum protocol to address the confidentiality needs of enterprises by adding privacy features (e.g., allowing for anonymity of both sender and recipient) as well as by offering users the ability to conceal the amounts or specifics of assets being traded.[40] JPMorgan planned to make such extensions available to third parties that could build vertical applications incorporating such privacy, such as Komgo's energy trading application (Komgo is a group of companies using blockchain to improve trade commodity finance and related applications). To increase acceptance and uptake across enterprises, JPMorgan's Quorum merged with Consensys to launch Consensys Quorum, to offer both public and private enterprise solutions as well as robust features attractive to enterprises while maintaining open-source development.[41]

In addition to JPMorgan's Quorum, which is a permissioned version of Ethereum, Hyperledger Fabric (from IBM) along with open-source protocols, such as Hyperledger Besu, are further examples of enterprise-friendly protocols. A 2019 report showed that Corda, Hyperledger Fabric, and Quorum accounted for 86 percent of all unique blockchain developers placing code on GitHub.[42] Over time, competing protocols will merge and a few surviving platforms will emerge as industry standards. A side benefit of fewer but dominant blockchain protocols is that it might be easier to achieve interoperability if the number of platforms is limited.

To be successful, these several competing DeFi innovations must go beyond early adoption by technology enthusiasts and achieve mass market adoption. In the next and concluding section, I outline issues that must be addressed to obtain DeFi adoption at scale.

DeFi: Growing the Market, Moving to Mass Adoption

Figure 4.5 spells out areas that DeFi must address to take off and be adopted at scale. A major priority is ensuring DeFi customers of digital currency stability. Again, the heart of DeFi is Ether, the ERC-20 token, whose value can and has fluctuated (Ether's value fluctuated from $1,416 to $4,620 over the February 2021–2022 period, dropped from $4,384 to $1,786 in the May–July 2021 period, and was priced at $2,790 on February 19, 2022). Stablecoin projects such as DAI have helped Maker command a leading position in the DeFi world, but DAI is not immune to instability, especially during a crisis. In the pandemic-induced March 2020 liquidity flight, for example, DAI could not maintain its parity link to the US dollar. Hence the availability and inclusion of fiat currency stablecoins such as CBDC is a critical step in growing DeFi and making it appealing to mainstream customers. If DeFi applications could be built on CBDC as they become available, that would facilitate mass market adoption and DeFi could seriously challenge and disintermediate traditional fractional reserve banking.

While blockchain protocols with robust encryption and consensus validation schemes are secure, digital custody wallets and digital currency sites represent possible points of failure. In an incident on April

DeFi Tokens Price Stability	Improved Security: Resolving DeFi Protocol Flaws to Prevent Hacker Attacks and Lost Funds	Overcoming Scalability Limitations	User-Friendly Interfaces, Overcoming Unfamiliarity with New DeFi Applications
• Stablecoins to reduce token volatility • DeFi based on central bank digital currencies (CBDCs) • Multicurrency capability, lower transaction costs	• Auditing DeFi ecosystem; e.g., Consensys Diligence • Open source software, continuously upgraded • DeFi insurance; Etherisc, Insurwave	• Improved transaction processing speeds • Faster consensus algorithms • Decentralization and governance tradeoffs	• Simplified user on-ramps to join, contribute to DeFi protocols • Fewer and standardized DeFi platforms • Attracting and educating newcomers about DeFi capabilities and benefits • Co-existing with legacy applications

Figure 4.5
The path to mainstreaming DeFi

19, 2020, nearly all of Lendf.me's funds—around $24 million—were drained using a reentrancy hacker attack that had been discussed at Consensys Diligence (digital insurance) almost a year earlier. Because the hacker inadvertently exposed an IP address during the attack, Lendf.me was able to be recapture the funds.[43] And in February 2022, Wormhole, a bridge linking Ethereum with the Solana blockchain was hacked, with about $320 million in losses.[44] As the number of distinct DeFi protocols increases, with several competing DeFi offerings in the same niche, flaws in the weaker, less well-tested protocols will be exploited, possibly discouraging potential new DeFi customers. At the same time, disclosure of such attacks can help the DeFi community learn about and better protect against such attack vectors.

Auditing the software code could help prevent attacks that exploit code flaws. DeFi ecosystems can be strengthened with objective audits of its software and by ensuring protective steps are in place when launching upgrades or changing the DeFi system's rules and standards. Open-source software could help too, as outsiders can monitor code upgrades, analyze attacks, and suggest improvements. Also helpful is the availability of several DeFi insurance products, such as Opyn Insurance, an Ethereum insurance protocol offering for DeFi users and Ether speculators that helps insure against Ether price volatility on deposits with Compound. Nexus Mutual is a mutual insurance firm, similar to Lloyd's of London, that offers insurance to customers investing in DeFi firms such as Compound and Synthetix. As the size of their investment in these protocols increases, larger customers might seek insurance coverage to protect against smart contract risk as well.

Competing against financial services incumbents offering legacy solutions, blockchains must contend with scalability limitations, such as slow transaction processing, and create user-friendly on-ramps that empower customers to interact confidently with unfamiliar blockchain platforms.[45] Better interfaces and user education can also help attract new, inexperienced users to these emerging DeFi platforms, and wider use of DeFi applications will familiarize consumers with blockchain as well as the benefits from using blockchain software.

Stablecoins, including CBDC, and DeFi applications as a group could be the "killer apps" that blockchain evangelists eagerly await and could bring blockchain into the consumer mainstream. DeFi applications may be the ones that finally persuade enterprises of the viability of using blockchain for their own internal and external applications. Next, in chapter 5, I consider another major area of blockchain application, global supply chains.

5   Global Supply Chains and Trade Finance

In chapters 4 and 5, I discussed blockchain pilots in stablecoins and DeFi that have met with some success and have the capability to gradually reach enterprise-scale adoption. This chapter considers another interesting application: global supply chains and their trade networks. I also consider the complementary role of trade finance and cross-border payments in facilitating the smooth functioning of such global trade networks. I examine blockchain pilot applications in these areas and the extent of their success.

Global trade connects supply chains, cross-border payments, trade financing, and marketplaces that match buyers with sellers.

Supply chains manage the movement of goods from supplier to buyer and enable contracting parties to deliver a finished product on time and in accordance with negotiated prices and contract conditions. Value chains (which chart the stages though which customer value is created, from R&D through manufacturing and marketing) are dispersed across multiple countries; materials, components, and subsystems need to be available in sequence to complete the finished product. Such a value chain benefits from participation of and cooperation from value-creating enterprises, transportation providers, and regulators monitoring compliance with differing regulations in multiple legal jurisdictions.

Cross-border payments are necessary to finalize payment across global supply chains. Arranging such payment is complex and slow and can involve high fees and delays from obtaining regulatory agency approvals. Progress along these steps may not be transparent to transacting parties. At each step, payment for services rendered is necessary for transfer of control and ownership to the next actor in the supply chain. Likewise, lag time in payment can delay onward transit and negatively affect supply chain performance.

Trade finance catalyzes global trade enacted through supply chains, whether conducted on an open account or through the more traditional LC. In other words, sellers may accept LCs furnished by buyers and obtain eventual payment or extend credit directly to the customer. When directly extending credit, the seller can collect from their customers at the end of the period of credit extension, or factor such receivables, collecting a discounted amount of their face value immediately to increase their liquidity. Similarly, buyers may need to obtain financing to offer acceptable payment terms to the seller, and access to such financing may be contingent on proof of contract fulfillment and receipt of goods.

Marketplace services, which match buyers and sellers who interact within supply chains, are a logical extension of services for both parties. Such matching would be based on needs delineated in search criteria and can also offer value to other service providers such as banks financing trade and insurance companies that help mitigate trade shipment risk.

Figure 5.1 illustrates this view of an integrated global supply chain.

Thus, an ideal global supply solution, as displayed in figure 5.1, should integrate efficient supply chain functioning, cross-border payments facilitation, trade financing to enable such payments, and, eventually, marketplaces that link buyers with suppliers and other supply chain actors as well as trade financing entities.

Initially, a basic supply chain solution can link with trade finance, cross-border payments, and marketplace solutions from third parties, creating an ecosystem. Over time, dominant firms in each segment may choose to enter the adjacent markets and provide integrated, one-stop

| Global Supply Chain Monitoring and Coordination | Cross-Border Payment Facilitation | Global Trade Financing | Marketplace: Matching Buyers, Suppliers, Financing Entities |

Figure 5.1
Integrated global supply chain

solutions, attempting to replace a decentralized collaborative ecosystem solution with a dominant hierarchy model that is controlled from the center. In the following sections, I discuss blockchain pilots that have been developed and tested in each of these critical components of global supply chains.

Global Supply Chains

Supply chains are an arena where numerous pilots of enterprise-level blockchain applications have launched and progressed to reach operational scale. Blockchain usage can satisfy many pressing supply chain needs, ultimately enhancing performance. For example, deploying blockchain can provide supply chains with timely accurate information, secure and free from tampering, and aid in detecting fraud and counterfeiting. Immutability and cryptographically assured security can save costs by reducing the involvement of intermediaries. Smart contracts triggered by data entering the blockchain, including from IoT devices, can automate transactions, including speeding up shipment flow and expediting payment. In addition, trusted data from the blockchain can verify provenance and bolster quality assurance, and the data accumulated within the blockchain can become the basis for analytical insights underlying future supply chain improvements.[1]

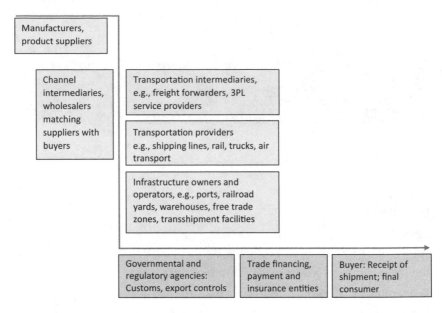

Figure 5.2
Supply chain participants and collaborators

Supply chains by their very nature consist of cross-industry partners, large and small, in a variety of industries. Actors come together and then drift apart on a regular basis, motivated by projects, be it a one-off supply contract or a longer-term procurement partnership. Figure 5.2 sets out the diverse actors who participate in the movement of goods across a global supply chain. All the parties listed above would need to be motivated (perhaps even cajoled) into joining the blockchain if the application is to provide benefits over legacy systems.

The Role of Documentation in Supply Chains

Complementing these actors as they connect along the supply chain is a significant volume of documentation that accompanies the goods being shipped. These documents verify ownership, stage in transit, regulatory compliance, and change in ownership. Complete and accurate documentation is essential to an uninterrupted shipment journey to the ultimate destination because correctly filled, verified, and duly assigned documentation is necessary for shipment clearance and hand-off to subsequent stages. Global supply chains function ponderously in large part because they rely on paper-based processes for most of their documentation. Conflicting information and lost documents lead to errors and suspend transaction approval. This creates a domino effect that results in long lead times, obscured status and location of a shipment, and inefficient capital allocation (due to higher investment in pipeline inventory).

When buyers finance their purchases with LC, proper documentation and verification is essential if the seller is to get paid. The issuing bank, acting for the buyer, issues an LC that the seller presents on completing a shipment. The bank honoring the compliant LC by releasing payment will in turn expect repayment from the buyer on the terms agreed. Hence, the issuing bank will not release payment unless it (or its representatives) has ascertained that the trade documents (e.g., the bill of lading) comply with the LC terms (description of goods, condition, quantity). Furthermore, the issuing bank will use its discretion in determining whether the LC terms have been met, and if it decides that there is a discrepancy, it must get the buyer's waiver or assent before payment is made. In other words, the issuing bank cannot make unilateral decisions.[2] Thus, documentation is essential, both for the smooth transfer of goods across intermediary points in the supply chain and for authorizing payment against proof of compliance with the sales contract and LC terms.

EDI has been the standard for document transmission in traditional supply chains; LCs are often issued as MT700 messages within the SWIFT network. Any changes in transit would require updated documentation consistent with the changes to permit continued processing and onward movement. Interruptions can result from changed contract terms or a lack of accurate updated information at both origin and destination. Obtaining the necessary modified documents can be a slow process that causes delays while raising costs. In many cases, supply chain actors have resorted to developing personal connections with expeditors at various locations to obtain such information and overcome bottlenecks.

Introducing blockchain architecture to supply chains would provide a revolutionarily secure, single source of truth. Immutable (tamper-evident) information that can be trusted would replace informal personal networks with continuously updated information, widely dispersed and available to all interested parties at decentralized nodes. Developing such a decentralized network involves working with and obtaining the participation of a large variety of potential ecosystem partners. There may be variations in each partner's (or node's) level of technical understanding and process capabilities. The network would be operating within different national jurisdictions, attempting to comply with different legal systems that might have conflicting requirements while implementing blockchain technology that is still evolving and by no means mature. And yet, there are pilots around the world whose success offers a glimpse of what global supply chains could be— error free, secure, with updated documents available in real time at a lower cost.

Configuring the Ideal Global Supply Chain

There are several desirable features that can result in the effective functioning of a global supply chain,[3] summarized in the following list:

- Link all parties to the supply chain
- Verified unique IDs for each of the actors, among them manufacturers, freight forwarders, customs and government agencies, transportation carriers (ships, trucks, rail, air, ports), third-party logistics (3PLs) service providers, and customers
- Use of IoT devices and sensors to monitor shipment conditions during transit and to continuously transmit information
- Timely (and eventually, real-time) information availability, updated for changes, covering shipment ID, location, storage characteristics such as temperature or humidity, changes in status (such as transfer of control), customs clearance completion, and duties assessed and paid

- Traceability related to provenance along the chain, custody tracking, and related documentation
- Controlled access to supply chain information, restricted to parties specific to an individual transaction
- Sharing of information, with data access restricted to relevant parties, maintaining competitive security and desired levels of privacy while avoiding silos and information redundancy
- Consistently high levels of tamper-evident security
- Common data and transmission standards for all involved supply chain entities, allowing for ease of access, coordination, collaboration, and verification
- Approvals and transfer of value facilitated for assets (goods, documents, payments) linked to contractual terms. Smart contracts can offer significant improvement over the current paper system, with contract execution triggered by data supplied by external events (oracles) and by information from IoT devices, with such updated information indicating fulfillment of contract terms.
- Greater efficiency and cost reduction from improved processes, fewer errors, fraud control, and reduced delays and time in transit
- Accumulated historic shipment data, which can serve as a basis for forecasting, capacity management, and pricing responsive to market conditions
- Ultimately, a single source of truth, leading to greater trust in partners and in supply chain efficiency and outputs

Deploying blockchain across the supply chain can offer several benefits. It would be possible to attach tokens to goods as they move along the supply chain, facilitating transfer of title between supply chain members as conditions are met. Such abilities would allow firms to find new markets and price risk accurately, ending up with "dynamic demand chains in place of rigid supply chains."[4] Such blockchain-enabled supply chains could also supply credentialed vendor personnel with unique traceable identifiers, allowing supply chain entities to monitor credentialed personnel in carrying out contractually required critical activities, such as sterilization and disinfection procedures in a food chain or verification of tamper-evident file downloads in an additive manufacturing environment.

In addition, digital control towers, which provide end-to-end visibility across the supply chain, including a central data dashboard of supply chain events and related business metrics, may be an alternative,[5] when embedded trust is less important and the number of players are few and do not change. From a legacy perspective, traditional database management systems may offer benefits without the cost and uncertainty of deploying new blockchain-based technology that is not mature or stable.[6] However, when high-volume transactions make speed and automation efficiency critical, blockchains offer a superior alternative.[7]

Given the potential that blockchain application has in surmounting supply chain deficiencies and improving their function, I now discuss TradeLens, a pilot application that is gaining traction.

Maersk, IBM, and TradeLens

TradeLens is a blockchain-based global supply chain "utility" jointly developed by Maersk and IBM. Maersk, a Danish shipping and logistics company, owned and operated by Maersk Lines, is the largest global container shipping firm, operating over seventy ports and terminals around the world. Maersk has an industry-leading market share of 16 percent, with the top five firms in the container shipping industry controlling 61 percent of the market, forming an oligopoly. Maersk formed an independent joint venture with IBM in 2014 to deploy blockchain technology and develop a global trade platform.[8] The product of their efforts became TradeLens, a blockchain solution designed as a permissioned network to serve the entire industry and remedy the deficiencies of current supply chain processes.

TradeLens was a joint venture, with Maersk owning 51 percent and IBM owning the remainder. Because ownership was centralized,

TradeLens differed from the normative blockchain preference for decentralized networks. However, the joint venture was intended to be independent from Maersk, with headquarters in New York, and with independent board members. The goal was to keep TradeLens neutral, with a firewall between the TradeLens platform and Maersk and other container ship competitors even while serving the various actors that collaborate within a supply chain, as set out in figure 5.2.

IBM, Maersk's partner, had experience using its Hyperledger blockchain protocol to develop blockchain solutions for various industry supply chain clients. IBM saw several benefits from using blockchain and its Hyperledger protocol in the supply chain context, including data consolidation and visibility, as supply chain information could be simultaneously and securely available to supply chain participants; enhanced shipment tracking, transparency, and trust in data provided by the network; shipment monitoring, such as confirming origin and provenance (bringing to light and preventing counterfeiting attempts),tracking storage conditions (e.g., temperature, humidity), and tracking dangerous or restricted materials; and real-time resolution of problems arising from supply delays, shortages, and faulty products (particularly useful in food chains, where food safety is paramount and timely knowledge can alert clients to suboptimal shipment conditions, contamination problems, and noncompliance with legal regulations). A well-known example of such outcomes is IBM's work with Everledger, which has digitally encrypted over one million diamonds on the blockchain, to facilitate tracking the journey of diamonds, both polished and rough, from mines to retail stores while also providing immutably linked diamond grading reports.[9]

TradeLens is intended to provide all supply chain data and information necessary to track and trace shipments, offering "end-to-end supply chain visibility to all actors involved in managing the supply chain to securely and seamlessly exchange information in real time."[10] Data privacy protection is a key feature of TradeLens, ensuring that only firms participating in a specific shipment have access to information relevant to that cargo. TradeLens aimed to deliver a paperless trade capability so that users could "securely submit, validate and approve documents across organizational boundaries," with access and approval permissions varying for sets of trusted stakeholders. Its usefulness to customers would increase as it expanded to include a wider range of supply chain constituents, including Maersk's competitors, and independent entities along the supply chain such as customs agencies and channel intermediaries. Therefore, to test and pilot TradeLens, IBM and Maersk had to recruit and persuade independent companies in several sectors to join the TradeLens blockchain. In addition, the TradeLens team had to develop long-term monetization strategies to recoup investment in building and operating the blockchain while also rewarding the various TradeLens members for their contribution to the value created.

TradeLens's design and implementation serves as a guidepost for successful blockchain application in the global supply chain area. TradeLens resolved several issues besetting global supply chains. It was able to meet the needs of each TradeLens supply chain member, thus increasing its usefulness and motivating key supply chain entities to join TradeLens, a critical factor when joining it is voluntary. TradeLens's architecture incorporates verified identity for each supply chain participant to determine transaction access and read-and-write privileges for each member, with cryptographic protection of data to enhance trust in the network. This works by having the TradeLens network select the relevant data to be collected from each network member, drawing on IoT devices and sensors to obtain real-time data, updated for state changes, covering shipment location, flow, and changes in status such as customs clearance and assessed duties.

Further, TradeLens uses mechanisms such as tokens and subsidies to supplement automated data collection and elicit timely data and updating from its members. Blockchain-derived immutability along with a timestamp and cryptographically linked data blocks create an audit trail and determine provenance, aiding traceability, custody tracking, and related documentation. Multiple privacy layers and access protocols determine which layers a member can access, restricting data access to the relevant counterparties in each transaction and providing competitive security while attempting to avoiding silos and information redundancy. Data sharing protocols between public ledgers allow supply chain data to be shared with external parties as and when needed.

As a business application operating in an environment of partial trust, TradeLens uses Hyperledger Fabric (the blockchain protocol) to create a permissioned voting-based approach to consensus, leading to rapid consensus and finality along with tamper-evident security. As joint owners, Maersk and IBM set common data and transmission standards, such as for APIs that allow third parties to add new modules and additional functionality to TradeLens. Such common standards are essential for ease of use, coordination, and collaboration across network members with varying IT configurations. In using Hyperledger Fabric, TradeLens can include a separate smart contract layer run in a container environment without direct access to the ledger state, with specific peer nodes (depending on the transaction), vouching for the correct execution of a given smart contract. The smart contract execution is triggered by data supplied by IoT devices distributed across the supply chain, and it can authorize the transfer of goods and documents as well as approve payments.

Using TradeLens can eliminate data silos and integrate data from multiple sources including shippers, 3PLs, ports, cargo terminals, ocean and inland carriers, customs authorities, and finance entities. This efficient data sharing can reduce errors, detect fraud, and reduce supply chain pipeline inventory and working capital, thus saving time and costs. As a collective, anonymized data from TradeLens, with member approval, can be linked to data analytics, providing insights into trade flows and logistics capabilities previously unavailable to the participants. Such historic shipment data, accumulated with increasing TradeLens use, can serve as a basis for forecasting, managing capacity, and pricing, with the aggregated data as a possible source of revenue if sold to interested industry constituents.

Of course, TradeLens faces competition, from other competing solutions, and it must overcome customer resistance to replacing tried and tested current practices. Further, TradeLens must persuade independent supply chain entities to collaborate through using its blockchain solution. The challenges associated with broadening TradeLens's market acceptance and getting firms from several related industries to work together in an ecosystem are discussed in more detail in chapter 6.

Intergovernmental Collaboration: eTradeConnect, Global Trade Connectivity Network

As discussed above, government agencies are critical to the smooth flow of goods through countries in a supply chain. Governments may bristle at allowing supply chains set up by private, for-profit firms to set conditions for network membership in a blockchain ecosystem and may refuse to cooperate. Without the participation of national customs agencies, the supply chain would slow down significantly, negating positive effects from improvements elsewhere in the chain. Hence, it is not surprising that some nation-states and their governments have sponsored with their own supply chain networks.

The Hong Kong Monetary Authority (HKMA) initiated a trade finance pilot—eTradeConnect—with international banks to address trade finance obstacles and reduce risk.[11] The features incorporated and tested in the pilot were similar to features incorporated in TradeLens, among them a permissioned blockchain to provide standardized digitized data to all members of the trade transaction and ecosystem and blockchain consensus-based validation of invoices, purchase orders, and bills of lading to prove authenticity. The network would spot attempts at "duplicate financing" and avoid fraud, and forging invoices would require forging related purchase orders and bills of lading, which are digitally signed by multiple participants who are parties to the transactions, alerting them to tampering attempts. Government sponsorship gave regulators influence over the trade finance application design, which motivated an increased emphasis on giving regulators access to continuously updated data to ascertain provenance and compliance with sanctions regimes and export controls. The MAS launched a similar Networked Trade Platform,[12] a one-stop trade and logistics network connecting domestic and foreign firms across the trade value chain.

The two nations have formed a Global Trade Connectivity Network (GTCN), linking Singapore's NTP and Hong Kong's eTradeConnect.[13] A governmental collaboration allows for jurisdictional and legal differences affecting trade between these two nations to be reconciled and for bringing on board banks specializing in trade finance for Asia. GTCN is a blockchain-based regional and global trading network that allows domestic firms in Hong Kong and Singapore to tap each other's domestic trade platforms, thus increasing their access to global trade opportunities while enhancing the transparency, integrity, and security of trade flows. Through GTCN, firms in Hong Kong and Singapore can interact with regulators and trade participants in both countries and obtain financing closer to receipt of goods, thus optimizing the use of working capital tied up in trade receivables.

IoT Sensors and Supply Chain: Ambrosus

There are many instances where data on ingredients and components used, provenance, manufacturing conditions, shipment conditions, and quality criteria are necessary to differentiate goods and to meet contract conditions and satisfy end users. Such data is also central to providing evidence of tampering and preventing counterfeiting. As noted earlier, goods being shipped cannot be cleared unless accompanying documentation is accurate and accepted by the relevant counterparties. Data-bonded tokens are one approach to tying together data and shipments: the tokens represent the shipment, and IoT sensors accumulate additional assembly line and shipping data. Examples of such data include provenance of goods and their ingredients, parts and components, data on manufacturing process conditions, and data on temperature, humidity, and other conditions of handling and storage during the shipping and delivery process.

These can all be attached to the token accompanying the goods in transit through the blockchain, available for changes of control and ownership across the supply chain. In the pharmaceutical industry, provenance and tracking shipments is crucial to detecting and guarding against counterfeit drugs and to monitoring the return of unsold drugs back to the manufacturer. In the case of controlled drugs, such as opioids, monitoring prescription data and refills are essential to prevent overuse and addiction with its harmful consequences.[14]

IoT sensors, if they can be made secure and tamperproof, can be a source of real-time data when linked to a blockchain network and used with smart contracts to automate transactions. Once online, they continually provide updated data to track shipments, monitor quality indicators, assess equipment conditions and readiness for maintenance, and help mitigate risk. IoT sensors communicate autonomously with other sensors and machines, creating possibilities for revenue from new services and monetization of data from the entire IoT sensor population deployed by the network.[15]

Ambrosus offers one such solution, linking IoT real-time sensors and electronic IDs with blockchain to improve supply chain visibility, provide quality assurance, and prevent counterfeiting.[16] Ambrosus is based on Ethereum and represents agreements between customers and their supply chains in smart contracts. Amber is the native token used to pay for activities and transactions, such as creating a digital asset representing a pallet or item being shipped. Data is bonded to an Amber token and is sent to the network, which follows a product or batch along the supply chain, acting as a digital ledger to ensure the secure and transparent transfer of information. Ambrosus's architecture consists of four interrelated modules. The Trace module generates data from IoT devices, and the Edge-Gateway collects and analyzes the IoT generated data and communicates with the third module, the Ambrosus blockchain, where the data is stored securely and is exchanged among the participants, as needed. The final module is a dashboard, which allows Ambrosus clients to retrieve, view, and further analyze their data.

Swiss cheese producers using Ambrosus can assure customers about the quality and provenance of the seventy thousand tons of cheese produced and exported from Switzerland every year. Consumers are concerned about safety and quality, and hence it is crucial to track the origin, production, and delivery conditions of raw milk cheese; track the temperature during the ripening and storage of cheese; and prevent contamination from the growth of harmful bacteria in the cheese. They also want information on the eco-friendliness of manufacturing procedures, employment conditions, animal welfare, livestock diet, and hygiene. Nutritive qualities of cheese are a differentiating factor, and they change depending on various conditions.

Ambrosus IoT sensors linked to the blockchain can provide data on all these factors. The multiple firms in the Swiss cheese industry can draw on the data from IoT sensors across the production value chain to offer verification of the provenance of the livestock, while IoT devices from the dairy farms and milk transportation tankers can verify the time and temperature at which the milk was collected and then received by the tankers. The dairy farm IoT sensors also attest to the levels of bacteria and antibiotics in milk as well as conjugated linoleic acid and Alphalinolenic acid, which are associated with anti-inflammatory effects and an important cheese quality consideration.

In addition, IoT sensors on milk tankers record the temperature and time in transit and the time of delivery at the cheese-producing facility. During cheese production, a variety of additional quality-related sensor data are captured during the various stages of cheese processing, such as the temperature when milk was curdled, conditions at pressing (to remove moisture), the duration and extent of salting, the duration and temperature during refining, and key measurements that point to the control of the fermentation process. The IoT data captured in the blockchain helps assure buyers of the quality of the Swiss cheese on offer.[17] Figure 5.3 illustrates the source and range of data available from secure IoT devices linked to a blockchain to help verify provenance and quality.

Food Trust: Addressing Safety, Freshness, and Waste in Perishable Foods

The Food Safety Modernization Act of 2011 increased regulation in response to an increased prevalence of foodborne illnesses. IBM's Food Trust[18] is a supply chain application that aims to address assurance of food safety by teaming with food industry leaders such as Dole, Kroger,

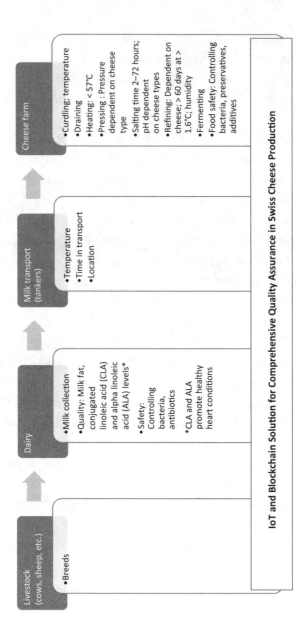

Figure 5.3

IoT and blockchain solution for the Swiss cheese industry. Source: Ambrosus, "Swiss Cheese: Protecting High-Quality Food Exports of Switzerland," p. 14 (May 2020).

Nestle, Tyson Foods, and Walmart to implement blockchain solutions along the supply chain. The project focuses first on food safety and seeks to securely trace products in seconds, help determine and mitigate sources of contamination, and reduce the economic burden of recalls that may become necessary. Second, the project emphasizes food freshness, using blockchain to increase supply chain visibility and optimize shelf life. Third, the focus on food freshness and early mitigation of contamination helps reduce food waste and maximize shelf life. These goals together help optimize the food supply chain and allow the industry to respond effectively to recalls. Such supply chain enhancement could also help meet sustainability goals, improve food quality, and certify provenance—the latter being an issue of growing importance in the organic and meat substitute markets.

A case in point is the use of the Food Trust blockchain application in New England's scallop fishing industry. The superior taste and quality of New Bedford scallops command a premium price. The industry was concerned about inferior scallops from other areas being misrepresented to consumers as hailing from New England and sold at premium prices, harming the New Bedford scallop reputation. Food Trust enabled provenance tracing, proving to restaurant owners, chefs, and their customers that the scallops were indeed from New Bedford. Another benefit was that the scallops could be traced to specific catches from individual fishing boats, and chefs concerned about problems such as overly sandy scallops could inform fishing boat captains who could then take steps to improve their fishing practices on future fishing expeditions.[19]

Cross-Border Payments

Cross-border payment flows are estimated to reach \$156 trillion in 2022.[20] They are inherently complex, resulting in a lack of transparency as to payment status (whether and when it has been completed), high costs to process payments (estimated at \$25–\$35 per transaction),[21] late payments, uncertainty as to the exact amounts to be paid out to recipients, trapped liquidity while payments are processed, and limited temporal availability of payment services due to time zone differences and limited operating hours in various recipient countries.

If the sender's bank does not have offices in the recipient's country, it will need to work with a correspondent bank that can channel payments through its network to that country. Since the payment is being made in a foreign country with funds that have been transferred to that country, the sender and their bank would like to guard against risk of settlement agent failure, which would lead to the payment not being made and the possibility of being unable to retrieve the transferred funds. One method of reducing settlement risk is to use the recipient country's central bank and its RTGS system. In this system, central bank reserves are used for real-time settlement, with obligations settled immediately as they are incurred. RTGS replaces deferred net basis settlement between individual banks, where the two banks total up all inflows and outflows over a defined period and settle the net amount owed by one party to the other. Such a deferred net settlement approach can accumulate credit risk. However, central banks restrict access to such RTGS accounts, and few banks have the global scale needed to justify operating RTGS accounts with central banks in several different countries. Further sources of complexity include the following:

- A lack of presence in the recipient's country requires finding correspondent banks that have the requisite in-country presence and obtaining access to RTGS systems with accompanying bank fees (eligibility conditions may restrict a bank from accessing a country's RTGS).

- The number of correspondent banks worldwide has been declining, necessitating the use of a chain of correspondent banks in sequence, with the final bank in the chain having the necessary in-country presence and ability to access the RTGS system. This lengthens the time it takes to process and finalize a cross-border payment.

- The multitude of banks involved in processing a cross-border transaction to finalize payment incurs processing costs at each bank node, raising total costs while also delaying payment.

- The use of varying messaging standards when communicating with other banks in the chain forces banks to use manual rather than automated processing to decipher message details, all of which can add to payment processing time. There are attempts to implement global payment messaging standards, such as the SWIFT GPI (global payments initiative, available to SWIFT member banks), ISO 20022, and use of a Legal Entity Identifier to uniquely identify each bank involved in global payments.

- A lack of transparency for senders: because of the number of banks that could potentially be involved in a cross-border payment, a sender may be unable to track the payment as it progresses through the chain of banks. The originating bank is often unable to track the payment as it enters the next link. This lack of transparency also extends to the fees charged by the chain of banks, the actual amount the beneficiary receives after conversion, and when such payment is completed.

- Restricted hours of operation of a central bank's RTGS system, together with time zone differences, leads to further delays in making cross-border payments.

- Interoperability issues arise from incompatible legacy systems (most banks use mainframes for high-speed, large volume transactions processing, with middleware layers to support interaction with newer applications) and from incompatibilities between new bank entrants using innovative new technologies and legacy RTGS systems. RTGS systems can be limited in their ability to accommodate the consensus validation algorithms used to verify transaction details in blockchain-based cross-border payment solutions.

- The slow and cumbersome payments process leads to trapped liquidity as entities involved in a funds transfer may need to set aside capital as required by regulations to cover settlement obligations. Entities may also need to prefund their "nostro" accounts as collateral and obtain foreign exchange funds in advance of the initiation of the cross-border transaction. (Nostro accounts are accounts that

banks hold at their correspondent banks overseas, and they function as collateral to cover risk while a foreign exchange transaction
is in process). Large banks have the scale to use continuous linked
settlement (CLS),[22] which facilitates settling foreign exchange trades
across time zones in a liquidity-efficient manner.

• Regulations concerning money laundering, customer identification,
  sanctions compliance, and cyber-risk controls and resilience vary
  across countries and raise the bank's total compliance costs when
  executing cross-border payments.

Governmental Efforts to Streamline Cross-Border Payments

Projects Jasper and Ubin[23] from the Bank of Canada and the MAS
(respectively) are pilots that tackle the cross-border payments problems described above. Jasper and Ubin explored the use of DLT-based
settlement for tokenized digital currencies across different blockchain
platforms. The project leaders noted there are alternatives to the DLT
technology used in the proposed model but that "DLT could offer an
easier and faster path toward adoption than a centralized approach
because it can leave the different jurisdictions involved in control of
their portion of the network while allowing for tight integration with
the rest of the network."[24] The pilot uses Hash Time Locked Contracts
(HTLCs, a type of smart contract) to ensure that all the events necessary
to justify a payment have occurred. HTLCs involve locking the asset,
which then requires the payment recipient to acknowledge receipt
with a cryptographic proof of payment within a set deadline or else
the payment is returned to the sender. HTLCs obviate the need for an
intermediary (i.e., the correspondent bank) to hold an escrow account
to ensure satisfactory transaction completion. Further, the pilot used
two different blockchain platforms—Corda in Canada and Quorum in
Singapore—to test interoperability issues.

The pilots considered various models including letting central bank
RTGS systems act as "super-correspondents,"[25] replacing the current chain
of intermediary correspondent (commercial) banks, and using CBDC

tokens available for wholesale interbank payment and settlement.[26] The project leaders noted that the wholesale CBDC model could be based on blockchain, but alternative technologies might also be workable.

In the wholesale CBDC model, the CBDC could be currency specific (i.e., linked to the Canadian dollar, the Singapore dollar, the British pound) and could be exchanged outside of the bank's or client's home country, with commercial banks holding multiple CBDC wallets (in different currencies) with their home central bank. Then, each central bank would need to support multiple CBDC tokens. An alternative to multiple CBDCs would be a universal CBDC linked to the basket of currencies of the participating governments and accepted by all these governments.

Implementing a wholesale CBDC model as stated would require the various governments to agree on procedures to set exchange rates for converting their domestic currency into the universal wholesale CBDC. An exchange would have to be set up to issue and redeem such CBDCs, with explicit rules allowing them to be used to settle cross-border transactions. The CBDC platform would need to operate 24/7 and in parallel with RTGS platforms to facilitate cross-border transactions in the CBDC between its banks and central bank within a country and across countries. Each country would have to set eligibility conditions for banks (or other settlement account holders) to hold a digital CBDC wallet in another country without having an RTGS account. Such a model would take time to implement as nations and central banks would need to implement legislation to accept a universal CBDC and manage their monetary policy to include a supply of the universal CBDC. Countries would need to agree on how the CBDC could be collateralized with central bank reserves, with the exchange rate risk as reserves in one country would be the collateral for a CBDC held in another country.

Furthermore, the universal CBDC, used simultaneously as a financial asset, a store of value, means of exchange, and for speculation, would introduce a single point of failure in the model. This is because the CBDC is controlled by a single entity, the central bank or equivalent, and if hacked it could compromise the foundational digital layer of a digital currency system. Canada and Singapore worked together on five successive stages of the Jasper and Ubin pilots, with the final phase report issued in July 2020 with the successful development of the prototype application, and described financial industry benefits. The project helped prove the business value of a blockchain-based payments network and established connectivity interfaces between the prototype CBDC network and other blockchain networks as well as support for specific use cases such as escrow for trade finance payments and delivery versus payment with private exchanges.[27]

A disruptive blockchain solution to address the problems endemic to cross-border payments would offer several features. First, upgraded, standardized payment messaging protocols would allow for sharing data. Second, it would end redundant repetition of steps involved in customer due diligence and verifying regulatory compliance. Third, blockchain would make it easier to accept and share data across the bank network, such as due diligence data furnished by counterparties, which would also require harmonized legislation across jurisdictions. Fourth, the extended availability of cross-border payments through the harmonization of RTGS systems with automated smart contract execution would nullify the impact of commercial banks' unsynchronized operating hours and provide broader access to RTGS systems, especially for smaller banks and nonbank payments providers.

Finally, blockchain solutions would provide greater scope for innovation from third parties (e.g., add-on Dapps for customer identification and due diligence). A successful application would offer outcomes such as lower cost and greater transparency for customers, a reduction in trapped liquidity at banks, and timely availability at central banks of data on the total volume of cross-border payments and their direction, which would lead to increased resilience, reduced systemic risk, and a better understanding of market trends in cross-border payments.

Ripple XRP and Cross-Border Payments

Sending money across borders, relying on the decades-old SWIFT interbank messaging system, is a process rife with problems. Cross-border remittance fees are high, it can take several days to complete the remittance, the sender does not know the actual F/X rate used in converting currencies, and the entire process is opaque, with remittance status unclear. In a complex and slow process, the sending bank must connect with correspondent banks in a chain across the global banking network, and the sender does not receive confirmation of completion of transfer for several days. Further, banks involved in facilitating such transfers must maintain liquidity balances in several foreign currencies on the various remittance corridors, increasing their working capital needs. Although the universal CBDC model discussed earlier presents a solution, the need for collaboration across several sovereign governments, and the accompanying additional monetary policy implications make private digital currencies an attractive alternative approach to smoothing cross-border payments, also making them less costly and increasing transparency. Private firms have entered this arena, attracted by the large addressable market and attendant profit opportunities—if they can successfully resolve cost, speed, transparency, and regulatory issues for customers.

Ripple is one such private sector start-up, offering its own digital currency, XRP, to make cross-border payments more efficient. Ripple is innovating with blockchain to better serve customers dissatisfied with existing solutions.[28] Ripple's blockchain solution has several components. It developed a digital currency, XRP, for use in transferring money across borders. In parallel, it developed XRP Ledger, a DLT network for its clients, to continually update and store clients' cross-border payment transactions and account balances. It then developed and implemented xRapid, an open-source blockchain protocol, to validate transactions, update ledgers, and complete transfers. Ripple also developed its unique node list (UNL),[29] with a UNL consisting of select trusted nodes that are the only nodes authorized to collectively validate and update the ledger with new transactions and balances.[30]

The XRP currency, XRP Ledger, the xRapid protocol, and UNL are integrated with RippleNet, Ripple's financial network, which banks and financial institutions join if they wish to use Ripple for initiating and managing cross-border payments. The key innovation of RippleNet is that clients can exchange the national fiat currency of their choice for XRP; transfer the XRP near instantaneously, securely, and at low cost; and then immediately convert the XRP received into local currency on the other end of the transaction. This is possible because Ripple persuaded cryptocurrency exchanges in multiple countries to list XRP for trading. This allows entities who participate in sending or receiving XRP to use the exchanges to purchase or sell XRP holdings for national currencies such as the US dollar or the euro. The emergence and growth in trading volume in XRP on such cryptocurrency exchanges gradually increases XRP liquidity, and ease of exchange with various fiat currencies at both ends of the remittance corridor, contributing to the willingness of counterparties to use XRP for their cross-border remittance needs.

As more banks join RippleNet, multiple routing pathways open for effecting transfers through different sets of correspondent banks. Correspondent banks form a network through which banks can operate with clients in a country in which they have no operations, using a chain of network banks to eventually reach the client. These bank groups, collaborating on a transfer through RippleNet, create a network, and different networks can compete to complete the transfer with lower fees. This results in a competitive transfer fee market, which gives sending clients access to lowest cost transfers. Clients first initiate a request to RippleNet to transfer XRP across borders, which uses the xRapid protocol to manage the transfer. The XRP Ledger maintains the transaction records (continually updated every two seconds), and once the latest state of the ledger is validated by most nodes, the XRP transfer is completed with payment finalized. Together, the various Ripple features enable it to disrupt the cross-border remittance market, increase its market share at SWIFT's expense, and become a major competitor in this payment segment.

Ripple competes with SWIFT, the global financial messaging system that banks have used since the 1970s for their cross-border remittances.

Ripple had to persuade regulators in each pair of countries along key remittance corridors to authorize XRP use in their markets and its conversion into local currencies. It also had to foster a trading market for XRP so that XRP owners could exchange it for fiat national currencies and other assets. Such a market is essential if Ripple clients are to accept XRP as the basis for cross-border payments.

While Ripple would prefer that its customers use XRP, Ripple also allows banks to use RippleNet and xRapid to transfer fiat currencies, for a fee lower than the cost of using SWIFT. Banks then manage their own liquidity balances in different currencies in each country instead of maintaining one pool of liquidity denominated in XRP across multiple remittance corridors. Banks can thus use RippleNet instead of SWIFT, getting the benefit of real-time settlement at a lower cost while still retaining their existing processes for KYC, AML, sanctions screenings, and regulatory compliance issues.

As banks become familiar and verify the benefits of using Ripple, they can decide whether to also start using XRP. Ripple offers its bank clients that use XRP its own On-Demand Liquidity service, for a fee, giving bank customers access to the required amount of XRP balances needed in any specific country. Bank customers would directly benefit from using XRP, as it would lower their working capital, by not having to establish nostro and vostro accounts in different foreign currencies in the respective remittance corridors. Transaction fees are paid in XRP, which is then burned (the XRP received in transfer fees is taken out of circulation), reducing XRP supply and gradually raising its price.

Once regulator and bank concerns about digital currency were satisfied, Ripple was careful to build an ecosystem of banks and nonbank financial institutions on RippleNet. However, the relative ease of becoming a node on RippleNet raises the possibility of reputational damage to banks in RippleNet: if darknet users formed nodes in RippleNet, they could submit and request validation for illegal transfers. Ripple's governance mechanisms (which is currently dominated by Ripple) would be the principal safeguard against such eventualities.

XRP's price appreciated as demand for using XRP grew, raising the value of Ripple's stock of the digital currency. This allowed Ripple to regularly convert XRP into operating funds, giving it capital to discount RippleNet and XRP Ledger usage fees, and subsidize lower prices, all of which helped attract new customers to the Ripple ecosystem. Thus, XRP, created and owned at Ripple's genesis, provides Ripple the wherewithal to seed the market to realize positive network effects. Figure 5.4 summarizes the flow of key events forming Ripple's disruptive business model.

Early Ripple adopters were mostly newer, smaller challenger banks and nonbank fintech firms. As the number of institutions using RippleNet increases, the RippleNet network becomes more attractive to new customers, increasing demand for XRP and stimulating volume XRP usage. Ripple's success threatens major banks as the increasing use of RippleNet would reduce the volume of cross-border remittances sent through Citi, Barclays, HSBC, and other major global banks dominating this market segment. SWIFT responded with its GPI, which will offer same-day cross-border transfers, transparency in fees, and end-to-end tracking of payments, reducing its bank clients' motivation to move to Ripple.

Hence, it is in Ripple's best interest to grow RippleNet as quickly as possible. Its aim to divert remittance traffic from the major banks and the SWIFT system to its own network before CBDCs and stablecoins, as well as an evolving SWIFT network, establishes it as an alternative to XRP. Ripple's disruption attempt is built on offering lower cross-border remittance fees, near-instantaneous transfer of funds, real-time verification of transfer and receipt, a known exchange rate at time of transfer, and a reduction in working capital needs if clients choose to replace multiple currencies with XRP in their transfers. Of course, private digital currencies such as XRP raise issues such as stability and systemic risk and a need for cross-border oversight, as discussed in chapter 3.

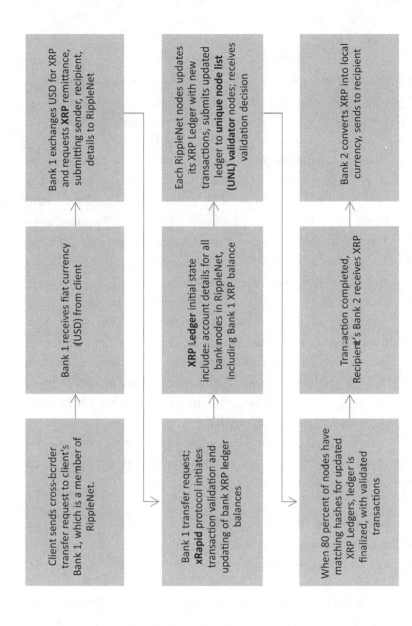

Figure 5.4
Ripple's disruptive process for cross-border remittances

Client sends cross-border transfer request to client's Bank 1, which is a member of RippleNet.

Bank 1 receives fiat currency (USD) from client

Bank 1 exchanges USD for XRP and requests **XRP** remittance, submitting sender, recipient, details to RippleNet

Bank 1 transfer request; **xRapid** protocol initiates transaction validation and updating of bank XRP ledger balances

XRP Ledger initial state includes account details for all bank nodes in RippleNet, including Bank 1 XRP balance

Each RippleNet nodes updates its XRP Ledger with new transactions, submits updated ledger to **unique node list (UNL) validator** nodes; receives validation decision

When 80 percent of nodes have matching hashes for updated XRP Ledgers, ledger is finalized, with validated transactions

Transaction completed, Recipient's Bank 2 receives XRP

Bank 2 converts XRP into local currency, sends to recipient

Trade Finance

Trade finance on open account terms is an increasingly popular payment arrangement in global trade.[31] Under open account terms, a
seller ships goods to a buyer, with payment to be made within a certain period, that is, thirty, sixty, or ninety days. The seller/shipper bears
the risk of nonpayment, leading sellers to obtain credit insurance, an
additional cost of global trade and trade financing. Furthermore, banks
are reluctant to finance global trade as an unscrupulous firm might
attempt to use the same purchase order (a paper document) and forge
such documents to obtain financing for the same shipment from multiple banks. As a result, small- and medium-sized enterprises (SMEs) are
less able to obtain trade financing from banks, stunting their growth.

DLT use could reduce such fraud with authenticated digitized versions of purchase orders, bills of lading, and invoices, alerting counterparties to attempts at duplicate financing of the same shipment. DLT
use permits tracing document flow, recording transaction evolution,
and—with links to smart contracts—releasing financing against proof
of shipment, of arrival, of exchange of title, to a bill of lading, and to
the goods themselves, all using real-time data. With greater certainty,
security, and fraud protection, banks would be able to lend to SMEs
with reduced risk and lower interest rates, furnishing both the sellers
and the banks with new sources of revenue growth.

HKMA Pilot in Trade Finance[32]

Given the pressing need to improve the trade financing environment,
the HKMA, operating as a regulator, teamed with several large global
banks in Hong Kong to develop a proof of concept for a DLT-based trade
financing platform. The goal was not only to develop a "technology
prototype, but also a thorough investigation of how DLT can potentially address a wide range of business, regulatory, legal, and technical
issues related to trade finance."[33]

The prototype trade finance solution design consists of a blockchain
base data layer to distribute data across actors and nodes and a business

application user layer, with end-to-end capture of the several steps in shipment movement and its financing, from supplier to customer. Banks could substitute their own internal "trade finance and trade systems" for the business application layer developed in the pilot and use their own user interfaces, linking to the blockchain-based data layer. Thus, the blockchain application can be linked with a bank's legacy systems as an intermediate solution.

The business user layer models the chain of events in trade finance. There are nodes for supply chain participants, logistics operators, and freight forwarders, similar to the TradeLens platform. Regulators, such as the HKMA, can join the platform to gain access to the data layer and for control and compliance purposes. Both SMEs and large corporations can request financing, furnish documentation, establish identity, and so forth.

Inclusion of both supply chain participants and regulators is essential for the effective provision of trade finance as they control events that can trigger smart contracts that release tranches of approved trade finance amounts. An integrated solution combining TradeLens and a trade finance platform would be a natural evolution and emerge as a highly useful blockchain application for both sellers and buyers in global trade.

Governance structures are an integral part of designing and implementing the trade finance solution and moving beyond pilots to commercial scale use. The trade finance prototype developed by the HKMA allows for the participation of financing entities, counterparties, regulators, and other parties necessary to verify that contract conditions are being met. Governance must offer a clear direction as to which data would be stored off-chain to speed network performance, protect data privacy, and lower costs (on-chain data storage in a blockchain is expensive).

Governance also extends to establishing dispute resolution, particularly in cross-border trade, which is characterized by multiple, distinct, and possibly conflicting international jurisdictions. (The fairness of a specific judicial system and enforcing compliance are pertinent matters.) Since a well-designed solution would interest most supply chain participants and increase public welfare through job creation, export earnings, and export sector competitiveness, public sector participation in ownership and governance that creates a public utility could be a worthy development.[34]

Trade Marketplaces

Before buyers and sellers can begin interacting through global supply chains, they need to find each other. Once they do, they negotiate to discover if they can arrive at a satisfactory sales agreement, spelling out contract terms agreeable to both sides. While buyers can be retail consumers, the focus here is on B2B transactions and on industrial buyers contracting in volume for internal use in their own processes or for eventual sale to end users. In such B2B situations, buyers are likely to choose sellers who can meet their detailed specifications.

For example, in the case of volume clothing buyers, specifications might cover the nature of fiber used, the weaving process resulting in finished cloth, specific dyes and colors used, the printing or finishing process for patterns, the design for finished garments, quality of stitching, sizes and quantities for each color, fabric and pattern, and ancillaries such as fasteners used, labels, and care instructions. Buyers may want the freedom to specify quantities to be included in each order under the total agreement, the destination of each shipment, storage conditions, trans-shipment points, and compliance with customs and other export regulations. Buyers may also want control over manufacturing conditions, environmental issues and proper disposal of hazardous waste, fair treatment of workers, avoidance of child labor, payment of fair wages, and equality in treatment of gender, ethic group, and religion.

Buyers may also want to ensure intellectual property protection (i.e., proprietary designs) and to manage the impact of foreign exchange fluctuations. As global supply chains involve contracting with suppliers in multiple geographic locations subject to varying legal jurisdictions, buyers may find it difficult to verify sellers' ability to comply with contract conditions, such as technological capabilities, range of production equipment and total factory capacity, availability of adequate working capital, staffing levels to ensure timely production of contracted output, a minimum level of experience with similar goods, the satisfaction of other customers with this seller, and overall general business reputation.

The difficulty that buyers may encounter in verifying seller capabilities, experience, and reputation leads to the use of intermediaries. Intermediaries can take over the critical function of qualifying sellers and matching buyers with sellers who can meet their desired profile and set of necessary capabilities. They charge fees for such services but reduce risk for buyers and increase the likelihood of buyers finding a satisfactory source of supply. Li & Fung,[35] based in Hong Kong, is one such intermediary, with over a hundred years of experience and a large pool of potential sellers and contract manufacturers in a wide range of countries in Asia and other regions.[36] Li & Fung uses its staff to audit and verify seller capabilities before offering them as potential supply sources matching their buyer clients' wish list.

Over time, disruptive online marketplaces have emerged to match buyers and sellers along the lines described above, competing with traditional matching services offered by firms such as Li & Fung. While Li & Fung concentrates on B2B applications, linking enterprise buyers with merchant suppliers, Alibaba (Taobao) and Amazon offer retail sellers the opportunity to establish web storefronts and connect with and sell to Alibaba and Amazon customers; Li & Fung has evolved to also offer similar functions. These online marketplaces function as platforms, often multisided and open to buyers, sellers, and other supply chain actors such as shippers, freight forwarders, financing entities, and insurance companies. They may offer free access to buyers or even subsidize them to attract them to their platforms while obtaining revenue by charging intermediary access fees and commissions to sellers and other parties.

As with other online platforms, these online marketplaces are subject to both same-side and cross-side network effects,[37] attracting more buyers as the number of sellers and contract manufacturers proliferate, and as other buyers (competitors) flock to these platforms and obtain satisfactory results in their search for potential supply partners. The quality and ease of use of application interfaces, privacy protection, and the degree of quality control exercised in enabling provider access to the network are all factors determining the extent of online plat-form usage. As with most platforms subject to network effects, a lim-ited number of platforms are likely to emerge as survivors and become oligopolies, with the potential to charge higher intermediary fees and capture a greater share of the value created by buyer-seller interaction and contracting.

It is in the context of preventing such platform marketplace oli-gopolies and avoiding the payment of rising intermediary fees that blockchain-based marketplaces appear as an alternative. The block-chain platform would allow buyers and sellers to interact with each other directly, avoiding or reducing intermediary fees. Such platforms can also offer escrow accounts, releasing payment against proof of per-formance. As discussed previously, HTLCs can be used to execute the simultaneous exchange of payment for performance completion. The data accumulated over multiple buyers and transactions can inform and lead to better forecasting of demand and market trends, aiding buy-ers in avoiding the need to discount excess merchandise.

For such aggregated data and associate forecasts to be available to net-work members, the blockchain's governance mechanisms would need consent from members to include their transaction data in the aggre-gated database, and then develop algorithms to conduct data analytics. Next, the managers would need to price such services, offering varying prices for member segments linked to their cooperation in aggregating the data necessary for forecasting and obtaining member consent to sell such trend analysis and forecasting services to nonmembers, for higher fees. Such fees from external clients can subsidize further development and upgrades to the blockchain solution. The platform can also help manage any tax consequences from such transactions.

The key difficulty in establishing such P2P blockchain platforms, however, is in qualifying sellers; certifying their experience, capabilities, and reputation; and guaranteeing performance. A recent attempt is the Trust Your Supplier network from IBM and Chainyard.[38] A common thread lies in using blockchain's ability to create and use tokens native to the blockchain to qualify sellers and their commercial reputation, with tokens awarded to a seller for high performance in meeting contractual commitments. A seller's accumulated tokens can serve as a proxy for reputation score, and buyers can use such reputation scores in choosing between alternative sources, patronizing higher-performing sellers or contract manufacturers. Suppliers can also reward loyal buyers and contract renewal with such tokens, as payment for loyalty and repeat business, with tokens exchangeable for seller services.

A platform such as Trust Your Supplier concentrates on enabling enterprises to find qualified trustworthy suppliers, with immutable supplier certification in meeting ISO standards, sustainability ratings, diversity, and reputation. The platform can help a merchant rapidly assess a potential supplier, drawing on their reliability record, performance ratings, and answers to FAQs from other users. It does this by using third parties such as Dun & Bradstreet to validate supplier records, EcoVadis for sustainability profile, and banks and entities such as RapidRatings that can verify account information and financial profile and risk. Clients can interact with the Trust Your Supplier application with web interfaces (APIs) and through procurement platforms such as SAP Ariba, and they can use a personalized dashboard to find and then select between qualified suppliers. Sellers who are not meeting their commitments, or acting in bad faith, can be denied access to the platform, with similar sanctions for buyers. IBM refers to these services as providing suppliers with a "blockchain-enabled digital passport."[39] Sharing such passport data reduces time to validate and onboard that supplier

This chapter surveyed blockchain application in three different industry sectors—digital currency and payments, DeFi applications using digital currencies, and global supply chains and trade finance.

These applications share a common element: they consist of multiple independent firms that come together to meet customer needs. This requires that they share information, trust each other, and collaborate in the best interests of the customer while remaining competitive and attempting to increase their profitability, forming ecosystems to provide customer solutions. Blockchains are uniquely suited to function effectively in ecosystems, and in chapter 6, I discuss the ecosystems framework and its strategic implications. I then draw on the varied results of several applications and pilots to discuss how enterprises can best leverage the ecosystem perspective to launch successful blockchain applications.

6 Blockchains as Ecosystems

The ecosystem form of organization has been growing in importance as an organizing principle for firms competing in a global digital economy. Rapid innovation and competitive advantage have stemmed from designing customer solutions that involve capabilities and contributions from multiple independent firms. It is useful to ask whether an ecosystem form of organization might be particularly appropriate for developing successful blockchain applications.

Blockchain nodes can be distributed across multiple firms in a single industry and/or across multiple industries. This introduces the possibility of interorganizational collaboration to develop blockchain-based customer solutions, which ultimately may perform better than individual competitor offerings. Such interorganizational solutions can draw on the multiple capabilities of disparate partners, cocreating highly modular, customized customer solutions. These interorganizational blockchain-based customer solutions contrast with platform-based solutions where strong network effects lead to a few firms, sometimes just one, dominating the platform with winner-take-all results. In contrast, blockchain applications based on voluntary cross-industry cooperation by independent firms can draw on each participant's distinct but complementary capabilities to create continuously improving customer solutions—"a proliferation of ecosystems of ecosystems."[1]

Such blockchain customer solutions do require that the firm step outside its organizational boundaries, but the blockchain value proposition increases when the blockchain network attracts ecosystem-wide participation. Thus, blockchain solutions will often require firms to coexist in an ecosystem, which collectively innovates and satisfies customers, enlisting each member firm in the ecosystem to choose roles such as orchestrator, innovator, supplier, complementor, intermediary, and regulator. Customers can choose between different ecosystem networks to solve their problems, and thus ecosystems compete with other ecosystems rather than firms competing against one another. However, ecosystems also require significant coordination by ecosystem orchestrators, which can be at odds with decentralization. As we have seen, some form of permissioned blockchain, with the orchestrator setting conditions of access to and levels of participation in the network, is often where enterprises have landed in their own pilots.

In this chapter, I first consider key aspects of ecosystem organization and how they might apply to blockchain-based solutions. I then consider examples of interorganizational blockchain pilots and the results they have achieved by adopting an ecosystem framework. The examples include autonomous vehicles in a sharing economy mode, health care application, and global supply chains. These examples allow us to assess the value of the ecosystem form of organization as a catalyst for successful enterprise-level blockchain implementation.

Firms initiating a blockchain-based ecosystem platform have to decide how to design an inclusive ecosystem model, and, conversely, firms within the ecosystem have to assess whether to join the ecosystem by weighing the potential benefits, their possible role in the ecosystem, and the risks of becoming dependent on and subordinate to the dominant blockchain orchestrator. Ecosystem complexity, stemming from several interacting subsystems, can be a motivator for likely members as membership in such blockchain networks allows the members to collectively offer solutions beyond the capabilities of any single member. At the same time, ecosystem members' preference for a more participatory governance blockchain may run counter to the design imposed by dominant network initiators and programmed into the specific blockchain rules and architecture.[2]

Strategic Thinking in an Ecosystem Perspective

Ecosystems consist of "partners who need to interact for a focal value proposition to materialize."[3] Ecosystems come in several forms. Andrew Shipilov and Annabelle Gawer identified multiple forms of ecosystems, outlined below:[4]

- *General ecosystem*: a set of actors who complement other ecosystem members with nongeneric complementary traits and capabilities
- *Business ecosystem*: a community of organizations, institutions, and individuals that impact the enterprise's customers and suppliers, with an intent to benefit both customers and suppliers
- *Innovation ecosystem*: a set of actors that contribute to the focal offer's user value proposition, with the possibility that an innovation ecosystem may evolve into a business ecosystem as products and solutions become mature enough to develop as economically viable business propositions
- *Platform ecosystem*: a core technology (typically, software together with network infrastructure and cloud storage) onto which members can connect their complementary products and services, often via standardized or open interfaces. Platform owners/operators may be a subset of the full ecosystem, who collectively control platform development, standards (data privacy, for instance), and revenue sharing and set the conditions to access the platform.

Blockchains are particularly capable of becoming platform ecosystems. Initially rooted in cocreation and shared value among primary ecosystem partners, the core platform ecosystem may evolve over time, with new ecosystem members further developing the platform and its offerings, continuously improving customer solutions and facilitating transactions between ecosystem members.

Ecosystem Design to Offer Successful Customer Solutions

Why is an ecosystem model needed? The enterprise considering an ecosystem model needs to weigh ecosystems against hierarchically organized supply chains and/or a vertically integrated firm with the enterprise playing a central role. When modular components are fitted to shape the customer solution, ecosystem models are likely to be superior to vertically integrated and hierarchical organizations. Putting together an ecosystem is complex, and the enterprise needs a strong rationale, a robust business case to justify the investment, and a path to monetization.

Ecosystem Interface Architecture

The interface would be shaped by the ecosystem's goals and by the need to allow a specific subset of members to collaborate to meet these goals. For example, an ecosystem might seek to establish industry-specific utilities, reducing friction from existing pain points. Members would need to agree to abide by shared processes and accept iterative and continuous improvement. Choosing a blockchain protocol is a fundamental step as the protocol needs to be adopted by all would-be ecosystem members. Ecosystem members as well as visitors and potential customers would be recognized by unique, verifiable digital identities. Members would agree on APIs facilitating visitor access and third-party add-ons and rules governing data flows, data analytics, links to IoT networks, and cloud infrastructure. Equally important are the products and services featured in the blockchain, with the intent to provide an integrated solution. However, as the number of users and providers grow, blockchain speed and scalability issues could be a hindrance to offering fast service and to providing quick, agile responses.

Ecosystem Membership

When the ecosystem is formed, its founding members could set minimum partner capabilities to join the ecosystem. Members would need to meet a minimum level of technological capability to manage nodes and data securely and to adopt the standard protocol. The governing members may establish partner tiers, depending on member contribution to the solution and levels of access and permissions. As independent entities join the ecosystem, they would have to negotiate the degree of interdependence they can accept. While ecosystems could vary in the number of partners, they are likely to grow over time if customers find their solution attractive and if future members meet the ecosystem's conditions of entry.

As the ecosystem is established, its viability would depend on "must-have" members, whose domain expertise, unique capabilities, and "gravitational pull" is essential to differentiating the ecosystem from competitors' and attracting customers. Founding members would need to identify desired partners and consider features that would persuade them to join. Designing a minimum viable ecosystem is the starting point to ensure an acceptable level of benefit for all ecosystem partners. This could involve choosing to subsidize particularly desirable partners (possibly for a predetermined initial period) and to attract early members to grow the ecosystem. The "ecosystem has to be a club that others want to join."[5]

As ecosystems are collaborative, a key question is who to collaborate with. Such collaboration could extend to erstwhile and future competitors or could transcend industry boundaries to include cross-industry partners. Collaboration is key because cocreation is an essential advantage of the ecosystem approach. Cocreation is a form of crowd sourcing that encourages multiparty innovation, hence the need for open interfaces that offer links between providers and enable customized solutions.

Ecosystems that address customers around the globe would also seek geographic diversity in their partner base. Global reach helps reach creative partners, beyond existing organizational, regional, and national boundaries. Ecosystem partners would necessarily play different roles, but among them the orchestrators would be key to building the network and recruiting partners, with other members joining an already-functioning ecosystem. After the ecosystem is established, growing the network would become a strategic consideration.[6] This is essential to expand content and capabilities, which can in turn generate new products and services. The growth path would cover evolving customer solutions, transaction facilitation, and entry into adjacent markets. Growth and scale can aid networks in competing against other networks, and positive network effects that help achieve scale can be accelerated by carefully assembling the partners in the network.

As the partner network is built up, it becomes important to "glue" the partners together by creating a sense of common purpose and community; partner exit could mean network deterioration. Keeping network partners together, then, depends on meeting partner expectations and recognizing and rewarding their disparate contributions. The total gains realized by partners collectively should have the characteristics of a positive-sum game rather than a winner-take-all profile; otherwise, the ecosystem could disintegrate, and its instability would in turn compromise the quality of customer solutions, negatively affecting the ecosystem's performance and survival.

An Ecosystem as a Platform

Ecosystems could feature a digital platform that enables interaction and transaction completion, serving enterprise and/or consumer markets. A platform ecosystem would likely be a many-sided platform with multiple providers. It would be able to integrate several platforms from its member industry subgroups and evolve to serve new markets and customer groups, becoming a multi-industry utility, with hubs at interconnection points between major providers and key industries. The modularity feature would allow individual ecosystem partners to weave together multiple value propositions in cooperation with a changing set of other ecosystem members, thus offering interorganizational and interindustry solutions. Providing open APIs and self-service portals could increase the chances of success by reducing barriers to attracting developers and customers.

Monetization

Ecosystem initiation can require significant up-front investments, and eventual return on investment would play a role in determining ecosystem launch approval. Likewise, monetization paths are an essential element of ecosystem strategy. A fundamental decision surrounds the question of who pays. Ecosystem orchestrators and members could choose between charging providers, users, or both. Charging providers implies that members derive significant benefit from participating in the ecosystem and are paying the ecosystem network for deal flow. Alternatively, customers could be charged a fee for service. The fees charged could vary over time with volume and usage, complexity of service provided, and value delivered. Further, ecosystems need both providers and partners, with network effects multiplying in a burgeoning symbiotic relationship between the numbers of providers and customers. Thus, motivating the early entry of multiple providers with subsidies, reduced fees, and a discount structure can hasten the generation of network effects.

Pricing could be linked to exclusivity offered select customers and providers (who may be competitors). Beyond ecosystem services, additional revenue could stem from the selling of data, marketing analytics findings, and consulting services based on ecosystem usage analysis. Aside from revenue, ecosystem governance would also need to manage finances, including initial investment decisions (and subsequent continuing investment in building ecosystem capabilities), and building up reserves. Maintaining ecosystem viability flows from effective ecosystem performance. Hence, baseline output metrics and comparison with desired performance standards are necessary to monitor ecosystem health and to take corrective action as needed. Common performance metrics worth considering are set out in figure 6.1 below.

Ecosystem Governance

Given the independent yet interdependent relationship between ecosystem partners who collectively provide the customer solution, governance is essential for setting goals, rules, standards, and fairness in assessing and rewarding partner contributions. It would not be a stretch to declare that without good governance, the ecosystem would dissolve, while fair governance would help achieve scale. Governance would likely be shared among ecosystem orchestrators and key providers, with avenues for ecosystem members to voice their opinions and

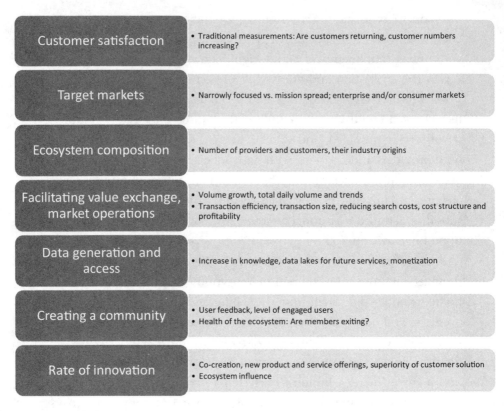

Figure 6.1
Ecosystem evaluation metrics

offer their assent or dissent. Ecosystem governance can be conceptualized as managing tensions between ecosystem members, varying across multiple dimensions, including standardization versus variety, control versus autonomy, and collective decision-making versus individualistic decision-making.

Ecosystems can evolve across these dimensions, balancing between openness (permissionless) and permission, giving the ecosystem orchestrator leverage over the ecosystem. Governance duties should include the following:

- Determining whether the ecosystem will be open or permissioned (the latter would have to set conditions for accessing services, for both providers and users)

- Coordinating innovation, particularly at the initial stages when early customer solutions are being developed, the goal being an efficient decentralized interactive collaboration system
- Fostering value creation to differentiate from competing ecosystems
- Setting customer service levels and safeguarding customer interests, inculcating ecosystem-wide standards of ethical behavior
- Assessing partner contributions to value creation and fair sharing of value created between members in proportion to contribution
- Resolving IP issues: IP ownership, IP sharing, and payment, and IP spillover into ecosystem offerings; compensation for IP absorbed into core value proposition
- Regulating patents and code ownership by members since a significant proportion of value creation would reside in code development and unique intellectual property
- Encouraging and retaining membership; aligning member activities toward common goals
- Deciding the composition of the regulatory body, with channels for ecosystem members at large to offer their opinions and assent on proposed regulations and revisions
- Setting rules and standards (e.g., data and service quality standards, error correction routines); data ownership and access, sharing, security, and maintenance; leveraging data analytics; sharing with ecosystem partners macro insights from collective anonymized data
- Imposing sanctions, including forced exit, when partner actions are deleterious to the continued growth and competitiveness of the ecosystem

Organizational Change: Implications

The ecosystem mode of organization runs contrary to well-established, hierarchically controlled organizations. Adopting the ecosystem framework would require significant organizational change as the organization and its members move from hierarchy to greater equality. A significant task is to establish trust among ecosystem members. Corporate culture must now modulate a competitive ethos of rivalry and pursue inter-organizational collaboration, following a path to informed consensus. Alongside the broader move to ecosystems, the organization must cope with the move to an unfamiliar technology—blockchain. Some fear and resistance to change is to be expected over replacing legacy solutions with blockchain-based solutions, and high-level organizational champions can help reduce anxiety over such moves. Education about blockchain is a necessary corollary to turn resistance into understanding and even informed enthusiasm. Well-designed pilots can be part of the educational effort, proving the concept and establishing functionality and the business case for a switch to blockchain. Enterprises often resort to temporary parallel tracks, with blockchain backstopped by legacy solutions. This helps reduce risk by protecting the enterprise against negative consequences from failure of the blockchain effort, at the cost of preserving redundancy.

Societal Implications

There may also be societal concerns over successful ecosystem organizations becoming oligopolies. Such concerns stem from fears of reduced access for some portions of the population and commercial dominance of the ecosystem at the expense of consumer welfare. As such concerns grow, calls for societal control over the ecosystem can affect their commercial viability and success. Ecosystem governance might extend, then, to include societal effects while formulating and assessing the quality and efficacy of customer solutions. Such a perspective would consciously seek to enhance public benefits and balance such achievement with private benefits to ecosystem providers and customers. Figure 6.2 summarizes key aspects of developing an ecosystem to guide interorganizational blockchain development and implementation.

I now consider some examples of how the ecosystem approach could shape blockchain-based solutions. I begin with autonomous vehicles (e.g., driverless cars) and then consider examples from health care and supply chains.

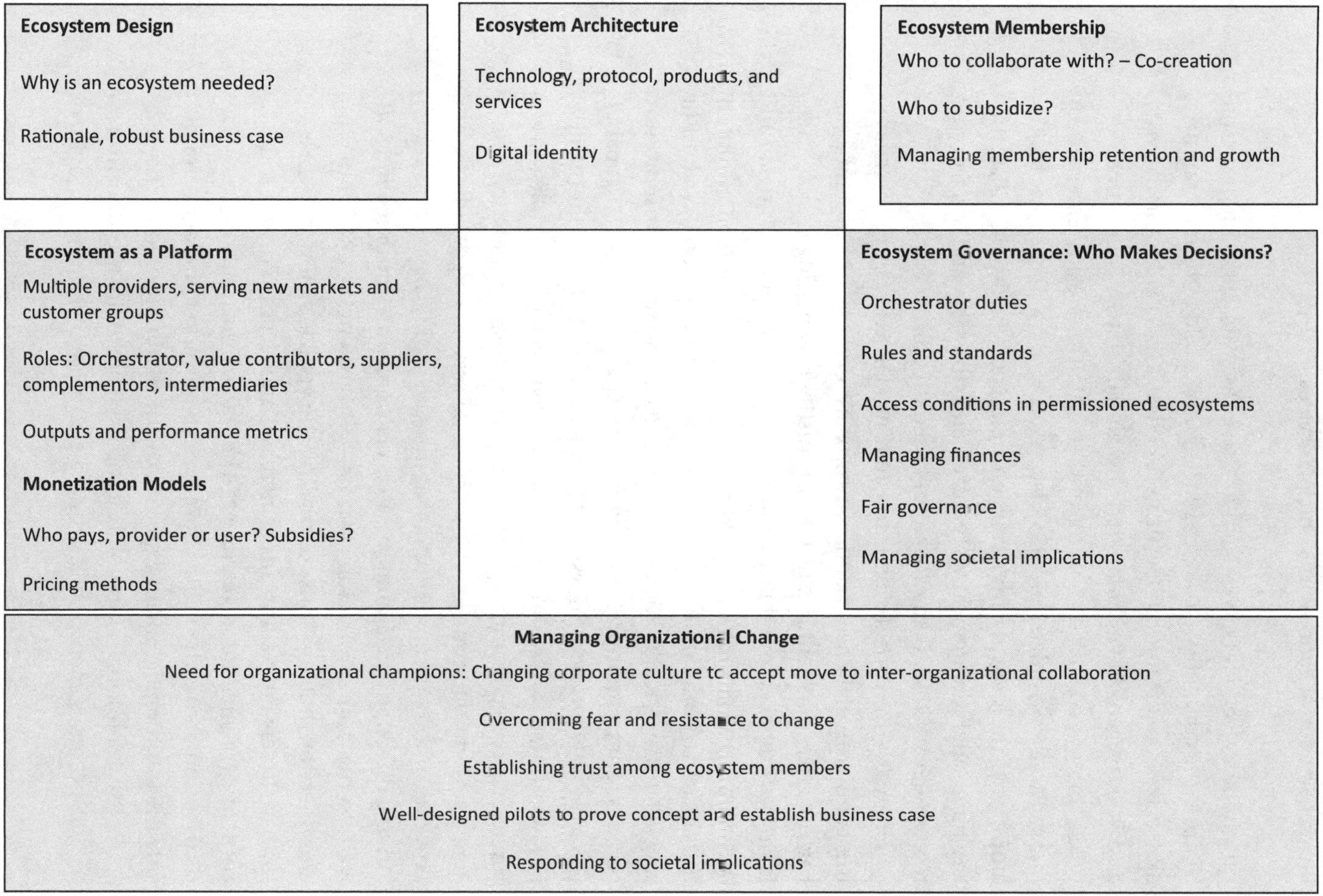

Ecosystem Membership

Who to collaborate with? – Co-creation

Who to subsidize?

Managing membership retention and growth

Ecosystem Governance: Who Makes Decisions?

Orchestrator duties

Rules and standards

Access conditions in permissioned ecosystems

Managing finances

Fair governance

Managing societal implications

Ecosystem Architecture

Technology, protocol, products, and services

Digital identity

Ecosystem Design

Why is an ecosystem needed?

Rationale, robust business case

Ecosystem as a Platform

Multiple providers, serving new markets and customer groups

Roles: Orchestrator, value contributors, suppliers, complementors, intermediaries

Outputs and performance metrics

Monetization Models

Who pays, provider or user? Subsidies?

Pricing methods

Managing Organizational Change

Need for organizational champions: Changing corporate culture to accept move to inter-organizational collaboration

Overcoming fear and resistance to change

Establishing trust among ecosystem members

Well-designed pilots to prove concept and establish business case

Responding to societal implications

Figure 6.2
Strategic thinking in an ecosystem perspective

Blockchains for Autonomous Vehicle Services

Autonomous vehicles (AVs), such as driverless cars, have the potential to upset the competitive balance in the automobile industry. Traditionally, a few major automobile firms, such as General Motors, Toyota, and Volkswagen, have dominated the global industry, with both vertically integrated manufacturing and distribution, complemented by hierarchically organized suppliers arranged in tiers. The move to AVs, along with the growing importance of electric vehicles, has disturbed the traditional hierarchically organized auto industry and has forced it to consider shifting to an ecosystem-based organization.

The reason to consider an ecosystem model stems from the changing competitive elements underpinning AV's emergence. Manufacturing driverless cars requires firms with distinct technology capabilities, from traditional automobile manufacturing to developing software and AI systems, and electronic and optical devices to voluntarily collaborate if they are to come up with a superior customer solution. AVs bundle several distinct technological innovations to provide transportation services. They require vehicle-driving software linked with AI capabilities to rapidly process and respond to the torrent of data about the driving environment in real time. The software links with multiple sensors such as vision recognition systems, navigation systems and their associated maps, mobile connectivity with cloud servers and data lakes, and powerful onboard computing capabilities (graphic processing units). Driving directions are communicated via onboard electronics and software to the car's mechanical systems—wheels, engine power, steering and direction, brakes—thus controlling the vehicle's motion. Replacing human drivers with automation increases the electronics and software content of vehicles and rearranges the value contribution and profit distribution across the value chain. These newer technologies are outside the traditional domain expertise of the major automobile firms.

As the traditional automobile industry moves in the direction of AVs, it becomes increasingly attractive to new technology providers.

For example, AV software leaders include Google's Waymo unit, which uses simulation and data derived from its pilot fleet of experimental AV cars driven in its Arizona test facility to continuously update its AV software. Tesla relies on AI machine learning, mining driving performance data from Tesla owners using their cars on the road to inductively develop its AV software. Car electronics to aid autonomous driving include Lidar units that use lasers to image the car's surroundings, RADAR to measure distances to objects surrounding the car, cameras to detect and recognize objects, and onboard computers and related cloud connectivity. These needs have attracted new competitors such as Intel (motivating its acquisition, Mobileye), Nvidia, Aptiv, Baidu, and Uber.

An additional complication is the growing importance of electric vehicles, with cities promoting electric vehicles to reduce urban pollution and move it upstream to electricity generation facilities. Tesla's emergence stems from its early mover ability to replace internal combustion engines with an electric powertrain driven by batteries. One consequence of the rise of electric vehicles is a reduced demand for internal combustion engines, which threatens to obviate the significant global investments in internal combustion capacity by the major car companies. These stranded factory investments could in turn reduce the ability of major auto firms to fund internally the range of new technologies needed for AV development, motivating them to consider cooperation and co-innovation with the newly powerful entrants in the AV world.

Given that cars are parked for roughly 90 percent of the time, and the estimated higher cost of driverless cars during their early stages of market introduction (primarily due to the higher prices for onboard computing power, electronics, sensors, and autonomous driving software[7]), it is thought that some individuals might prefer to hire the services of a driverless car rather than own one. Boston Consulting Group estimated that in 2030, an AV with an electric powertrain could cost 75 percent more that of its internal combustion engine counterpart in

2017 and about 25 percent of all auto passenger miles in 2030 would come from shared autonomous electric vehicles.[8]

Furthermore, McKinsey forecasted that one in ten cars sold in 2030 could be a shared vehicle.[9] They also suggested that such shared vehicles would be more likely to be used in densely populated cities, where "congestion fees, a lack of parking, traffic jams, etc. mean car ownership is more of a burden for many, and shared mobility presents a competitive value." The sharing economy approach may be a creative solution to overcome "sticker shock" and increase AV market share relative to traditional automobiles. This transformation is portrayed in figure 6.3, which illustrates how the accelerating interest in AVs motivates the shift from hierarchy to the ecosystem model.

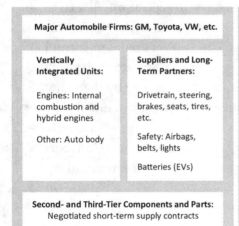

Traditional Automobile Industry
Vertically Integrated and Hierarchical
Global Supply Chain

Driverless Cars
The Move to a Mobility Ecosystem

Major Automobile Firms: GM, Toyota, VW, etc.		Traditional Competitors	New Entrants
Vertically Integrated Units:	**Suppliers and Long-Term Partners:**	**Incumbent Automobile Firms**	**New Automobile Entrants:** Electric vehicles (e.g., Tesla, BYD)
Engines: Internal combustion and hybrid engines	Drivetrain, steering, brakes, seats, tires, etc.	**Power:** Internal combustion engines, hybrids, electric	**Power:** Batteries for EVs
Other: Auto body	Safety: Airbags, belts, lights	**Suppliers:** Automobile sub-assemblies, parts, and components	**Autonomous driving software, navigation**
	Batteries (EVs)		
Second- and Third-Tier Components and Parts: Negotiated short-term supply contracts		**Distribution:** Dealer network, fleet sales, direct-to-consumer, online; car-sharing; after-sales service, maintenance	**On-board computing power, GPUs, electronics**
Distribution: Dealer network, fleet sales, direct-to-consumer online; after-sales service, maintenance			**Sensors:** Radar, lidar, vision
Infrastructure: Insurance, financing, government regulations		**Infrastructure:** Insurance, financing; government regulations	**Connectivity:** Wi-Fi, cloud; apps **Content:** Onboard consumption

Figure 6.3
From hierarchy to ecosystem: The move to autonomous vehicles

Blockchain Benefits for the AV Industry

In a sharing economy application, as in the case of AV, a principal objective is to maximize recurring revenue from the shared AV assets. AV manufacturers as a group could own these shared vehicle assets and recover their costs and earn a return on their investment from the profit annuity stream of shared vehicle use. Blockchains could manage the sharing economy demand for driverless car services and AV transportation, ensure fleet availability, and handle payments. Both annuity and public utility models, discussed further below, could be used in provisioning AV transportation services through a blockchain.

In an annuity model, the ecosystem of value-adding content providers could band together on a blockchain platform to offer driverless cars for hire. The value-added contributions of each ecosystem provider to the completed driverless car would represent their ownership stake in each car, with the stake size varying depending on the chosen final configuration for each car. Such ownership stakes could be retained or traded, with ownership state changes recorded in the blockchain. APIs would allow individuals to summon a driverless car, and smart contracts would calculate and bill each user with proceeds shared among providers in relation to their ownership stake. Tokens native to that blockchain could be developed and serve as the means of payment for the transportation services offered. The tokens, representing revenue earned from driverless car usage by customers, would be distributed among the fleet owners in proportion to their ownership stake, representing an annuity earned over the useful life of each driverless car.

The blockchain could extend to scheduling and paying for regular maintenance and to insurers, who could offer insurance for the fleet of driverless cars as it grows or offer reinsurance to a self-insured fleet. Loyalty tokens could be offered to users based on the accumulated volume of use. Blockchain data for each car in the fleet could monitor usage and manage routine scheduled maintenance as well as unusual events such as accidents. It could also cover the entire useful life of each driverless car in the fleet, from initial production and introduction into use to end-of-life recycling, with tokens incentivizing and rewarding the recycling of the total value added.

As an alternative to the manufacturing ecosystem owning and earning revenue from deploying the AVs in a sharing economy, private entrepreneurial firms could purchase and similarly deploy AVs, seeking similar profit annuity streams. A third possibility is private individual ownership of AVs, with revenue and profit annuities going to these individual owners; this third scenario seems less viable economically given the significantly higher purchase prices per AV, the scale economies from fleet ownership, and the higher maintenance demands from more intensive usage. Nevertheless, all three ownership modes could rely on an annuity model blockchain.

The public utility model is based on public sector ownership, similar to how public transportation is offered. Local governments providing public transportation services to their citizens could also consider deploying AVs in a sharing mode as one of many transportation options; AVs could be efficient for low-demand routes and in off-peak hours. Such a public utility model could use blockchains with some adaptations to meet public service considerations.

AVs could be offered as a public utility, with local government ownership of autonomous vehicles offered for sharing use through a blockchain. This would be analogous to public ownership of bus or train transportation, with services offered to users with unique ID as municipal residents of a city or region. Such transportation as a utility service could be fee based, with a progressive fee structure possible, tied to income, while also offered as a free or reduced-price service for specifically identified segments of the population. The blockchain could use each traveler's unique ID, together with travel route parameters, to calculate and bill that user for the transportation service rendered, similar to other utilities billed, such as public water provision. Such utility models could also be hybrid, with public/private partnerships, and with private owners receiving fees from use until fleet costs plus a predetermined return on investment are earned, at which point fleet ownership would revert to municipal ownership and the transportation services could be offered at lower prices, covering operating costs.

Challenges to Blockchain Adoption in AVs

Since many different industries would need to collaborate to successfully introduce AVs to mass markets, one or more of the leaders from each of the distinct industries would need to initiate such cooperation. At the same time, a respected neutral firm from the IT sector, with blockchain expertise, would need to participate in these initial talks, as an "honest broker," to add credibility and overcome reluctance to harness an unfamiliar technology. City public transit administrators would also need to participate to clarify rules and regulations governing AV introduction. Subsidies to transportation users to increase demand could be necessary to creating the rapid growth essential to a successful AV launch.

The multi-industry consortium backing the blockchain-based system for AV deployment would need to invest in developing and piloting new software modules, such as a solution that offers secure communication from IoT devices on each AV, to verify its digital identity, record usage, and link associated charges with specific transportation customers. Additional modules would match available AVs with customer demand, and allocate revenue earned, as well as associated AV costs to the appropriate AV supplier account. AV owners would need to be motivated to make their AV fleets available for use within the blockchain, with acceptable pricing formulas. To reduce risks for both AV customers and providers, the consortium would need to establish a market for tokens used within the system, obtain their listing on digital currency exchanges, and manage their value so that they function as stablecoins. These are not insurmountable challenges but indicate the tasks that must be addressed if the AV blockchain is to gain traction and increasing adoption.

As AV demand develops at scale, a next step would be to coordinate next generation innovation of AVs since synchronous innovation within the various subsystems offered by the various ecosystem partners would be needed to fully realize AV capabilities and maintain a competitive edge. Otherwise, AV innovation would be constrained to the pace of the laggard innovators. And once AV innovation is managed within a blockchain, the blockchain could extend to overseeing manufacturing and supply chain operations.

Blockchain Implementation Issues in the AV Industry

Blockchain applications can have value in AV manufacturing, in AV usage, and in communications between AVs and independent entities such as regulatory bodies, insurance firms, and in business and leisure applications. In AV design and manufacturing, traditional auto firms need to collaborate with electronics and software firms, at a minimum. At minimum, the blockchain-based production system should treat each AV as a token moving through the value chain, with individual firm contributions to AV value added updated in the ledger attached to the token, enabling tracking and rewarding of contributions.

On the user side, the blockchain can register AV usage, with a token specific to each car registering state changes, such as usage of a specific vehicle by a specific clients. The blockchain can also register related data such as the AV's present location and changes in location, linking such data to user billing. Furthermore, IoT sensors onboard each AV can monitor operational readiness. Such information could be linked to billing- and maintenance-related data including ordering parts and maintenance charges, resulting in an AV maintenance log over the AV's entire useful life. Ownership-related data such as loans, leases, updated ownership equity, and depreciation charges could be similarly recorded. It is entirely possible for an AV to continue to be owned by the consortium of manufacturers, with usage charges billed in the blockchain accruing back to the AV owner over the AV's useful life. Insurance companies could offer parametric insurance based on immutable, continually updated driving records and permissioned data access offered with differentiated access rights for owners, lenders, manufacturers, and government agencies.

A fear with AVs is that they can be hacked by malicious actors, causing accidents and endangering life and property. Blockchain-based AV communication with other vehicles, IoT devices, and other service providers through cloud connectivity could provide significant protection against such risks. Such security could also provide data privacy and secure content delivery as AV passengers interact with shopping, entertainment, and other business and leisure apps. In preparation, blockchain pilots would need to explore attackers and vulnerabilities and develop robust solutions before moving to implementation at scale.

The biggest obstacle will be obtaining satisfactory performance at scale. As the number of AVs in operation increases, the blockchain application will need to manage many connections in a situation where real-time data provisioning is necessary for safe AV operation. On the manufacturing side, developing AV manufacturing across an ecosystem governed with a blockchain will require orchestrators akin to the role of Maersk and IBM in TradeLens, and an AV supplier side blockchain will face similar challenges of recruiting network members, establishing fair governance, and evaluating and rewarding contributions fairly. Such blockchains will also have to obtain regulatory approval when regulatory variation and multiple jurisdictions are likely to be the norm in early stages of AV introduction.

Blockchain and Health Care Delivery

There are a diverse group of entities collaborating and innovating in the value chain to offer health care delivery in the United States. A critical element of providing quality care is continuous access to the latest patient information, with accuracy, availability, and timeliness, all paramount. However, the US health care system has had difficulty with this primary responsibility of providing up-to-date patient health care records to medical providers as and when needed. The reasons for the breakdown in fulfilling this basic and necessary service are manifold. Process variations impede the smooth transfer of health care records across organizational boundaries, which is further stymied by disparate standards and formats. Legal barriers stand in the way of such data handover, principally HIPAA provisions that motivate health care providers to err on the side of caution and delay such data transfer until complete assurance of compliance with HIPAA rules. The US health care system is fragmented, divided between governmental and private sector responsibilities; some segments of the private sector are for-profit entities and must balance profit maximization with health care provision, which affects these providers' willingness to share health care records in a complete and timely fashion.

There are also competing value propositions and opposing goals among the ecosystem members. Health care records inform actuarial calculations that indicate insurability and the appropriate premium rate, setting health insurers and employers at possible odds with individual patients and their medical care providers. Similarly, individual genomic data can offer deep insights into susceptibility to disease incidence, but that would require legislative protection against invidious treatment to guard against individual consequences of health care record transparency across the ecosystem. Some of these impediments stem from ideological choices that underpin US health care provision. These impediments may not exist in countries that offer nationalized health care and single payer systems, where ecosystem members are more likely to share similar goals.

For ecosystems to provide a cocreated customer solution, they need to share common goals. When ecosystem members diverge in their goals, the ecosystem may take on more characteristics of a zero-sum game, with some network members benefiting at the expense of other members. Ecosystem members might prefer to run their own centralized ecosystem, preferring a central, orchestrator role in a smaller ecosystem. Such an orchestrator would want to manage the network, set objectives, and control access to their network; such central direction could also lead to constrained innovation and reduced customer satisfaction and be seen as acting in one's own self-interest.

The US health care delivery ecosystem has two sides, with the patient at the center of the ecosystem, interacting with both patient care providers and payers. On the patient care side, there are several independent entities who are beginning to merge into integrated entities in response to cost reduction pressures and to better coordinate and thus improve patient outcomes. These entities include medical providers such as primary care physicians, nurses, and physician assistants, often organized into physician practice groups, community health centers, and newly emergent pharmacy-based clinics. They interact with specialist medical providers such as surgeons and oncologists, who all might be further grouped into hospitals, emergency rooms and intensive care units, rehabilitation facilities, assisted living, hospices, and other entities.

These medical providers are supported by laboratories and specialized testing services (MRI, CT scans) and by monitoring and IoT devices and sensors, with health data summarized in patient electronic health records (EHRs) and with AI-based data analytics to aid in diagnostics. New developments include the growing use of telemedicine providers and health care navigators, acting as intermediaries between the patient and patient care providers. Overseeing patient care are regulators, such as the US Food and Drug Administration (FDA) and the US Department of Health and Human Service to ensure safety, efficacy, and compliance.

On the payer side, there are government entities including Medicare and Medicaid, with covered services determined under the Affordable Care Act, and by the Veterans Administration. Private payers are numerous, with total health care payments apportioned between private health insurers and individuals making copayments on their covered health care costs; health insurance premiums from both individuals and employers that offer health insurance benefits offset, to an extent, insurance company outlays on covered costs. In addition, government and private sector foundation grants, together with corporate and venture capital funding, enable drug development and health care–related R&D, essential to the longer-term improvement of health care delivery. These funding sources distribute their outflows among pharmaceutical drug and generic drug manufacturers, medical equipment and device producers, medical supplies firms, health care information technology and software providers, and health care research organizations including universities. Other beneficiaries are health care intermediaries such as contract research organizations, insurance brokers, pharmacy benefit managers, drug distributors and pharmacies, and providers of legal services. Altogether, the US health care system accounts for nearly 20 percent of US GDP.

The Promise of Blockchain in Health Care

Blockchain offers tantalizing promise for the health care industry, listed below.

Payments: In addition to resolving the problem of health care record availability, blockchain can make payments more efficient and reduce administrative costs, with superior claims management linked to blockchain-validated medical procedures, drug prescriptions, and so forth. For example, a health care blockchain could incorporate smart contracts to activate next steps in the health care delivery process, triggered by updated information such as test results and procedure outcomes. As the various steps are completed, with proof of completion, smart contracts could automate payments from government entities such as Medicare and from private insurers for services rendered. Smart contracts could consult pharmacy benefit management formularies, link payments to patient outcomes rather than the current procedure-based billing, and use anonymized and aggregated patient data analytics and AI to offer patient care improvement suggestions.

Drug development: Blockchain can also play a role in drug manufacturing and supply, guarding against counterfeiting, ensuring that drugs have been properly stored, monitoring the sale of controlled substances (e.g., opioids), and removing expired drugs from inventories. Blockchain also has a potential role in developing new drugs, by monitoring patient enrollment, capturing and storing data from drug trials, ensuring data security, and shepherding data through FDA submissions for Investigational New Drug and marketing approvals.[10]

Patient health records: With blockchain at the heart of this ecosystem to record and transmit patient data, it could provide distributed availability of immutable patient health care records—a single source of truth—with traceable provenance to all relevant health care providers. The blockchain could offer patients sovereignty and control over their data, allowing them to consent to access by authorized health care providers. Native tokens could reward patients for allowing access to their data, for example, to pharma companies seeking candidates for their drug trials.[11]

Challenges in Adopting Blockchain in Health Care

The difficulty in deploying blockchain is less technological than economic and organizational. Private sector incumbents with dominant legacy solutions for managing health care records—firms such as Epic Systems, Cerner, Meditech, and Allscripts—create data silos. Integrating such disparate databases creates high switching costs and is likely to slow down potential blockchain disrupters, giving current EHR firms time to decide whether to offer their own blockchain-based electronic health records solutions. This results in incompatible processes and data standards across provider ecosystem, and together with legal barriers stemming from the need to comply with HIPAA privacy regulations, it slows progress toward blockchain solutions. Thus, disagreement over organizational goals, legal barriers, and profit motives are greater barriers, as discussed above.

Given these impediments to deploying blockchain within the health care ecosystem, it is not surprising that, in a recent survey, 44 percent of health care responders indicated that blockchain was the technology they were the least excited about.[12] There was even greater skepticism among investors, with 64 percent of them expressing similar disdain for blockchain application in health care. Furthermore, health care firms may be reluctant to approve risky new technology investments such as blockchain when the US health care system is exposed to political risk and is buffeted by uncertainty surrounding reimbursements, payers, and health care industry regulation.

With all these difficulties, a more likely development, at least in the short term, is innovation within a subset of the entire ecosystem. Martin Ihrig and Ian Macmillan[13] point out that in an ecosystem, innovation should create value propositions that other stakeholders can contribute to. They offer an example of a new treatment for patients with a metabolic disorder that would remove the need for surgery but would reduce surgeons' income and make obsolete the investments that hospitals had made in the traditional approach to treatment. The innovating company would need to decide if it was willing to create a new profit-sharing physician-staffed treatment clinic network while disrupting hospitals and surgeons in the ecosystem.

More broadly, ecosystem innovation will affect outcomes differently for each group of ecosystem players. Innovators need to plan to manage the resultant tensions. Ihrig and Macmillan go on to suggest that ecosystem innovation can succeed if it enhances differentiation for other ecosystem members, compensating in total for the negative consequences for other constituencies. Thus, in the case of introducing blockchains for patient data records, there should be positive effects for doctors and other medical practitioners, hospitals, regulators, insurers, pharma companies, and drug distributors to overcome possible negative consequences for current incumbents dominating the electronic health record sector. There needs to be an innovation coalition[14] within the ecosystem to promote risky new directions such as blockchain introduction.

Blockchain and Global Supply Chains: TradeLens as an Ecosystem

TradeLens, discussed in chapter 5, is an example of an ecosystem perspective application in implementing interorganizational supply chain solutions.[15] Supply chain actors benefit if everyone trusts the data, works from the same copy of the data, and are confident that the data is secure and private.[16] As independent firms, they need to be motivated and persuaded to join the blockchain if the application is to provide benefits over legacy systems.

As is common with any digital platform, as more supply chain participants join TradeLens, positive networks effects lead to greater benefit. Given that TradeLens is controlled by Maersk and IBM, governance arrangements that separate TradeLens from its owners is critical to attracting Maersk's competitors, whose collective participation is needed to make TradeLens effective. Onboarding assistance is necessary to induce smaller supply chain firm participation to overcome fears that their relative lower level of technological and organizational preparedness might reduce their ability to function as equal members in the network. Pricing TradeLens's services involves balancing the cost–benefit of participation with the need to recoup investments and create positive cash flow to fund continuing sustainable operations. And TradeLens must show continuous evolution and upgrades to attract members who might prefer to join newer supply chain networks such as the Global Shipping Business Network (GSBN) with more advanced blockchain protocols. GSBN includes some of the largest Chinese and Asian shipping firms, which together control about 30 percent of global container traffic (Maersk itself controls about 20 percent).

IBM and Maersk, as joint owners, and orchestrators, made several architectural choices to motivate TradeLens adoption across the supply chain ecosystem.

Attracting buyers: Open access for users with shipments to track, a form of user subsidies, to encourage rapid adoption. Fostering user loyalty, by giving access to a large set of potential supply chain providers, and accumulated historic shipment data are intended to make TradeLens the platform of choice.

Value for ecosystem members: Customers who have placed orders and are awaiting shipment delivery obtain value from visibility and transparency of their shipment flow, with positive effects on pipeline inventory and working capital levels and reducing losses from stock-outs. Supply chain providers similarly derive value from knowledge about shipment location, status, and possible delays. Such data can increase market share from loyal, satisfied customers. Such customer loyalty eases supplier willingness to pay for using TradeLens, whether through a subscription fee, through a volume fee based on usage levels, or through charges for access to shipment status data.

Encouraging collaborative innovation: IBM and Maersk can set rules to reward innovators before the innovation is absorbed as a standard feature.[17] Such rules encourage the blockchain's continuous evolution, for example, through integrating IoT devices with software and AI capabilities to track shipments. Such open innovation can help TradeLens compete with other similar emergent platforms.

Thus, fostering open standards, encouraging new entrant acceptance, giving data security primacy, decentralizing governance, and developing metrics to measure progress helped successful TradeLens blockchain adoption. After completing satisfactory initial trials, IBM and Maersk introduced TradeLens in January 2018 and by year-end had signed up over "100 organizations, including four ocean carriers, three inland carriers, more than forty worldwide ports and terminals, large freight forwarders, and eight customs authorities spanning the globe from Rotterdam to Bahrain."[18] TradeLens drew users such as Dow Chemical and Du Pont, which relied on TradeLens members to ship their cargo.

Blockchain offers the possibility for entities and individuals who do not know each other to share data and transact in a trustless setting. The machine—the blockchain—provides the trust. Blockchain technology also offers significant benefits within ecosystems, evidenced by the number of blockchain pilot applications[19] underway at various organizations. As its value as an ecosystem utility increases, so does the momentum for widespread adoption. Helping other firms create and share value on fair terms is the best approach to encouraging participation in an emerging ecosystem.[20] Blockchain use can catalyze collaborative value creation, transparently allocating and recording the distribution of that value. Participants can judge for themselves whether their rewards are commensurate with their efforts.

In the next and final chapter, I build on the insights from the various industry and ecosystem application examples to outline strategic steps for enterprises to decide whether blockchain is appropriate for the problems they wish to solve, and if so, how to develop and implement such blockchain applications.

7 Realizing Blockchain's Potential: A Strategy Road Map for Enterprises

In the previous chapters, I discussed how blockchain's disruptive capabilities have been used in several industries. I also addressed the reasons why blockchain adoption has not yet taken off in enterprises. I now consider how enterprises can decide whether or not to develop and use blockchain in their operations.

How Should a Firm Strategically Approach the Promise of Blockchain?

Enterprises can follow a stepwise approach in deciding whether and how to deploy blockchain. The first step is to determine whether existing legacy solutions are unsatisfactory and need replacing. If so, firms need to assess whether blockchain is the answer. Then, they should map out the business case for developing blockchain-based solutions to gain support and resources (capital, personnel, time, etc.) to develop and test the project. This leads to designing the blockchain solution, which should capitalize on blockchain's unique features and capabilities. The last step is preparing the organization to work with blockchain so that managers, technologists, and other employees unite to become successful with it.

Do Existing Legacy Solutions Need Replacing?
If legacy solutions are working well, and customers are satisfied, there may be little need to move to a blockchain-based solution. Before blockchains, firms used centralized databases to secure data and control

access. The centralized firm controlled subordinate units and managed suppliers. A control tower or dashboard that summarized updated, timely information with exception reporting on key metrics has served top management and key decision-makers well in the past and may be still serviceable—at least for as long as the firm continues to operate hierarchically, to dominate its hierarchy, and can rely on its own data for sound long-term decision-making.

As an industry expert at Capital One commented, "keep in mind that a chain is only as strong as its weakest link, which is equally true of blockchains. If one node has performance, scale or security problems, they can impact the other nodes. A blockchain can be a powerful solution, but organizations should use it only when they have challenges that aren't addressed well by existing technology."[1] It is when industry structure changes so that the firm has to collaborate to satisfy customers—and needs accurate, timely data from independent parties—that blockchain becomes attractive. I have previously referred to the credit scoring industry, with three dominant firms in the US market, including Equifax. And as noted, centrally controlled deep repositories, as at Equifax, can and have been hacked, creating considerable collateral damage to customers. In such circumstances, blockchain-based decentralized creditworthiness determination, with individuals in control of their credit data, is the disruptive innovation with long-term potential.

Is Blockchain the Answer?

Can blockchain lead to a better solution? If customers are dissatisfied with existing (legacy) solutions, it may be a suitable alternative. Blockchain use is particularly appropriate for achieving certain goals:[2]

- replacing intermediaries and their fees with direct interaction between the transacting parties to lower costs;
- safeguarding digital assets by clearly recognizing unauthorized copies, forgeries, and counterfeiting attempts, thus offering tamper-evident security;

- preserving an immutable record of transactions specific to a digital asset;
- protecting against counterparty risk when exchanging valuable assets through simultaneous settlement and payment finality;
- accessing, updating, and sharing accurate, real-time updated information between multiple entities involved at various stages of a transaction, when such transparency is needed;
- conducting online transactions with unknown parties, where no previous trusted relationship exists;
- cocreating customer value with multiple independent firms; and
- sharing governance, accepting decentralization, and relinquishing hierarchical control of application design and functionality.

For example, EHR portability across different health care providers could allow health care teams to spread across different health care organizations for better patient outcomes and care. Sharing EHRs across health care nodes within a blockchain could achieve this goal, a reason for health care providers to work with ecosystem partners and pilot a blockchain application.

Problems with internal business processes may result in similar dissatisfaction from internal "customers." For example, construction contractors must deploy and move heavy equipment from one contract location to another, and a breakdown of critical equipment at a remote construction site could delay operations and increase costs. Using a blockchain with smart contracts linked to IoT sensors to track equipment readiness and usage would help forecast and detect imminent equipment breakdown. It could also launch preemptive parts requests and preventive maintenance steps, including timely ordering and positioning of key spare parts at the relevant site. Enterprises moving to blockchain might still need to combine legacy solutions with blockchain, as an intermediate stage, with blockchain complementing legacy solutions. For example, Santander Bank was an early adopter of Ripple to lower cross-border remittance costs for its customers but still had to continue using legacy remittance transfer systems. Some customers did not or were not able to use Santander's One Pay FX mobile app, and several governmental authorities did not approve XRP transfers for their remittance corridors.

A Forrester study of the total economic impact of using an IBM Blockchain[3] notes that blockchain participants need to be patient with blockchain introduction. First, it takes time to reach scale operations and begin reaping benefits. Second, blockchain application development benefits from collaborating with an expert partner that is chosen for expertise, has a proven track record, and a good reputation. Finding, negotiating, and beginning to work with such a partner can be time-consuming. Third, cost–benefit outcomes need to be acceptable across a range of projections. To support a positive recommendation, projections should include both pessimistic and optimistic scenarios alongside a base case, and even lower cost–benefit forecasts, based on a pessimistic scenario, should be seen as acceptable before a go-ahead by the enterprise decision-makers.

Blockchain use is problematic when high-volume transaction processing is essential (as blockchain has scalability limitations, though these are gradually being overcome). Enterprises may also be deterred by blockchain's inherent transparency and hence prefer permissioned blockchains where they can control data access and sharing. Furthermore, data storage within a blockchain is costly, rendering it uneconomic for applications requiring continuous access to large databases. (The cost rises because the same data is stored at multiple nodes, with increased processing costs from using blockchain consensus validation algorithms to update data and ledgers at multiple nodes).

Developing the Business Case for Blockchain Solutions

Firms need to ensure that a proposed blockchain solution will ultimately enhance its profitability and efficiency. Hence, it is important to start with the business case for applying blockchain by setting out expected benefits (such as new revenue streams and eventual profits from new services/products), profit margin improvements from efficiency gains, and reduced costs. Both internal applications and external, customer-facing blockchain applications can be candidates to replace current solutions, and developing both kinds of blockchain applications can be bolstered by making a business case for their adoption. Monetizing data accumulated through blockchain usage is an additional longer-term revenue source: firms can offer forecasts and consumer needs analysis, based on analyzing the accumulating data lakes of ecosystem-wide data.

Finding large, addressable markets is key to earning significant revenue from new blockchain applications. For example, given the large volume of total cross-border remittances using SWIFT, it made sense for Ripple to develop a better cross-border remittance solution using blockchain. Ripple could grow significantly even with a small initial market share of the global market. Competitive fees for access to RippleNet and the continuing sales of XRP as the digital currency of choice for making remittances helped grow their share. One of blockchain's drawbacks is difficulty in ascertaining the cost–benefit outcomes for the enterprise, which can limit blockchain rollout at scale in enterprises. In the next section, I take a closer look at economic barriers and how they can be addressed.

Economic Barriers to Implementation   From an economic perspective, firms may be uncertain about committing to blockchain technology due to uncertainty over the cost–benefit tradeoff from using blockchain, high development costs of investing in equipment and software to run blockchain networks, and a scarcity of talent to lead and build blockchain applications. Firms can decide that existing technologies such as distributed databases are satisfactory in the short term and can estimate that blockchain does not offer enough improvement to justify switching to a new unfamiliar technology.

Assessing the Economic Returns from Using Blockchain   Given the economic barriers discussed above, it is essential to assess economic returns to the firm. Quantifying blockchain's impact should include cost impact, considering both costs incurred from blockchain adoption and cost reduction from greater efficiency. There may also be revenue gains from fees from users of the blockchain, and, more broadly, from

Revenues and Inflows $+$	Costs and Outflows $-$
a) Introductory entry membership: one-time fees, annual subscription renewal fees; less churn	a) Blockchain development costs: software development, blockchain platform licensing fees, consultation and legal fees to experts such as IBM or Consensys, contract negotiations among ecosystem members
b) Usage fees based on number of transactions, value of transactions, volume of data flows, software licensing fees, etc.	b) Specialist personnel such as blockchain developers and project managers
c) Cost savings from avoiding duplication of records, reduced expenditures on reconciling conflicting data; capital expenditures avoided	c) Initial and continuing IT costs for network node creation, security, and management
d) Cost reduction in arbitration and legal costs of resulting disputes	d) Training, onboarding, and monitoring costs
	e) Governance and dispute resolution, and regulatory compliance costs
e) Efficiency gains: productivity gains from speedy processing, increase in transactions processed; time saving from reduction in delays; value realized from real-time access to continually updated data; reduced labor costs from reduced paperwork; savings in back-office tasks such as data reconciliation	**NOTE:** Projections from a pilot may vary from results obtained from implementation at scale. Hence, firms should introduce risk factors to obtain a range of possible cost/benefit forecasts varying from low to medium to high degree of confidence in projections.
f) Revenue gains from increased market share, introduction of new products and services and enhanced competitiveness	

Figure 7.1
Relevant factors for cost–benefit analysis

market share gains due to enhanced competitiveness and the introduction of new products and services.[4] Figure 7.1 outlines factors relevant for conducting a cost–benefit analysis.

Since blockchain applications, if successful, involve ongoing costs, total cost of ownership (TCO) is a useful metric as it allows for a more complete better cost–benefit analysis.[5] TCO assumes that blockchain applications are an asset that yields returns over several years while also depreciating and requiring ongoing maintenance to deliver high performance. TCO includes IT costs such as hardware, licenses and software purchases and development, IT support by skilled personnel, end-user training and help, communications and costs of downtime, legacy interfaces and data migration, and costs of software bugs and upgrades. Other TCO costs include management resources and time commitments and associated staffing for administration and continual improvement.

An alternative approach is to model different scenarios that can result from deploying a blockchain solution. Patara Panuparb[6] considers a blockchain use case within supply chain finance, estimating the cost–benefit for different ecosystem members, namely suppliers, buyers, and supply chain finance providers. The model considers several parameters:

- savings to the supplier from obtaining a lower interest rate from the supply chain finance providers against the cost of joining the blockchain platform and paying a percentage of the invoice as transaction fees;

- quicker payment facilitated by trust in supply chain information due to greater blockchain security and immutability of transaction execution;

- the redistribution of the profit pool in favor of the blockchain with lower-rate supply chain financing replacing the supplier's high-cost finance sources;

- disintermediation resulting in diverting part of the interest savings from lower-rate financing to the blockchain in the form of blockchain transaction fees; and

- benefit to the buyer, who may not directly benefit from the interest rate reduction but can benefit from the supplier offering longer-duration payment terms since his interest rates are lower.

The model can consider different scenarios, with and without blockchain use, to evaluate the net benefits from using blockchain in this supply chain finance setting. The model compares traditional supply chain finance with alternatives within a supply chain blockchain that offer lower-cost financing and extended payment terms, with enhanced supply chain efficiency from blockchain platform use leading to a reduction of days in shipment transit and in turn resulting in an earlier realization of the shipment invoice amount. Figure 7.2 sets out the model and its parameters.

Such detailed modeling can help enterprises experiment with different blockchain configurations of fee structure and services, feeding data

---

Buyer Benefit: Value of extended payment terms: number of additional days × interest rate × invoice amount

Supplier Benefit: Percentage of invoice amount financed × interest rate reduction × early realization (by number of days) of invoice amount

Supply Chain Financier Benefit: Percentage of invoice amount financed × interest rate spread × early realization (by number of days) of invoice amount

Blockchain Platform Benefit: Percentage of invoice amount financed × platform service fee (%) × early realization (by number of days) of invoice amount

Model variables include:

• Invoice Amount

• Interest rate for suppliers and buyers

• Interest rate spread for the supply chain financier (difference between interest rate charged and paid)

• Difference in number of days between extended payment and original payment terms

• Platform service fee

• Number of days by which earlier payment is realized

• Percentage of invoice amount financed (assuming a buyer downpayment)

Benefits for all concerned parties can then be compared under different scenarios, including with and without blockchain platform use.

Figure 7.2
Model to assess cost–benefit of blockchain application in supply chain. Adapted from Patara Panuparb, "Cost–Benefit Analysis of a Blockchain-Based Supply Chain Finance Solution" (master's thesis, MIT Center for Transportation and Logistics, May 2019).

from the different pilots to the models to compare the cost–benefit of alternatives.

Estimating Cost–Benefit from Switching to Blockchain Applications over Legacy Systems Blockchain pilot projects can provide proof of concept but be unable to demonstrate clear economic benefits over legacy applications, making it difficult to get budget approval for large-scale implementation. Blockchain development can also incur high costs, discouraging the funding of multiple pilots with disparate objectives.

A banking industry application noted that blockchain solutions might work best in a mainframe-centric computing network, requiring significant incremental investment. Banks are able take advantage of the "speed, cryptography and reliability of z Systems (new generation IBM mainframes) for hosting blockchain while seamlessly integrating with transactional data and applications already running on the mainframe."[7] Costs also mount from distributed storage of a copy of continually updated information at every node. As an example, in examining the potential cost–benefit of using blockchain solutions in supply chains,[8] there were benefits from the improved efficiency of invoice processing, which reduced working capital; these were offset by blockchain platform costs and usage fees. Further, benefits accrued to the supplier but not the buyer, discouraging some ecosystem members from joining the blockchain.

Preference for Centralized, Permissioned Networks   Blockchain was not developed with enterprises in mind. As used by Bitcoin, it is an unpermissioned network, open to anyone who wishes to join the network. Such openness is not seen as desirable in corporate DLT applications, for example, in an investment banking network focused on flotation and life cycle management of a corporate bond issue like the one DB piloted. In such circumstances, firms such as loan-seeking clients or investment banks managing bond issuance might prefer to restrict membership in the network. The Nakamoto whitepaper explicating the Bitcoin concept[9] assumed that a decentralized distributed network designed to track ownership and state change of digital assets (Bitcoin) would need to work in the presence of ill-intentioned actors, for example, nodes seeking to double-spend or introduce counterfeit assets.[10]

The additional steps to protect against malfeasance can be cumbersome to enterprises that might prefer to work with a few trusted nodes in their blockchain, in a permissioned network. Enterprises could then avoid using computation and time-intensive consensus validation approaches, increasing blockchain's speed of execution. This centralization of governance nodes, however, is contrary to the fundamental blockchain principle of decentralization and can compromise security. Opting for centralized networks in permissioned networks reduces benefits from trust intermediation, raising network administration and governance costs.

Costs of Addressing Interoperability Barriers between Multiple Blockchain Protocols Enterprise-level blockchains, to be useful, often require that third parties external to the firm join the blockchain network. Blockchain participants cannot all be expected to adopt and use the same protocol, security features, and algorithms, leading to the use of multiple blockchain protocols. Firms could find themselves belonging to multiple blockchain networks, each using a unique blockchain protocol, with differences in transaction processing, smart contract features, security of communication across blockchains, and consensus approaches.

Costs of Smart Contracts Flaws Bugs in smart contract code, as well as deliberate errors introduced to counter contract terms, can raise the costs of using smart contracts in blockchain solutions. For example, smart contracts can be tampered with to release digital assets to an arbitrary address (prodigal contracts), kill contracts by an arbitrary account (suicidal contract), and program contracts to lock in resources indefinitely, with no conditions that can release these impounded funds (greedy contracts). Tools such as MAIAN can detect such malicious contracts[11] but require additional spending.

Designing the Blockchain Application

Successful blockchain applications develop from business models that leverage blockchain capabilities to overcome customer pain points. In other words, enterprises must determine which capabilities will create value for customers.

Permissioned or Permissionless Blockchains? Enterprises are unlikely to choose *classic* blockchain configurations (unpermissioned, decentralized) in developing their blockchain solutions. Initially, they are likely to opt for closed permissioned systems, prioritizing internal applications that emphasize process improvements and efficiency gains. When developing external customer-facing solutions, they are likely to prefer ecosystems where they can exercise an orchestrator role, with significant voice in investment, monetization, and governance decisions. In such permissioned blockchains within ecosystems, the enterprise and its ecosystem partners set conditions for entry and decide which entities are allowed as nodes into the blockchain.

For example, the DTCC piloted a customized permissioned blockchain for managing $11 trillion of credit derivatives that were previously stored in its Trade Information Warehouse. The permissioned application, built in collaboration with IBM, R3, and Axoni's AxCore blockchain protocol (a version of Ethereum), enabled DTCC partners such as Barclays, Citi, DB, UBS, and JPMorgan to move record keeping, life cycle events, payments, and settlement of credit default swaps to the blockchain platform, yielding a single set of records for regulators and counterparties.[12] The project was then extended to additional DTCC clients but with permissioned access. Controlling access leads to faster validation of transactions and greater data privacy. Further, a limited number of nodes can more easily agree on common data standards and governance as in this case of credit derivatives. The downside is that fewer nodes result in less robust security. It is likely that enterprise platforms will evolve in the direction of public permissionless blockchains as scalability, speed, privacy, and finality questions are resolved. Also, private blockchains can be linked with public permissionless decentralized blockchains, drawing on blockchain protocols with privacy layers built on base public platforms and computational trust executed off-chain.

Which Blockchain Protocol? The specific use cases will influence the blockchain protocol selection, based on whether to create permissioned networks, the degree of interoperability, and relative performance on scalability, speed, finality and privacy protection, ease of secure linkage to decentralized secure storage and cloud integration, and off-chain networks (e.g., to oracles).

Ethereum has become the protocol of choice for financial applications due to its smart contract capability linked to Ether, the widespread acceptance of Ether as tokens, and network effects from widespread use across fintech ecosystems. Other widely used protocols such as Hyperledger, R3/Corda, and Consensys may be better suited to certain use cases because of results from deployment in specialized vertical industry segments in a variety of industries. Infura, for example, allows enterprises and their developers to connect an application to a blockchain via an Infura node, permitting rapid proof of concepts pilots and making inexperience with blockchain development less of a barrier. Newer protocols such as Quant Overledger (discussed in chapter 2) offer greater flexibility, such as simple APIs that allow legacy applications to communicate with Dapps.

Identity Verification   Blockchain's strength is in preventing fraud, being both tamper evident and tamper resistant. A critical step in fraud prevention is using verified identity. SSI deployed and verified within a blockchain gives individuals control over their identity and data. Individuals can then decide how much to disclose and to whom, preventing losses from data hacks such as the pilfering of 140 million individual credit records from Equifax. A major pain point for network members in supply chain and trade finance ecosystems is complying with KYC regulations,[13] and SSI can reduce the complexity and burden associated with identifying clients and complying with KYC requirements.

A German start-up, evan.network,[14] developed an identity and trust infrastructure for blockchain ecosystems, integrating individual and organizational identities, identities for physical objects, and external identities provided by third parties (such as digital signatures and data authentication)[15] so that ecosystem members could rely on evan.network as an identity verifier. Network effects are critical to evan.network's growth since the larger the number of identities it can verify, the more useful it becomes, thereby attracting additional members.

As a German firm initially focused on building comprehensive verified identity data, evan.network's scalability outside Germany is dependent on licensing and collaboration with blockchains in other large markets with similar strategic intent. Applications such as Komgo and we.trade draw on blockchain's ability to ensure secure, transparent, real-time, tamper-resistant, immutable digitized documentation and transaction records. As a result, credit risk and loan defaults are reduced, and they can offer smart contract–based automated credit and collection. These applications target new customer segments such as SMEs and connect to new customers who join via their we.trade member banks. Komgo and we.trade can rely on evan.network identity tools and specialize in improving their trade finance applications, collaborating in an emerging ecosystem.

Catalyzing Ecosystem Formation for Delivering Customer Value   Blockchain works well in bringing together ecosystem members to collaborate and develop customer solutions that are a significant improvement over existing legacy solutions. Blockchain solutions enable firms in the ecosystem to draw on each other's complementary capabilities and cooperatively develop innovative solutions. Blockchain, with its decentralized node architecture, and transparent and immutable record of transaction and information flow across various nodes, is uniquely suited to facilitate interorganizational cooperation and problem solving. For example, the ecosystem that has been developed around cryptocurrencies, digital wallets, DEXs, and distributed app providers can provide services using digital currencies, such as lending and portfolio management.

For growth to gain traction, successful consortia must be neutral and fair to all members and keep the consortia together during early years of losses from continued investments. Of course, early success in showing improved efficiency and reduced costs will also stimulate positive network effects, and more firms will seek to join the ecosystem. An essential step is harmonization so that all ecosystem parties can interact on a single platform, reducing interoperability issues and make joining the consortia more attractive.[16] Consortia need to balance standardization with accommodating unique member differences, such as customized clauses in smart contracts. Voltron, a trade finance platform built on R3/Corda, came up with a unique approach—creating a core smart contract base with an additional layer for custom additions.[17] Figure 7.3 sets out a process to help enterprises assess different blockchain features in deciding whether to include them when designing the blockchain application.

Preparing the Organization

Organizations are naturally resistant to change, meaning project leaders will need to prepare the organization for the transition to blockchain, deploying education and training to develop the necessary human resources and knowledge base and to help with onboarding. It takes investment and time to develop the necessary expertise in-house, and efforts may need to be supplemented with external contract help as needed. If the enterprise is prioritizing internal applications, it will need to motivate different organizational units to work together to apply and realize blockchain benefits. Top management support will need to provide funding and time to establish proof of concept before moving to larger-scale implementation. The organization also needs realistic expectations as blockchain implementation is difficult, particularly in initial efforts, and pilots may not be able to establish proof of concept at first try. Finally, a top management champion who understands the technology and can act as a liaison with C-suite executives can be a make-or-break appointment.

Organizational readiness can be bolstered with launching and learning from pilot projects. Chapter 1 discussed the value of pilot projects with commercial operations in mind in giving the organization a lead over its competitors when it becomes time to launch implementation at scale. In comparing Chinese and US blockchain efforts, Gartner noted that Chinese companies that already have blockchain technology infrastructure in place are taking the lead in using blockchain applications to help businesses and consumers who need faster payments and access to (increased) credit lines.[18] The key point is that an enterprise that waits

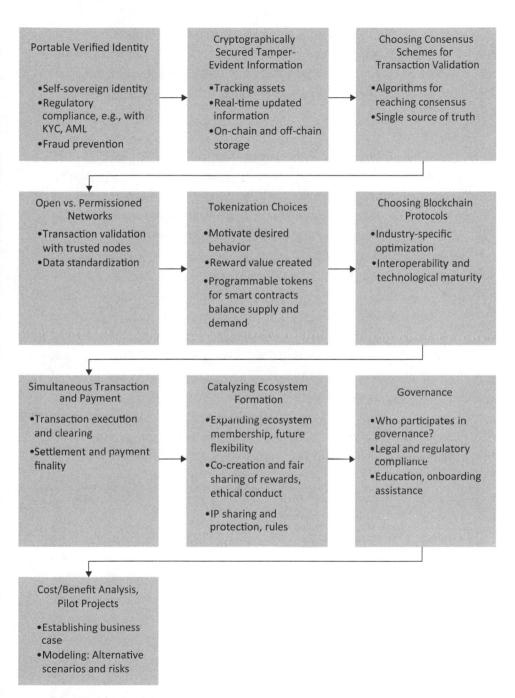

Figure 7.3
Designing the blockchain application

until blockchain's promise is fully evident can fall behind as it will still be building blockchain infrastructure and developing familiarity while its competitors are implementing time-tested blockchain commercial efforts, resulting in a serious loss of competitiveness.

Resistance to Change

Upper management may be resistant to efforts to replace legacy systems with blockchain application, due to their unproven nature, the paucity of significant positive results from blockchain usage among industry peers, and the risks inherent in being pioneers. Internal champions that have credibility with upper management need to spearhead blockchain development efforts, obtaining budgets and shielding project teams from interference while gaining adequate time to complete a pilot and assess outcomes. Recruiting capable designers and programmers to deliver workable solutions that can be deployed in the pilot efforts can enhance credibility and reduce resistance. The need and perceived value of the blockchain solution, weighed against switching costs, and individual readiness to change are some determinants of organizational acceptance and resistance.[19]

Knowledge, Financial, and Human Capital Resource Constraints

Enterprise knowledge built on legacy systems and experience can get in the way of understanding blockchain's potential for disrupting their business processes and existing ecosystems and creating new business models.[20] Accumulated knowledge and heritage can generate resistance to a blockchain-based replacement of legacy systems and ways of doing business. In addition, enterprises may try and fit blockchain into existing business paradigms. Blockchain start-ups have an advantage as they have no legacy heritage and can approach business problems afresh, using the power of DLT to improve efficiency and generate new business models while transcending traditional organizational boundaries.

Scarcity of experienced blockchain programmers and designers who have the necessary blockchain domain skills as well as an understanding of the needs of users and of the organization at the enterprise level remains a constraining issue. Talent shortages raise employment costs, further (negatively) affecting blockchain cost–benefit calculations. As a new technology, DLT also requires new technology skills such as identity verification and cryptography, token incentive design, inserting privacy controls, linking with decentralized large volumes of cloud data storage, and integration with a permissioned network governance structure.[21] All of these create bottlenecks for enterprise adopters until they can gradually ramp up investments, hiring, and training to obtain the necessary talent and knowledge capabilities. Recruiting developers and project managers as well as investing in software and networks to run blockchain can involve significant investment, with corporate financial constraints determining the level and duration of funding available to undertake such pilot projects and the subsequent implementation at scale. Cost–benefit analysis is critical in persuading top management and boards to approve funding what are seen as risky projects.

User Reactions

Users have become accustomed to web-based user interfaces, point-and-click navigation and drop-down option boxes. The continual use and familiarity gained from years of use, on desktops, tablets, and smartphones, makes users reluctant to learn new interfaces and expect new applications to offer similar convenience and ease of use. Potential users may reject blockchain because they find it difficult, find the interface to be unfriendly, and are unfamiliar with the technology, which then limits adoption. Blockchains are unfamiliar to most users; their interfaces have yet to match the ease of use and transparency of legacy applications.

Further, blockchains place novel demands on users, for example, requiring them to use both public and private keys in ensuring identity and gaining access to the blockchain. Secure private key storage and retrieval is essential to the continued access and use of blockchain applications, and novice users can unintentionally mislay or give access to their private key to ill-intentioned actors and thus be denied access to the applications and possibly lose assets and information. Blockchain user interfaces can be improved by involving subsets of potential users while the application and interface are being designed—"participatory design."[22] In contrast, negative experiences with blockchain pilots and applications lead users to question the utility of switching to blockchain and to increase support for the status quo, relying on legacy applications that meet their current needs, even if imperfectly.

Dominant Network Member Control of Blockchain

Blockchain governance in open public networks—like the one used for Bitcoin—is democratic. In permissioned networks, dominant members have more centralized control and can direct the future of their blockchain networks. They can shape new member entry, transaction fees, monetization strategies, and member rewards to suit their needs. They can also approve erasure of past transactions by fiat, contravening the immutability of a blockchain, and grant varying levels of control to different network nodes over issues such as changing blockchain architecture, standards setting, features evolution, and acceptance of future protocol changes. Other ecosystem members might then be less willing to join the network in a subordinate position. Viewing blockchains as encompassing entire ecosystems and drawing on ecosystem governance principles can help resolve some of the tension surrounding dominant member control and create greater decentralized autonomy.[23]

Regulatory Uncertainty

Nation-states and their governments have mixed attitudes toward blockchain, with varying levels of government support for blockchain initiatives. They are uncomfortable with decentralizing economic transactions because it moves valuable exchanges out of their tax jurisdiction. Some countries such as China and India have banned cryptocurrency use, while other governments have encouraged blockchain evolution, among them Switzerland and Estonia. Without regulatory clarity, enterprises may adopt a cautious wait-and-see attitude toward blockchain.

The lack of a clear regulatory framework matters. For example, as discussed in the introduction, cross-border remittances incur high fees, costing 6–7 percent of transfer amounts, and can take several days and be opaque, with clients unable to ascertain when the transaction would be completed or the exchange rate used for conversion. Blockchain applications aim to resolve these problems, with the goal of faster fulfillment, lower costs, and greater transparency. However, implementing successful cross-border remittance applications needs timely cooperation from multiple governments, whose jurisdictions are involved in cross-border money transfers. Governments have to be persuaded to collaborate with each other and accept harmonized cross-national regulations. And enterprises and their banks must work alongside central banks, regulators, and payments infrastructure operators, in a slow and sometimes bureaucratic process, to arrive at a satisfactory solution.[24]

The speed of blockchain evolution has also outpaced legal oversight, as in the case of ICOs, which were estimated to have raised over $50 billion worldwide by 2018. In the absence of regulation, ICO investors lacked knowledge about who the ICO issuers were, how the funds raised were to be spent, and whether an external auditor had reviewed the offering.[25] Such gaps in information left ICO investors open to fraud and price manipulation. ICO issuance in the United States declined dramatically after the SEC stepped in and held that ICOs could be subject to, and be required to, comply with US securities law. For example, Telegram Group, an ICO, was forced by the SEC to return $1.2 billion to US investors because it was determined that its ICO offering violated US securities law.[26]

Regulatory bodies may insist on more power over blockchains. For example, in a blockchain-based global supply chain, customs officials might require access to blockchains to ensure compliance with import/export regulations and tariffs, which would give them visibility into private sector transactions. Firms then might choose not to participate in the blockchain to avoid such governmental oversight. Another example of the impact of regulatory uncertainty is the debate over the fiduciary role and responsibility of blockchain programmers and project leaders.[27] The debate is whether or not developers of blockchain networks maintain a governance role that should have a fiduciary obligation toward the network's digital asset holders (owners of cryptocurrencies and tokens). Enterprises would have reason to be wary of blockchain usage if such a direction opened them up to claims for damages from errant blockchain execution.

Blockchain and Legal Responsibility: Accountability for Transaction Completion

Intermediaries can protect interests of counterparties, for example, holding funds in escrow until contractual conditions are fulfilled before releasing the escrowed funds in payment. In a centralized network such as Airbnb, if the accommodations that a user has contracted and paid for are not available, Airbnb, as the network intermediary, undertakes the search for alternative accommodation. In a blockchain, with decentralized nodes, immediate accountability and make-whole response may be lacking. A smart contract may not provide similar accountability for inadequate performance. It can provide for repayment and possible adjudication in case of nonperformance, but damages incurred from nonperformance or defective performance would have to be awarded by a court. The judicial system in force would need to decide whether smart contracts are legally enforceable. Thus, a smart contract cannot easily substitute for the legal system and for commonsense judgment of "reasonable care" or "good faith."[28] Enterprises also must contend with flaws in reporting or misrepresentation of off-chain events (by oracles) which can trigger automated contract execution and associated payment or exchange in error. Thus, doubts over transaction or service completion, service quality, and payment disputes, can forestall user adoption of blockchain solutions.

I now briefly compare FedNow, a pilot project from the Federal Reserve Bank of Boston, with Ripple, for insights into strategy for developing blockchain projects.

FedNow: The Federal Reserve Pilot Project

Currently, the US financial system takes an average of three days to clear and finalize payments, leading to pressure from customers for faster payments. Blockchain-based payments offer near-instantaneous settlement and payment finality. The building buzz around blockchain led the Federal Reserve Bank of Boston to ask whether blockchain could help it advance its task of ensuring monetary stability and financial system integrity, improving its overall effectiveness. It began experimenting with blockchain in 2019,[29] its goal being to understand, "through trial and error," how blockchain use could help it better perform central bank services.

The FedNow program, planned to launch in 2023, is the Federal Reserve response to the standard elongated payment settlement window—it attempts to provide payment settlement within the day, multiple times a day.[30] The Federal Reserve banks began developing FedNow to provide safe and efficient instant payment services in real time, around the clock, every day of the year. Incumbent banks might find FedNow, when available, acceptable and satisfactory, and it may possibly reduce the impetus to move to digital currency–based blockchains.

The Boston Fed wanted to test blockchain functionality in carefully circumscribed, simple test cases. It did not want to overreach given the resource constraints in technological knowledge, programming language, business expertise, and cybersecurity. Its goal was to learn, establish proof of concept, determine scalability, ascertain protocol limitations, and test the feasibility of using open-source tools. It first set up an insulated sandbox for the pilot in parallel with ongoing operations; however, they did not have the pilot interact with the legacy systems in order to reduce risk from harmful errors during implementation.

The Boston Fed then conducted two experiments. The first one involved managing a limited number of accounts that financial institutions held with the Fed. The blockchain pilot would be used to record transfers and the corresponding general ledger entries and updates and then to verify reconciliation of transfers and ledger records. In a second experiment, it modeled a supervisory node among the set of nodes within the blockchain. This second use case tested a specific requirement: a supervisory node needed access to all transaction details, while counterparties specific to a transaction were restricted via dedicated channels to their interactions alone. The Fed wanted to determine scalability limitations when using blockchain since a rising number of such transactions, each with a set of counterparties, implied a continually increasing number of dedicated channels and possible deterioration in performance. Such side channels, with the relevant counterparties in full control of the data (whether and whom to share with and on what terms), are features that the Boston Fed's blockchain needed to provide to be accepted and make inroads in critical business applications.

Their pilot results helped the Boston Fed decide that it was too early for it to commit to blockchain. Blockchain technology was not considered mature enough and too technologically incomplete to meet its needs for resolving customer pain points—mainly shortening the transaction finalization and payment settlement window from two or three days to same-day and real-time settlement. It also had to implement permissioned networks to be able to use membership services, and Ethereum versions available at that time were not deemed able to handle its membership and permissioning requirements. It was also able to assess the pros and cons of using open-source protocols; it was difficult getting help and expert advice, and the constantly evolving protocol created a burden of rewriting code to accompany newer versions.

The Boston Fed also found scalability deficiencies: to ensure data privacy, counterparties to a specific transaction were privy to specific ledgers that validated and recorded their transactions. It needed to ensure that business critical data was only available to the interested parties in that particular transaction, which required setting up private channels. The Fed found setting up channels complicated in both Ethereum and Hyperledger, and those channels did not scale easily. Of these efforts, the Fed said, "When there are hundreds of entities on a given network, the number of potential channels multiplies exponentially, as does the effort to manage them."[31]

Ripple's Blockchain Strategy

Ripple provides a sharp contrast to FedNow. Ripple was able start with a clean slate and develop its blockchain payments system from scratch. It used specific blockchain features to craft its disruptive application and offer customers advantages over the existing SWIFT messaging system–based legacy alternative. Ripple, unlike Bitcoin, departed from a fully decentralized network and restricted validation to a few trusted validator nodes, the UNL. This leads to faster processing and settlement. However, relying on a few trusted nodes makes RippleNet vulnerable to a single point of failure, that is, Ripple itself. Further, Ripple does not mint XRP using Bitcoin's slower and energy-intensive PoW approach. Instead, it premined XRP, creating one hundred billion XRP at the firm's outset in 2012, and released (gifted) eighty billion XRP to the Ripple company for use in funding its operations (the founders kept twenty billion XRP as their share).[32] Ripple has noted that XRP is independent, and while XRP liquidity and acceptance is critical to Ripple's growth, its principal responsibility is to its shareholders, not to XRP owners and market makers.

In summary, Ripple addressed a major use case—customer dissatisfaction with costly, opaque, and slow cross-border remittances—and used blockchain to create its faster, secure, and lower-cost application. Its use of trusted nodes, listed on UNL, enabled both rapid transaction authentication and simultaneous payment finality. It relied on blockchain's ability to continuously update the ledger with transaction state and account balances to offer clients immutability and a timestamped audit trail. And as XRP use grows, network effects could persuade clients to use the Ripple network over the incumbent SWIFT solution. This would further grow Ripple's business by expanding XRP use as the medium of exchange in cross-border transfers and would benefit clients by reducing their multicurrency working capital needs.

Strategy Roadmap for Choosing and Implementing Blockchain Solutions

Considering the Boston Fed's experience with its blockchain pilots, while the pilot did not achieve the desired results, the bank learned enough to determine that blockchain had potential and would be of future value as the technology matures, creating an impetus to continue to learn and experiment with blockchain innovation. Ripple shaped blockchain to suit its use application, departing from the classic open-source, fully decentralized node form used by Bitcoin. Hence, the critical step is having a compelling use case. Blockchain can be adapted for the specific use case, and adoption can occur in stages and vary in degrees.[33]

Firms can start with blockchain-enabling technologies, such as encryption algorithms, and then develop blockchain-inspired solutions that use some aspects of blockchain technology and a limited size network (i.e., a few nodes) restricted to internal trusted nodes. Next, firms could pursue blockchain complete solutions that include and comply with full blockchain specifications. Firms could then move to blockchain-enhanced solutions that combine blockchain with complementary technologies, such as AI and IoT. Last, they could develop an ecosystem, encouraging and leveraging third-party distributed apps (Dapps), which build on a blockchain platform and offer additional functionality. Blockchain thus enables a new business model, with the firm developing new services built on a decentralized system, collaborating with and available to ecosystem members.

Firms attempting blockchain pilots could experiment with using different protocols for the same use case and then choose the protocol with superior results. For example, blockchain member firms could gain insights from secure data flowing from the blockchain application. But without blockchain pilots, organizations would not be able to assess benefits and decide on the right architecture and application features. Enterprises will also become aware of human capital gaps through their pilots. As mentioned above, specialized human resources are needed

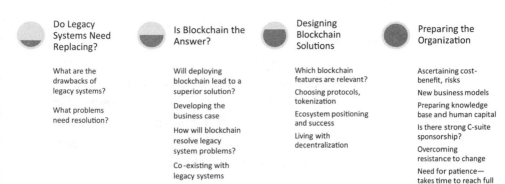

Do Legacy Systems Need Replacing?	Is Blockchain the Answer?	Designing Blockchain Solutions	Preparing the Organization
What are the drawbacks of legacy systems? What problems need resolution?	Will deploying blockchain lead to a superior solution? Developing the business case How will blockchain resolve legacy system problems? Co-existing with legacy systems	Which blockchain features are relevant? Choosing protocols, tokenization Ecosystem positioning and success Living with decentralization	Ascertaining cost-benefit, risks New business models Preparing knowledge base and human capital Is there strong C-suite sponsorship? Overcoming resistance to change Need for patience—takes time to reach full implementation Ensuring regulatory compliance

Figure 7.4

A strategic approach to enterprise blockchain

to develop and implement blockchain projects. Such resources might be scarce, difficult to locate and recruit, and costly. User education to reduce unfamiliarity with blockchain and providing user-friendly interfaces can lead to support for replacing legacy applications with blockchain solutions. Experimentation can also help ascertain the cost–benefit advantages from switching to blockchain and help make the case for switching from legacy applications. Figure 7.4 summarizes the key strategic steps for enterprises as they contemplate blockchain application.

For Enterprises, There Is Everything to Gain, and the Time Is Now

What this survey of blockchain underlines is that blockchain is a world in ferment, undergoing rapid transformation. While cryptocurrencies might be sidelined by national digital currencies and stablecoins, the underlying blockchain technology is forming deep roots, spreading into various industries. Consumers of all ages are becoming comfortable with the idea of blockchain, as NFTs such as NBA Top Shot and blockchain games such as *Axie Infinity* become part of the everyday vernacular, with large numbers of retail clients and gameplayers. Firms such as Visa and Square offer easy online ramps for payment with digital currencies, with customers becoming accustomed to securing their private keys and holding digital wallets.

DeFi start-up firms allow enterprises and individuals to hold and trade tokens and convert idle digital assets into working assets by staking them as collateral to underpin loans, investments, and derivatives. Governmental agencies and organizations are similarly experimenting, with the European Investment Bank (EIB) issuing a €100 million two-year zero-coupon bond on the public Ethereum blockchain, in collaboration with Goldman Sachs, Santander, and Société Générale, with Banque de France partnering to make funds available to the EIB in the form of CBDCs.[34] Meanwhile, start-ups are competing to outdo each other in offering new blockchain protocols that are faster, secure, more scalable and privacy preserving, and interoperable so that different blockchains can be mashed together to create customized solutions.

Governments are getting in on the act, with China making a national commitment to becoming the global leader in blockchain development and use. Not only has China launched a national digital currency, but it has also developed and offered a low-cost blockchain infrastructure,[35] the Blockchain-Based Service Network (BSN), with low-cost servers, programming tools, and standard templates to promote interoperability. BSN is available to both Chinese and foreign firms, which could host their blockchain nodes and information transmission on this network. The Chinese government's control of servers in BSN is fundamentally different from permissionless and decentralized classic DLT as it is fully centralized, with the government visibility into blockchain operations taking precedence over privacy. An open question is the degree to which China's oversight of BSN would allow it to control access and thus deny BSN use permission to individuals and enterprises it deemed inappropriate.

In addition to the US with its myriad start-ups, other countries are similarly engaged, such as Switzerland, Singapore, Estonia, Russia, the EU, Japan, South Korea, and India. National central banks around the world are experimenting with CBDC pilots, while private firms such as Coinbase and Ripple XRP are lobbying in Washington, DC, and in other capitals to influence regulation so that it is not onerous and does not stifle their creativity and freedom of action. The world that emerges will be one where private stablecoins coexist with national digital currencies and gain ground as an increasingly acceptable vehicle for payments, lending, and investments.

Advantages such as privacy protection, tamper resistance, and identity verification can bring about social benefits, such as voter access and transparent elections, efficient and corruption-free provision of government services, and increased financial inclusion. And blockchain, by being decentralized, can shake up traditional hierarchical enterprises and confront them with an existential dilemma—can they function in an ecosystem, where interdependence is the norm and cooperation is a basis for offering creative customer solutions and developing competitive advantage?

Blockchain has been unleashed for some time and is taking off in different directions. Startups such as Audius are attempting to more amply reward musicians and other creators at the expense of central intermediaries. With the introduction of the digital Chinese yuan, stablecoins and CBDCs are even more likely to become a means of payment, sidelining volatile cryptocurrencies. Ethereum, although dominant in business blockchain applications, is losing ground because of higher processing costs ("gas") and slower processing speed at higher transaction volumes, making room for newer protocols such as Polygon, Polkadot, Algorand, Avalanche, and others. *Axie Infinity*'s Ronin blockchain is one such effort, seeking to become the blockchain standard for other game developers, with its RON token serving as the basis for decentralized Ronin governance. As dissatisfaction with the internet increases, stemming from poor privacy controls, the spread of false information, the rise of dominant oligopolies, and misbehavior such as cyberbullying and hiding behind anonymity, blockchain shows promise as the bedrock on which Web 3.0 can be built, centered on secure, decentralized peer-to-peer interaction, freed from control by centralized entities.

Enterprises can best benefit from joining this ride. They can benefit from replacing intermediaries, saving on their commission or charges. They can rely on secure customer and counterparty identification to transact globally while being compliant with KYC and other legal requirements across multiple jurisdictions. They can also develop new markets and revenue sources, collaborating with independent cross-industry partners in an emergent ecosystem, with blockchain-based information sharing and the use of tokens motivating and rewarding cocreation.

As the World Economic Forum stated in its "Building Value with Blockchain Technology" report, "when done right, blockchain is all about rethinking business models, rethinking relationships between companies and between companies and customers, and is, at its heart, a strategic change effort."[36] Experimentation allows enterprises to assess different alternative configurations for their proposed solution, such as choosing between open-source and customized blockchain protocols. They can resort to sandboxes, with a limited number of participants, separated from mainstream legacy operations, to control risk. They can try out different governance arrangements to pinpoint accountability and maintain quality and equity. They can also explore the implications of instant settlement with different payment rails, ranging from accepting cryptocurrency payments to private stablecoins such as USDC or DAI as well as CBDCs, as they become available.

Experimentation also allows enterprises to give attention to regulatory acceptance and compliance, for example, blockchain compatibility with privacy regulations, such as the EU's GDPR and the "right to be forgotten," which would seem to be at odds with blockchain's tamperproof and immutable nature. Balance-based blockchains that validate the updated account balances, such as Algorand, provide one approach to complying with right-to-be-forgotten privacy demands.[37] Such experimentation, with evaluating different protocols and with issues such as instant settlement, is essential, and urgent, if enterprises are to learn about the nuances of blockchain development and implementation and to keep abreast of a rapidly evolving technology, one in which both start-up challengers and their incumbent competitors are present.

Blockchain offers improved customer solutions, but they will also change the firm, destabilizing its centralized and hierarchical pillars. Enterprises are accustomed to being at the center, choosing subcontractors and suppliers, outsourcing partners, and making the final determination regarding pursuing new products and markets. Blockchain inverts this hierarchy, offering exciting new possibilities for combining technologies and capabilities across industries but with the expectation that governance will be similarly shared across partners and industries. It is Janus faced, with customer-facing and internal organizational impact. Enterprises that face this challenge expeditiously will emerge better prepared for the new blockchain world.

Notes

Introduction

1. Collin Eaton and Dustin Volz, "US Pipeline Cyberattack Forces Closure," *Wall Street Journal*, May 8, 2021, https://www.wsj.com/articles/cyberattack-forces -closure-of-largest-u-s-refined-fuel-pipeline-11620479737.

2. Collin Eaton and Dustin Volz, "Colonial Pipeline CEO Tells Why He Paid Hackers a $4.4 Million Ransom," *Wall Street Journal*, May 19, 2021, https:// www.wsj.com/articles/colonial-pipeline-ceo-tells-why-he-paid-hackers-a-4-4 -million-ransom-11621435636.

3. Juan Carlos Olivares-Rojas, Enrique Reyes-Archundia, Jose A. Gutierrez-Gnecchi, Jaime Cerda-Jacobo, and Johan W. Gonzalez-Murueta, "A Novel Multitier Blockchain Architecture to Protect Data in Smart Metering Systems," *IEEE Transactions on Engineering Management* 67, no. 4 (November 2020): 1271–1284, https://doi:10.1109/TEM.2019.2950410.

4. Wei Ren, Xutao Wan, and Pengcheng Gan, "A Double-Blockchain Solution for Agricultural Sampled Data Security in Internet of Things Network," *Future Generation Computer Systems* 117 (April 2021): 453–461, https://doi:10.1016/j.future .2020.12.007.

5. Chris Hoffman, "The Ultimate Defense: What Is an Air Gapped Computer?," How to Geek, September 3, 2020, https://www.howtogeek.com/687792/the -ultimate-defense-what-is-an-air-gapped-computer/.

6. "Together, We Can Set Trade Free," TradeLens, accessed February 18, 2022, https://www.tradelens.com/ecosystem.

7. Bank of Canada, Bank of England, and Monetary Authority of Singapore, *Cross-Border Interbank Payments and Settlements: Emerging Opportunities for Digital*

Transformation (Singapore: KPMG Services Pte. Ltd., 2018), 36, https://www
.mas.gov.sg/-/media/MAS/ProjectUbin/Cross-Border-Interbank-Payments-and
-Settlements.pdf.

8. World Bank, "Migration and Development Brief 33," table 1.1, p. 33,
accessed February 18, 2022, https://www.knomad.org/sites/default/files/2020
-11/Migration%20%26%20Development_Brief%2033.pdf.

9. "Berklee Partners with MIT to Help Students Get Paid for Their Music,"
Berklee College of Music, September 14, 2020, https://college.berklee.edu/news
/berklee-now/berklee-partners-mit-help-students-get-paid-their-music.

10. Dan Gallagher, "Apple and Google Can Hold Out Longer Than a Fortnite," *Wall Street Journal*, August 14, 2020, https://www.wsj.com/articles/apple
-and-google-can-hold-out-longer-than-a-fortnite-11597413750.

11. "Blockchain Technology in Gaming: Transforming the Way We Play
Online Video Games," Game Designing, accessed February 18, 2022, https://
www.gamedesigning.org/gaming/blockchain.

12. "Data: Blockchain-Based Gaming Booms with Help from Axie Infinity,
Outpacing NFTs, DeFi," Yahoo Finance, August 18, 2021, https://news.yahoo
.com/data-blockchain-based-gaming-booms-outpacing-nf-ts-de-fi-174617791
.html.

13. Andrew Hayward and Stephen Graves, "What Is *Axie Infinity*? The Play-to-
Earn NFT Game Taking Crypto By Storm," February 2, 2022, https://decrypt.co
/resources/what-is-axie-infinity-the-play-to-earn-nft-game-taking-crypto-by
-storm.

14. William Foxley, "How Hashmasks Are Setting the Standard for Digital Art,"
Coindesk, February 26, 2021, last updated September 14, 2021, https://www
.coindesk.com/hashmasks-set-standard-digital-art-nft.

15. Willim Mougayar, *The Business of Blockchain* (Hoboken, NJ: John Wiley and
Sons Inc., 2016), 65–82.

16. Jacques Bughin, Tanguy Catlin, Martin Hirt, and Paul Willmott, "Why Digital Strategies Fail," *McKinsey Quarterly*, January 25, 2018, https://www.mckinsey
.com/business-functions/mckinsey-digital/our-insights/why-digital-strategies
-fail.

17. Maxwell Wessel and Clayton H. Christensen, "Surviving Disruption," *Harvard Business Review* 90, no. 12 (December 2012), 56.

18. Alexis Kriykovich and Zac Townsend, "Seven Ways for Financial Institutions to React to Financial-Technology Companies," McKinsey & Company, July 27, 2020, https://www.mckinsey.com/industries/financial-services/our-insights /banking-matters/seven-ways-for-financial-institutions-to-react-to-financial -technology-companies.

19. Clayton M. Christensen, *The Innovator's Dilemma: When New Technologies Cause Great Firms to Fail* (Boston, MA: Harvard Business School Press, 1997); Clayton Christensen, Michael Raynor, and Rory McDonald, "What Is Disruptive Innovation?," *Harvard Business Review* 93, no. 12 (December 2015), 44–53.

20. Filecoin, accessed February 18, 2022, https://filecoin.io.

21. Dennis Grishin, Kamal Obbad, Preston Estep, Kevin Quinn, Sarah Wait Zaranek, Alexander Wait Zaranek, Ward Vandewege, Tom Clegg, Nico César, Mirza Cifric, and George Church, "Accelerating Genomic Data Generation and Facilitating Genomic Data Access Using Decentralization, Privacy-Preserving Technologies and Equitable Compensation," *Blockchain in Healthcare Today* 1 (2018), https://doi.org/10.30953/bhty.v1.34.

22. Avivah Litan, David Groombridge, Chrissy Healey, and Adrian Leow, "Blockchain Unraveled: Determining its Suitability for Your Organization," Gartner Research, 2019, https://www.gartner.com/en/doc/3913807-blockchain -unraveled-determining-its-suitability-for-your-organization.

Chapter 1

1. Clayton Christensen, Michael Raynor, and Rory McDonald, "What Is Disruptive Innovation?," *Harvard Business Review* 93, no. 12 (December 2015), 44–53.

2. Jai S. Arun and Alexander Carmichael, *Trust Me: Digital Identity on Blockchain* (Somers, NY: IBM Corporation, 2017), 3–4.

3. "Sovrin: A Protocol and Token for Self-Sovereign Identity and Decentralized Trust," Sovrin Foundation, January 16, 2018, https://sovrin.org/library /sovrin-protocol-and-token-white-paper/.

4. Vincent Gramoli, "From Blockchain Consensus Back to Byzantine consensus," *Future Generation Computer Systems* 107(2020): 760–769, https://doi.org /10.1016/j.future.2017.09.023; Lucas Mearian, "The Way Blockchain-Based Cryptocurrencies Are Governed Could Soon Change," *Computerworld*, June 12, 2018.

5. Arvind Narayanan and Jeremy Clark, "Bitcoin's Academic Pedigree," *Communications of the ACM* 60, no. 12 (2017), 36–45; Shaan Ray, "Merkle Trees," Hackernoon, December 14, 2017, https://hackernoon.com/merkle-trees -181cb4bc30b4.

6. Gideon Greenspan, "Payment and Exchange Transactions in Shared Ledgers," *Journal of Payments Strategy and Systems* 10, no. 2 (2016): 172–180.

7. Tobias Meyer, Marlene Kuhn, and Evi Hartmann, "Blockchain Technology Enabling the Physical Internet: A Synergetic Application Framework," *Computers and Industrial Engineering* 136 (2019): 5–17.

8. Qiuyun Shang and Allison Price, "A Blockchain-Based Land Titling Project in the Republic of Georgia," *Innovations* 12, no. 3/4 (2018): 72–78; Mitchell Weiss and Elena Corsi, "Bitfury: Blockchain for Government," Harvard Business School Case 818–031, October 2017.

9. "Improving the Security of a Government Land Registry," Exonum, accessed Februay 19, 2022, https://exonum.com/story-georgia.

10. "This Video Game Is Turning the Pandemic Jobless into Crypto Traders," *Bloomberg News*, August 25, 2021, https://www.bloomberg.com/news/articles /2021-08-25/axie-infinity-how-game-is-turning-pandemic-jobless-into-crypto -nft-traders.

11. Rafael Ziolkowski, Gianluca Miscione, and Gerhard Schwabe, "Decision Problems in Blockchain Governance," *Journal of Management Information Systems* 37, no. 2 (2020): 316–348, https://doi.org/10.1080/07421222.2020.1759974.

12. "About CHESS Replacement," ASX, accessed February 18, 2022, http://www .asx.com.au/services/chess-replacement.htm.

13. "ASX's New Blockchain-Based CHESS System: A Marathon Not a Sprint," ZDNet, July 30, 2019, https://www.zdnet.com/article/asxs-new-blockchain-based -chess-system-a-marathon-not-a-sprint/.

14. "BNP Paribas Securities Services and TCS Join Forces to Transform Asset Servicing Industry Using Blockchain Technology," Tata Consultancy Services, October 16, 2017, https://www.tcs.com/tcs-bnp-paribas-securities-services-join -forces-transform-asset-servicing-industry-blockchain-technology.

15. "Market Capitalization, XRP Volume and Settlement Speed," Ripple, accessed October 22, 2021, https://ripple.com/xrp/market-performance/.

16. "Role of Akshaya Patra," Akshaya Patra Foundation, accessed February 18, 2022, https://www.akshayapatra.org/our-role.

17. Sanjay Podder, Pradeep Roy, Praveen Tanguturi and Shalabh Kumar Singh, *Blockchain for Good: 4 Guidelines for Transforming Social Innovation Organizations* (Bangalore, India: Accenture Labs, 2017) 7–17.

18. "Blockchain for Social Impact: Moving beyond the Hype" Center for Social Innovation, Stanford Graduate School of Business, 2019, https://www.gsb .stanford.edu/sites/gsb/files/publication-pdf/study-blockchain-impact-moving -beyond-hype.pdf.

19. "The Natural Capital Marketplace," Veridium Labs, accessed February 18, 2022, https://www.veridium.io.

20. Jesse Lund, Shanker Ramamurthy, and Bridget van Kralingen, *Moving to a Token-Driven Economy—Enabling the Digitization of Real-World Assets* (Armonk, NY: IBM Corporation, 2018), 5.

21. Mike Orcutt, "IBM Thinks Blockchains Can Help Reduce Carbon Emissions," *MIT Technology Review*, July 19, 2018, https://www.technologyreview .com/2018/07/19/141404/blockchain-explainer-tokenizing-carbon-credits/.

22. "Design Your Dream Home at Your Fingertips," DecorMatters Inc., accessed February 18, 2022, https://www.company.decormatters.com.

23. Avivah Litan, Adrian Leow, and Nadine LeBlanc, *Cool Vendors in Blockchain Business* (Stamford, CT: Gartner, 2020), 6–8.

24. "Form S-1 Registration Statement Coinbase Global Inc.," Securities and Exchange Commission, February 25, 2021, https://www.sec.gov/Archives/edgar /data/1679788/000162828021003168/coinbaseglobalincs-1.htm.

25. Sam Eifling, "Coachella Is Canceled. Catch a Show on Fortnite," *Experience Magazine*, October 28, 2020, https://expmag.com/2020/10/coachella-is-canceled -catch-a-show-on-fortnite/.

26. "NBA Top Shot Sales Marketplace," Cryptoslam, accessed February 18, 2022, https://cryptoslam.io/nba-top-shot.

27. Kellen Browning, "How 'Put That on Top Shot!' Became a New N.B.A. Mantra," *New York Times*, May 20, 2021, https://www.nytimes.com/2021/05/13 /business/nba-top-shot-moments.html.

Chapter 2

1. Kevin Wack, "BofA, Wells Fargo Sour on Blockchain," *American Banker*, March 28, 2019, https://www.americanbanker.com/news/bofa-wells-fargo-sour -on-blockchain.

2. David Furlonger and Rajesh Kandaswamy, *Understanding the Gartner Blockchain Spectrum and the Evolution of Technology Solutions* (Stamford, CT: Gartner, 2020), 12; Rajesh Kandaswamy and David Furlonger *Blockchain-Based Transformation: A Gartner Trend Insight Report* (Stamford, CT: Gartner, 2019), 5.

3. "Examining the Blockchain Trilemma," Hackernoon, February 28, 2020, https://hackernoon.com/examining-the-blockchain-trilemma-from-algorands -prism-2kcb32qd.

4. Christian Catalini and Joseph S. Gans, "Some Simple Economics of the Blockchain," *Communications of the ACM* 63, no. 7 (202): 80–90.

5. Kenny Li, "The Blockchain Scalability Problem and the Race for Visa-Like Transaction Speed," Hackernoon January 26, 2019, https://hackernoon.com /the-blockchain-scalability-problem-the-race-for-visa-like-transaction-speed -5cce48f9d44.

6. Gianluca Miscione, Rafael Ziolkowski, Liudmila Zavolokina, and Gerhard Schwabe, "Tribal Governance: The Business of Blockchain Authentication," Hawaii International Conference on System Sciences, January 3–6, 2018, https://doi.org/10.2139/ssrn.3037853.

7. Lucas Mearian, "Sharding: What It Is and Why Many Blockchain Protocols Rely on It," *Computerworld*, January 28, 2019, https://www.computerworld .com/article/3336187/sharding-what-it-is-and-why-so-many-blockchain-proto cols-rely-on-it.html

8. Toshendra Kumar Sharma, "A Comprehensive Guide on Sidechains, RSK and Liquid," Blockchain Council, accessed February 18, 2022, https://www.block chain-council.org/blockchain/a-comprehensive-guide-on-sidechains-rsk-liquid.

9. Patrick Murck, "Who Controls the Blockchain?," *Harvard Business Review* (April 2017).

10. Jesus Leal Trujillo, Steve Fromhart, and Val Srinivas, "Evolution of Blockchain Technology: Insights from the GitHub Platform," Deloitte, November 6, 2017, https://www2.deloitte.com/us/en/insights/industry/financial-services /evolution-of-blockchain-github-platform.html.

11. Vijay Madisetti and Arshdeep Bargha, "Method and System for Tuning Blockchain Scalability for Fast and Low-Cost Payment and Transaction Processing" US Patent 10102265B1, October 16, 2018, https://patents.google.com/patent/US10102265B1.

12. Toju Ometoruwa, "Solving the Blockchain Trilemma: Decentralization, Security and Scalability," Coinbureau, May 16, 2018, https://www.coinbureau.com/analysis/solving-blockchain-trilemma/.

13. David Schwartz, "Beyond Proof of Work: The XRPL Consensus Solution," Ripple Insights, October 28, 2020, https://ripple.com/insights/beyond-proof-of-work-the-xrpl-consensus-solution/.

14. Todd Kronenberg, "Why Bitcoin's Lightning Network Is Ingenious," Coinmonks, June 7, 2018, https://medium.com/coinmonks/why-bitcoins-lightning-network-is-the-ingenious-10dc1ad9ccae.

15. "Algorand Initial Specs," Algorand Foundation, May 30, 2019, https://github.com/algorandfoundation/specs/blob/master/overview/Algorand_v1_spec-2.pdf.

16. "AssetBlock and Algorand: Modernizing Real Estate Investment and Leveraging Digital Assets," Algorand Blog, May 23, 2019, https://www.algorand.com/resources/blog/assetblock-and-algorand-modernizing-real-estate-investment.

17. Catherine Turcker and Christian Catalini, "What Blockchain Can't Do," *Harvard Business Review* (June 2018); Alexander Savelyev, "Some Risks of Tokenization and Blockchainization of Private Law," *Computer Law and Security Review* 34, no. 4 (2018): 863–869, https://doi.org/10.1016/j.clsr.2018.05.010.

18. "Top 5 Enterprise Blockchain Protocols You Need to Know," EC-Council, March 2021, https://blog.eccouncil.org/top-5-enterprise-blockchain-protocols-you-need-to-know/.

19. Gilbert Verdian et al., "Quant Overledger Whitepaper," Quant Network, January 31, 2018, 5–16, https://uploads-ssl.webflow.com/6006946fee85fda61f666256/60211c93f1cc59419c779c42_Quant_Overledger_Whitepaper_Sep_2019.pdf.

20. "Quant Network's Overledger: Part Two—The Layers of Overledger," CryptoSeq, March 26, 2019, https://medium.com/@CryptoSeq/quant-networks-overledger-part-two-the-layers-of-overledger-ea23a7148af1.

21. Avivah Litan et al., "Cool Vendors in Blockchain Technology," Gartner, May 21, 2020, 7–8.

22. "Quant Network's Overledger: Part Three—TrustTag and the Tokenisation of Data," CryptoSeq, April 3, 2019, https://cryptoseq.medium.com/quant-networks -overledger-part-three-trusttag-and-the-tokenisation-of-data-71b325f4247d.

23. Gavin Wood, "Polkadot Light Paper An Introduction to Polkadot," Polkadot, April 2020, 6, https://polkadot.network/Polkadot-lightpaper.pdf.

24. "Polkadot FAQ," Polkadot, accessed February 18, 2022, https://polkadot .network/faq.

25. Rafael Belchior et al., "A Survey on Blockchain Interoperability: Past, Present, and Future Trends," ArXiv, May 28, 2020, https://arxiv.org/pdf/2005 .14282.pdf.

26. "1.1 Billion 'Invisible' People without ID Are Priority for New High Level Advisory Council on Identification for Development," World Bank, October 12, 2017, https://www.worldbank.org/en/news/press-release/2017/10/12/11-billion -invisible-people-without-id-are-priority-for-new-high-level-advisory-council -on-identification-for-development.

27. "Equifax Data Breach Settlement," Federal Trade Commission, January 2020, https://www.ftc.gov/enforcement/cases-proceedings/refunds/equifax-data -breach-settlement.

28. John Hagel III and Jeffrey F. Rayport, "The Coming Battle for Customer Information," *Harvard Business Review* (January–February 1997).

29. "Sovrin: A Protocol and Token for Self-Sovereign identity and Decentralized Trust," Sovrin Foundation, January 16, 2018: 13, 25, https://sovrin.org /library/sovrin-protocol-and-token-white-paper.

30. David Mahdi, Jonathan Care, and Michael Kelley, "Innovation Insight for Decentralized and Blockchain Identity Services," Gartner, June 25, 2019, 8–11.

31. Danielle Enwood, "Zero-Knowledge Proofs—A Powerful Addition to Blockchain," Blockhead Technologies, June 1, 2021, https://blockheadtechnologies .com/zero-knowledge-proofs-a-powerful-addition-to-blockchain/.

32. Jack Shaw, "Making Smart Contracts a Reality with Blockchain Technology," Oracle Blockchain Blog, January 27, 2020, https://blogs.oracle.com/block chain/making-smart-contracts-a-reality-with-blockchain-technology.

33. "What Is a Blockchain Oracle?," Chainlink, September 14, 2021, https://chain.link/education/blockchain-oracles.

34. "The 3 Levels of Data Aggregation in Chainlink Price Feeds," Chainlink, December 21, 2020, https://blog.chain.link/levels-of-data-aggregation-in-chainlink-price-feeds.

35. Ricardo Marcacini, "How to Use Machine Learning Algorithms as Oracles in Smart Contracts?," Medium, July 1, 2019, https://medium.com/artificial-intelligence-for-blockchain-smart/how-to-use-machine-learning-algorithms-as-oracles-in-smart-contracts-238c6353526a.

36. Josh Fruhlinger, "The Mirai Botnet Explained," CSO/IDG Communications, March 9, 2018, https://www.csoonline.com/article/3258748/the-mirai-botnet-explained-how-teen-scammers-and-cctv-cameras-almost-brought-down-the-internet.html.

37. Ahmed Banafa, "IoT and Blockchain Convergence: Benefits and Challenges," *IEEE Internet of Things*, January 10, 2017, https://iot.ieee.org/newsletter/january-2017/iot-and-blockchain-convergence-benefits-and-challenges.html.

38. Zia Yusuf et al., "Are Blockchain and the Internet of Things Made for Each Other?," Boston Consulting Group, July 30, 2018, 4.

39. Mark Hung, *Leading the IoT* (San Francisco: Gartner, 2017), 13.

40. "People-Powered Networks," Helium Systems Inc., https://www.helium.com/.

41. "What is LoRaWan Specification?," LoRa Alliance, https://lora-alliance.org/about-lorawan/.

42. Shayan Eskandari, Seyedehmahsa Moosavi, and Jermey Clark, "Transparent Dishonesty: Front-Running Attacks on Blockchain," ArXiv, April 9, 2019, https://arxiv.org/abs/1902.05164.

43. "Blockchain Security and Ethereum Smart Contract Audits," Consensys, accessed February 18, 2022, https://consensys.net/diligence.

44. "EY Blockchain Analyzer: Smart Contract and Token Review," EYGM Ltd., 2020, https://www.ey.com/en_cz/blockchain-platforms/smart-contract-token-review.

45. "Continued EY Investments in Blockchain Market to Support Increased Demand," EY, May 17, 2021, https://www.ey.com/en_gl/news/2021/05/continued-ey-investments-in-blockchain-market-to-support-increased-demand.

46. John Mardlin, "Questions DeFi Users Should Be Asking DeFi Developers," Consensys Diligence, March 2, 2020, https://consensys.net/diligence/blog/2020 /03/questions-defi-users-should-be-asking-defi-developers.

47. "Smart Contract Vulnerability Coverage," Consensys MythX, accessed February 18, 2022, https://consensys.net/mythx.

48. Andrew Gillick, "The Future of the Firm," Brave New Coin Ltd., June 24, 2019, 6.

49. "Aragon Whitepaper," GitHub, July 18, 2019, https://github.com/aragon /whitepaper.

50. Nancy Baym, Lana Swartz, and Andea Alarcon. "Convening Technologies: Blockchain and the Music Industry," *International Journal of Communication* 13, no. 9 (2019): 402–421.

51. Nick Balkin, "Berklee Partners with MIT to Help Students Get Paid for Their Music," Openmusic Initiative, September 14, 2020, https://open-music.org /blog/2020/11/12/berklee-partners-with-mit-to-help-students-get-paid-for-their -music.

52. Thomas Hardjono et al., "Towards an Open and Scalable Music Metadata Layer," ArXiv, November 20, 2019, 15, https://arxiv.org/pdf/1911.08278.pdf.

53. Balkin, "Berklee Partners with MIT to Help Students Get Paid for Their Music."

54. Hardjono et al., "Towards an Open and Scalable Music Metadata Layer," 7–8.

Chapter 3

1. John Lanchester, "The Invention of Money," *The New Yorker*, July 29, 2019.

2. "China's Mobile Payments Market Grows over 15 Percent in Q3 2019, Alipay's Market Share Exceed Half," China Banking News, January 21, 2020, http://www.chinabankingnews.com/2020/01/21/chinas-mobile-payments -market-grows-over-15-alipays-market-share-exceed-half/.

3. "Triennial Central Bank Survey," Bank for International Settlements, September 16, 2019, 3–5, https://www.bis.org/statistics/rpfx19_fx.pdf.

4. Paul Vigna, "Bitcoin Looks to Gain Traction in Payments," *Wall Street Journal*, December 31, 2020.

5. Kelly Crow and Caitlin Ostroff, "Digital Image Sells for $69.3 Million," *Wall Street Journal*, March 12, 2021.

6. "JP Morgan Creates Digital Coin for Payments," JP Morgan, updated February 1, 2021, https://www.jpmorgan.com/global/news/digital-coin-payments.

7. "Fed Chair Powell Reveals US Response to China's Digital Yuan, Libra, Public Payments Ledger," Bitcoin.com News, February 12, 2020, https://news.bitcoin.com/fed-china/.

8. Paul Vigna, "Tether's $5 Billion Error Exposes Crypto Market's Fragility," *Wall Street Journal*, July 16, 2019.

9. Tobias Adrian and Tommaso Mancini-Griffoli, "Digital Currencies: The Rise of Stablecoins," IMF Blog, September 19, 2019, 6–7, https://blogs.imf.org/2019/09/19/digital-currencies-the-rise-of-stablecoins/.

10. "Addressing the Regulatory, Supervisory and Oversight Challenges Raised by 'Global Stablecoin' Arrangements," G20 Financial Stability Board, April 14, 2020, 34–40.

11. *Big Tech in Finance: Opportunities and Risks* (Basel: Bank of International Settlements, 2019).

12. "Addressing the Regulatory, Supervisory and Oversight Challenges Raised by "Global Stablecoin" Arrangements," G20 Financial Stability Board, April 14, 2020, 3, 34–40.

13. President's Working Group on Financial Markets, "Report on Stablecoins," US Treasury, November 2021. accessed February 19, 2022, https://home.treasury.gov/system/files/136/StableCoinReport_Nov1_508.pdf.

14. Michelle F. Davis & Alastair Marsh, "JPMorgan to Use Cryptocurrency in Corporate Payments," Treasury&Risk, February 14, 2019, https://www.treasuryandrisk.com/2019/02/14/jpmorgan-to-use-cryptocurrency-in-corporate-payments.

15. "JP Morgan Creates Digital Coin for Payments," last updated February 1, 2021, accessed February 19, 2022, https://www.jpmorgan.com/solutions/cib/news/digital-coin-payments.

16. "Powering the Future of Finance, Together," Fnality International, accessed February 18, 2022, https://www.fnality.org.

17. "An Introduction to Libra White Paper," Libra Association Members, revised July 23, 2019, https://sls.gmu.edu/pfrt/wp-content/uploads/sites/54/2020/02/LibraWhitePaper_en_US-Rev0723.pdf.

18. Letter to Mark Zuckerberg, Sheryl Sandberg, and David Marcus, US House of Representatives, Committee on Financial Services, July 2, 2019, https://financialservices.house.gov/uploadedfiles/07.02.2019_-_fb_ltr.pdf.

19. William Mougayar, "Thoughts and Recommendations on the Facebook Libra Congressional Hearings," Medium, July 19, 2019, https://medium.com/@wmougayar/thoughts-and-recommendations-on-the-facebook-libra-congressional-hearings-dac7aa8909d7.

20. AnnaMaria Andriotis and Peter Rudegeair, "Mastercard, Visa, eBay Drop Out of Facebook's Libra Payments Network," *Wall Street Journal*, October 11, 2019.

21. "Libra White Paper V 2.0," Libra Association Members, April 2020, accessed February 19, 2022, https://developers.diem.com/docs/technical-papers/the-diem-blockchain-paper.

22. Peter Rudegeair and Liz Hoffman, "Facebook's Cryptocurrency Venture to Wind Down, Sell Assets," *Wall Street Journal*, January 26, 2022, https://www.wsj.com/articles/facebooks-cryptocurrency-venture-to-wind-down-sell-assets-11643248799.

23. Federal Reserve, "The FedNow Service Readiness Guide," accessed February 19, 2022, https://www.frbservices.org/binaries/content/assets/crsocms/financial-services/fednow/prepare-for-fednow/fednow-service-readiness-guide.pdf.

24. Adrian and Mancini-Griffoli "Digital Currencies," 14.

25. Rohan Grey and Jonathan Dharmapalan, "Case for Digital Legal Tender: The Macroeconomic Policy Implications of Digital Fiat Currency," eCurrency, March 27, 2017, 17, https://www.ecurrency.net/post/the-case-for-digital-legal-tender-the-macroeconomic-policy-implication-of-digital-fiat-currency.

26. Committee on Payments and Market Infrastructures, "Central Bank Digital Currencies," Bank for International Settlements, March 12, 2018.

27. Ulrich Bindseil, "Tiered CBDC and the Financial System," Working Paper Series no. 2351, European Central Bank, January 2020, 7.

28. Jesse Lund et al., "Charting the Evolution of Programmable Money," IBM Institute for Business Value, March 17, 2019.

29. Digital Monetary Institute, "DMI Annual 2022," OMFIF 2022, accessed February 19, 2022, https://www.omfif.org/dmiannual2022.

30. Board of Governors, the Federal Reserve System, "Money and Payments: The U.S. Dollar in the Age of Digital Transformation," January 2022, accessed February 19, 2022, https://www.federalreserve.gov/publications/files/money-and -payments-20220120.pdf.

31. Office of Congressman Tom Emmer (MN-06), "Emmer Introduces Legislation to Prevent Unilateral Fed Control of a U.S. Digital Currency," press release, January 12, 2022, https://emmer.house.gov/2022/1/emmer-introduces-legisla tion-to-prevent-unilateral-fed-control-of-a-u-s-digital-currency.

32. Grey and Dharmapalan, "Case for Digital Legal Tender," 36.

33. Michael Kumhof and Clare Noone, "Central Bank Digital Currencies—Design Principles for Financial Stability," *Economic Analysis and Policy* 71 (September 2021): 553–572.

34. Tobias Adrian, Stablecoins, *Central Bank Digital Currencies, and Cross-Border Payments: A New Look at the International Monetary System* (Zurich: IMF-Swiss National Bank Conference, May 2019).

35. Grey and Dharmapalan, "Case for Digital Legal Tender," 31.

36. Ian Allison, "Inside the Standards Race for Implementing FATF's Travel Rule," Coindesk, Feb 4, 2020, https://www.coindesk.com/inside-the-standards -race-for-implementing-fatfs-travel-rule.

37. David Riegelnig, "OpenVASP: An Open Protocol to Implement FATF's Travel Rule for Virtual Assets," Bitcoin Suisse, November 14, 2019, https://www .openvasp.org/wp-content/uploads/2019/11/OpenVasp_Whitepaper.pdf.

38. "Central Bank Digital Currency, Opportunities, Challenges and Design," Discussion Paper, Bank of England. March 2020, https://www.bankofengland .co.uk/-/media/boe/files/paper/2020/central-bank-digital-currency-opportuni ties-challenges-and-design.pdf.

39. "The Rijsbank's e-krona pilot," Sveriges Rijsbank, February 2020.

40. "Cross-Border Interbank Payments and Settlements," Bank of Canada, Bank of England, and Monetary Authority of Singapore, November 2018, https:// www.mas.gov.sg/-/media/MAS/ProjectUbin/Cross-Border-Interbank-Payments -and-Settlements.pdf.

41. "Virtually Money," *The Economist*, April 23, 2020, 67–68.

42. William Foxley, "President Xi Says China Should 'Seize Opportunity' to Adopt Blockchain," *CoinDesk*, October 25, 2019, https://www.coindesk.com

/markets/2019/10/25/president-xi-says-china-should-seize-opportunity-to
-adopt-blockchain.

43. Rita Liao, "China's Digital Yuan Wallet Now Has 260 Million Individual
Users," *TechCrunch*, January 18, 2022, https://techcrunch.com/2022/01/18
/chinas-digital-yuan-wallet-now-has-260-million-individual-users.

44. "Addressing the Regulatory, Supervisory and Oversight Challenges Raised
by 'Global Stablecoin' Arrangements," G20 Financial Stability Board, April 14,
2020.

45. "Central Bank Digital Currency, Opportunities, Challenges and Design,"
25–30.

46. Jack Meaning et al., "Broadening Narrow Money: Monetary Policy with a
Central Bank Digital Currency," Staff Working Paper No. 724, Bank of England,
May 18, 2018.

47. Committee on Payments and Market Infrastructures, "Central Bank Digital
Currencies," Bank for International Settlements, March 12, 2018, 13.

48. Meaning, "Broadening Narrow Money," 3.

49. Yaya J. Fanusie and Trevor Logan, "Crypto Rogues US State Adversar-
ies Seeking Blockchain Sanctions Resistance," Foundation for Defense of
Democracies, July 11, 2019, https://www.fdd.org/analysis/2019/07/11/crypto
-rogues/.

50. "The Dollar's Dominance Masks China's Rise in Finance," *Economist*, April
16, 2020.

51. Deutsche Bank, "Digital Yuan: What Is It and How Does It Work?," July
14, 2021, https://www.db.com/news/detail/20210714-digital-yuan-what-is-it-and
-how-does-it-work.

52. Eswar Prasad, "China's Digital Yuan—Premiering Globally at the Beijing
Olympics—Could Become a Model for Other Countries," *Fortune*, February 1,
2022, https://fortune.com/2022/02/01/china-digital-yuan-beijing-winter-olympics
-cbdc-pboc-renminbi-eswar-prasad.

53. "Does the US Need a National Digital Currency?," *Wall Street Journal*, February 23, 2020.

54. Board of Governors of the Federal Reserve System, "Money and Payments."

55. Adrian and Mancini-Griffoli, "Rise of Digital Money," 6.

56. Darrell Duffie, "Digital Currencies and Fast Payment Systems: Disruption Is Coming," Paper presented at the Asian Monetary Policy Forum, May 2019.

57. "Financial Inclusion—A Phoneful of Dollars," *Economist*, November 15, 2014.

58. Christine Lagarde, "Mexico: An Opportunity for Financial Inclusion," International Monetary Fund, May 28, 2019, https://www.imf.org/en/News /Articles/2019/05/29/sp052919-mexico-an-opportunity-for-financial-inclusion.

59. Jason Davis, Minh Vo, and Anne Yang, "Alibaba in Blockchain—Integrating Blockchain-Based Remittances in Cloud Services," INSEAD, 2018.

60. Guillermo Jesús Larios-Hernández, "Blockchain Entrepreneurship Opportunity in the Practices of the Unbanked," *Business Horizons* 60, no. 6 (2017): 865–874.

61. Phil Lucsok, "Social Recovery on Substrate," Parity Technologies, April 15, 2020, https://www.parity.io/social-recovery-on-substrate/.

Chapter 4

1. "Blockchain in Capital Markets," Consensys, accessed February 18, 2022, https://consensys.net/blockchain-use-cases/capital-markets.

2. "DeFi Dashboard," DeFi Llama, accessed October 24, 2021, https://defillama .com/home.

3. "The Q2 2021 DeFi Report," Consensys Codefi, https://consensys.net/reports /defi-report-q2-2021.

4. "Why 'HODL'ing' Your Bitcoin Pays Off," *Forbes*, December 7, 2020.

5. Nathan Reiff, "What Crypto Users Need to Know: The ERC20 Standard," Investopedia, updated August 24, 2021, https://www.investopedia.com/tech /why-crypto-users-need-know-about-erc20-token-standard/.

6. "Maker Protocol 101," Maker Foundation, December 9, 2019, 2, https:// docs.makerdao.com/getting-started/maker-protocol-101.

7. "The Maker Protocol: MakerDAO's Multi-Collateral Dai (MCD) System," Maker Foundation, accessed February 18, 2022, https://makerdao.com/en /whitepaper.

8. Andrew Gillick, "2019 Money Markets Review: MakerDAO and the Federal Reserve," Brave New Coin Research, January 7, 2020, 16–17.

9. "Total Value Locked (USD) in Maker," DEFI Pulse, accessed February 19, 2022, https://defipulse.com/maker.

10. "Total Value (USD) Locked in Compound," DeFi Pulse, accessed February 19, 2022, https://www.defipulse.com/projects/compound.

11. Robert Leshner and Geoffrey Hayes, "Compound: The Money Market Protocol," Compound Labs Inc., February 2019, https://compound.finance/documents/Compound.Whitepaper.pdf.

12. Julia Wu, "Compound: The Money Market on Ethereum," Hackernoon, June 30, 2020, https://hackernoon.com/compound-the-money-market-on-ethereum-zm113yxb.

13. "Maximize $COMP Mining," Instadapp, accessed February 18, 2022, https://dsa.instadapp.io/recipe/comp-max.

14. "Blockchain Makes Inroads into the Stock Market's $1 Trillion Plumbing System," *Wall Street Journal*, November 7, 2019; "Paxos, Credit Suisse Claim First Blockchain-Based Settlement of US Equities," *CoinDesk*, February 20, 2020, https://www.coindesk.com/paxos-credit-suisse-claim-first-blockchain-based-settlement-of-us-equities.

15. Fernando Martinelli, "Calculating Value, Impermanent Loss and Slippage for Balancer Pools," Balancer, June 19, 2020, https://medium.com/balancer-protocol/calculating-value-impermanent-loss-and-slippage-for-balancer-pools-4371a21f1a86.

16. Fernando Martinelli, "80/20 Balancer Pools," Balancer, March 16, 2020, https://medium.com/balancer-protocol/80-20-balancer-pools-ad7fed816c8d.

17. "Synthetix Litepaper v1.4," Synthetix, March 2020, 2, 5–6, https://www.digitalcoindata.com/whitepapers/synthetix-whitepaper.pdf.

18. Yan Chen, "Blockchain Tokens and the Potential Democratization of Entrepreneurship and Innovation," *Business Horizons* 61 (2018): 567–575.

19. James Clayton, "Statement on Cryptocurrencies and Initial Coin Offerings," US Securities and Exchange Commission, December 11, 2017, https://www.sec.gov/news/public-statement/statement-clayton-2017-12-11.

20. Vitalik Buterin, "Explanation of DAICOs," ethresearch, January 5, 2018, https://ethresear.ch/t/explanation-of-daicos/465.

21. Alex Kleydints, "Top 10 Reasons Why the ICO Model Failed," Medium, October 31, 2018, https://medium.com/@kleydints/top-10-reasons-why-the-ico -model-failed-48024bc819ff.

22. "DeFi Project Orion Protocol," Crowdfund Insider, July 22, 2020, https:// www.crowdfundinsider.com/2020/07/164366-defi-project-orion-protocol -secures-over-3-million-in-capital-via-dynamic-coin-offering-or-dyco/.

23. Martin Leibi, "A Primer on the Regulation of Trading in Cryptocurren-cies and Asset Management Related to Cryptocurrencies in Switzerland," PWC Switzerland, March 27, 2018, 2–3, https://www.pwc.ch/en/insights /regulation/a-primer-on-the-regulation-of-the-trading-in-cryptocurrencies-and -the-asset-management-related-to-cryptocurrencies-in-switzerland.html.

24. Kadan Stadelmann, "What Is an Initial DEX Offering (IDO) and Why Do We Need Them?," *CoinMarketCap*, May 10, 2021, last updated December 5, 2021, https://coinmarketcap.com/alexandria/article/what-is-an-initial-dex-offering -ido-and-why-do-we-need-them.

25. "Syndicated Loans and Blockchain Webinar," Consensys, July 16, 2020, https://pages.consensys.net/enterprise-ethereum-syndicated-loans.

26. Lynda Applegate, Roman Beck, and Christoph Muller-Bloch, "Deutsche Bank: Pursuing Blockchain Opportunities (A)," Harvard Business School Case 817–100, April 11, 2017.

27. Lynda Applegate, Roman Beck, and Christoph Muller-Bloch. "Deutsche Bank: Pursuing Blockchain Opportunities (B)." Harvard Business School Case 817–101, April 11, 2017.

28. "Project Bond-i: Bonds on Blockchain," Commonwealth Bank of Austra-lia, accessed February 18, 2022, https://www.commbank.com.au/business /business-insights/project-bondi.html.

29. "CBA Chosen by World Bank to Deliver World's First Blockchain Bond," Commonwealth Bank of Australia, August 10, 2018.

30. "World Bank and CBA Partner to Enable Secondary Bond Trading Recorded on Blockchain," Commonwealth Bank of Australia, May 16, 2019.

31. Yanfen Zheng, "Lemonade: 'Juicy' Flavor Insurtech," Asia Case Research Centre, University of Hong Kong, November 18, 2019, 8.

32. "Blockchain in Insurance," IBM Corporation, accessed February 18, 2022, https://www.ibm.com/blogs/blockchain/category/blockchain-in-financial -services/blockchain-in-insurance.

33. Dante Disparte, "Blockchain Could Make the Insurance Industry Much More Transparent," *Harvard Business Review* (July 2017).

34. Nicky Morris, "EY Maersk Blockchain Marine Insurance Platform Goes Live," Ledger Insights, May 25, 2018, https://www.ledgerinsights.com/block chain-marine-insurance/.

35. "Digital Transformation for reinsurance Is Here," B3i, accessed February 18, 2022, https://b3i.tech.

36. "Amica Mutual Insurance Company," IBM Corporation, March 2018, https://www.ibm.com/case-studies/amica-mutual-insurance-company.

37. "Insurance Reimagined with Groupama," IBM Corporation, accessed February 18, 2022, https://mediacenter.ibm.com/media/t/1_709756n4.

38. "Etherisc, Aon and Oxfam in Sri Lanka on a Mission: To Expand Inclusive Insurance in Sri Lanka" Etherisc, November 29, 2018, https://blog.etherisc .com/etherisc-aon-and-oxfam-in-sri-lanka-on-a-mission-to-expand-inclusive -insurance-in-sri-lanka-696b51c98d9b.

39. "The Policy That Pays Out Cash after a Hurricane," Raincoat LLC, accessed February 18, 2022, https://www.getraincoat.com.

40. Ian Allison, "JPMorgan Adds Privacy Features to Ethereum-Based Quorum Blockchain," Coindesk, May 28, 2019, https://www.coindesk.com/jpmorgan -adds-new-privacy-features-to-its-ethereum-based-quorum-blockchain.

41. "ConsenSys Acquires JP Morgan's Quorum to Advance Enterprise Blockchain Adoption," Consensys, August 25, 2020, https://consensys.net/blog/news /consensys-acquires-jpm-quorum/.

42. Adrian Zmudzinski, "Hyperledger Fabric Sees More Dev Activity Than Corda in Q3 2019: Report," Cointelegraph, January 22, 2020, https://cointele graph.com/news/hyperledger-fabric-sees-more-dev-activity-than-corda-in-q3 -2019-report.

43. Catalin Cimpanu, "Hackers Steal $25 Million Worth of Cryptocurrency from Lendf.me Platform," ZDNet, April 19, 2020, https://www.zdnet.com/article /hackers-steal-25-million-worth-of-cryptocurrency-from-uniswap-and-lendf-me/.

44. MacKenzie Sigalos, "More Than $320 Million Stolen in Latest Apparent Crypto Hack," February 2, 2022, https://www.cnbc.com/2022/02/02/320-million -stolen-from-wormhole-bridge-linking-solana-and-ethereum.html.

45. Dan Morehead, "Pantera Blockchain Letter," Pantera Capital, December 10, 2019, 4, https://panteracapital.com/wp-content/uploads/2019/12/Pantera -Blockchain-Letter-Dec-2019.pdf.

Chapter 5

1. Amit Ganeriwalla et al., "Does Your Supply Chain Need a Blockchain?," Boston Consulting Group and MIT Media Lab, March 16, 2018.

2. Lata Varghese and Rashi Goyal, "Blockchain for Trade Finance: Payment Method Automation Part 2," Cognizant, October 2017, 4–8, https://www .cognizant.com/whitepapers/blockchain-for-trade-finance-payment-method -automation-part-2-codex3071.pdf.

3. David Simchi-Levi, *Designing and Managing the Supply Chain* (New York, NY: McGraw-Hill, 2005); Soonhong Min, Zach G. Zacharia, and Carlo D. Smith, "Defining Supply Chain Management: In the Past, Present, and Future," *Journal of Business Logistics* 40, no. 1 (2019): 44–55; Sangeet P. Chaudhary et al., "Plat-forms and Blockchain Will Transform Logistics," *Harvard Business Review* (June 2019).

4. Michael J. Casey and Pindar Wong, "Global Supply Chains Are About to get Better, Thanks to Blockchain," *Harvard Business Review* (March 2017).

5. Katie Devlin, "What Is a Supply Chain Control Tower?," IBM Supply Chain Blog, January 13, 2021, https://www.ibm.com/blogs/supply-chain/what-is-a -supply-chain-control-tower.

6. Alex Pradhan, Andrew Stevens, and John Johnson, "Blockchain Fundamen-tals for Supply Chain," Gartner, February 2018.

7. Ganeriwalla and Casey, "Does Your Supply Chain Need a Blockchain?."

8. Rajiv Lal and Scott Johnson, "Maersk: Betting on Blockchain," Harvard Busi-ness School Case 518–089, revised July 2018.

9. Leanne Kemp, "Everledger's Pioneering Blockchain Work for Diamonds," IBM, May 23, 2018, https://www.ibm.com/blogs/think/2018/05/everledger/.

10. Lal and Johnson, "Maersk: Betting on Blockchain," p. 7.

11. "What is eTradeConnect," Hong Kong Trade Finance Platform Company Limited, https://www.etradeconnect.net/Portal.

12. "The One Stop Trade Platform That Helps Businesses," Government of Singapore, last updated April 20, 2021, https://www.ntp.gov.sg/home/.

13. "Trade Finance," Hong Kong Monetary Authority, updated October 21, 2021, https://www.hkma.gov.hk/eng/key-functions/international-financial-centre /fintech/research-and-applications/trade-finance/.

14. Helen Partz, "US FDA Partners with IBM and Walmart to Improve Drug Supply Chain Using Blockchain," Cointelegraph, June 13, 2019, https://coin telegraph.com/news/us-fda-partners-with-ibm-and-walmart-to-improve-drug -supply-chain-using-blockchain.

15. Zia Yusuf, Akash Bhatia, Massimo Russo, Usama Gill, Maciej Kranz, and Anoop Nannra, "Are Blockchain and the Internet of Things Made for Each Other?," Boston Consulting Group and Cisco, July 30, 2018.

16. "Welcome to Ambrosus," Ambrosus Inc., accessed February 18, 2022, https://ambrosus.com.

17. Team Ambrosus, "Swiss Cheese: How Ambrosus Protects High-Quality Swiss Food Exports," Ambrosus, August 13, 2017, https://blog.ambrosus.com/swiss -cheese-how-ambrosus-protects-high-quality-swiss-food-exports-d318dda720d7.

18. "IBM Food Trust: A New Era in the World's Food Supply," IBM Corporation, accessed February 18, 2022, https://www.ibm.com/blockchain/solutions /food-trust.

19. Dan McQuade, "Blockchain-Traced Seafood: Helping Historic New England Fisheries Thrive," IBM Corporation, October 17, 2019, https://www.ibm.com /blogs/blockchain/2019/10/blockchain-traced-seafood-helping-historic-new -england-fisheries-thrive.

20. Florian Seeh, "How New Entrants Are Redefining Cross-Border Payments," Ernst & Young Global Ltd., February 23, 2021, https://www.ey.com/en_us /banking-capital-markets/how-new-entrants-are-redefining-cross-border -payments.

21. "Global Payments 2016: Strong Fundamentals Despite Uncertain Times," McKinsey & Company, September 2016, 21–23, https://www.mckinsey.com /~/media/mckinsey/industries/financial%20services/our%20insights/a%20 mixed%202015%20for%20the%20global%20payments%20industry/global -payments-2016.ashx.

22. "Settlement," CLS 2021, accessed February 18, 2022, https://www.cls-group .com/products/settlement.

23. "Jasper–Ubin Design Paper Enabling Cross-Border High Value Transfer Using Distributed Ledger Technologies," Bank of Canada, Monetary Authority of Singapore, and Accenture, 2019; "Delivery versus Payment on Distributed Ledger Technologies: Project Ubin," Deloitte, Singapore Exchange, and Monetary Authority of Singapore, 2018.

24. "Jasper—Ubin Design Paper," 4.

25. Bank of Canada, "Cross-Border Interbank Payments and Settlements," 30.

26. Bank of Canada, "Cross-Border Interbank Payments and Settlements," 32–36.

27. "Project Ubin: Central Bank Digital Money Using Distributed Ledger Technology," Monetary Authority of Singapore, last updated December 8, 2020, https://www.mas.gov.sg/schemes-and-initiatives/project-ubin.

28. Joe Kendzick, "Ripple XRP Analysis," May 4, 2018, https://medium.com/@jkendzicky16/ripple-xrp-analysis-cc4f440d0604.

29. Lara Mauri, Stelvio Cimato, and Ernesto Damiani, "A Formal Approach for the Analysis of the XRP Ledger Consensus Protocol," Proceedings of the 6th International Conference on Information Systems Security and Privacy, February 25–27, 2020, 52–63.

30. Dave Cohen, David Schwartz, and Arthur Britto, "XRP Ledger Consensus," XRP Ledger, accessed February 18, 2022, https://xrpl.org/consensus.html.

31. "Trade Finance Is Going Open Account," Nordea, Mar 21, 2018, https://insights.nordea.com/en/ideas/trade-finance-is-going-open-account/.

32. "Whitepaper 2.0 on Distributed Ledger Technology," Hongkong Monetary Authority, October 25, 2017, https://www.hkma.gov.hk/media/eng/doc/key-functions/finanical-infrastructure/infrastructure/20171025e1a1.pdf.

33. "Whitepaper 2.0 on Distributed Ledger Technology," 5.

34. "Whitepaper 2.0 on Distributed Ledger Technology" 51–52.

35. Danielle Yew and Boon-Soong Neo, "Li & Fung Navigating through Disruptive Changes," Nanyang Tech University, June 16, 2017.

36. "Partner with Us," Fung Group, accessed February 18, 2022, https://www.funggroup.com/en/our_businesses/partner_with_us.

37. Thomas Eisenmann, Geoffrey G. Parker and Marshal. W. van Alstyne, "Strategies for Two-Sided Markets," *Harvard Business Review* (October 2006).

38. Lucas Mearian, "IBM, Chainyard Unveil Blockchain-Based 'Trust Your Supplier' Network," *Computerworld*, August 5, 2019.

39. "Trust Your Supplier: A Case Study in Faster, More Secure Vendor Onboarding through blockchain," *Hyperledger*, May 28, 2020, https://www.hyperledger .org/blog/2020/05/28/trust-your-supplier-a-case-study-in-faster-more-secure -vendor-onboarding-through-blockchain.

Chapter 6

1. Mary C. Lacity, *Blockchain Foundations for the Internet of Value* (Arkansas: Epic Books, University of Arkansas Press 2020): 461–462.

2. Avivah Litan and William Clark, "The Future of Blockchain: 8 Scalability Hurdles," Gartner, September 2018.

3. Ron Adner, "Ecosystems as Structure: An Actionable Construct of Strategy," *Journal of Management* 43, no. 1 (2017): 39–58.

4. Andrew Shipilov and A. Gawer, "Integrating Research on Interorganizational Networks and Ecosystem." *Academy of Management Annals* 14, no. 1 (2020), https://doi.org/10.5465/annals.2018.0121.

5. Nikolaus Lang, Konrad von Szczepanski, and Charline Wurzer, "The Emerging Art of Ecosystem Management," Boston Consulting Group, January 16, 2019.

6. Michael G. Jacobides, "In the Ecosystem Economy, What's Your Strategy?," *Harvard Business Review* (September–October 2019).

7. Brian Collie et al., "The Reimagined Car—Shared, Autonomous, Electric," Boston Consulting Group, December 18, 2017, 12.

8. Brian Collie et al., "The Reimagined Car," 3.

9. "Automotive Revolution—Perspective towards 2030," Advanced Industries, McKinsey & Company, January 1, 2016.

10. Karalee Close et al., "A Prescription for Blockchain in Healthcare" Boston Consulting Group, April 2018.

11. Andrew Lippman et al., "MedRec: Patient Control of Medical Record Distribution," IEEE Blockchain Technical Briefs, July 2018.

12. "Healthcare Technology: 2020 Outlook" Credit Suisse Report, January 8, 2020, 19–20.

13. Martin Ihrig and Ian C. Macmillan, "How to Get Ecosystem Buy-In," *Harvard Business Review* (March–April 2017).

14. Sharon Hakkennes and Mike Jones, "A Healthcare Provider CIOs Playbook on Lessons Learned from Global Electronic Health Record Projects," Gartner, April 30, 2021.

15. Nikolaus Lang, Konrad von Szczepanski, and Charline Wurzer, "The Emerging Art of Ecosystem Management," Boston Consulting Group, January 16, 2019; Jonathan Wareham, Paul B. Fox, and Josep L. C. Giner, "Technology Ecosystem Governance," *Organization Science* 25, no. 4 (2014): 1195–1215.

16. Alex Pradhan, Andrew Stevens, and John Johnson, "Blockchain Fundamentals for Supply Chain," Gartner, February 2018.

17. Geoffrey Parker, Marshall Van Alstyne, and Xiaoyue Jiang, "Platform Ecosystems: How Developers Invert the Firm" *MIS Quarterly* 41, no. 1 (2017): 255–266.

18. Todd Scott, "TradeLens: How IBM and Maersk Are Sharing Blockchain to Build a Global Trade Platform," IBM THINK Blog, November 27, 2018, https://www.ibm.com/blogs/think/2018/11/tradelens-how-ibm-and-maersk-are-sharing-blockchain-to-build-a-global-trade-platform.

19. Madhusudan Singh and Shiho Kim, "Branch-Based Blockchain Technology in Intelligent Vehicle" *Computer Networks* 145 (2018): 219–231.

20. Ulrich Pidun, Martin Reeves, and Maximilian Schüssler, "How Do You 'Design' a Business Ecosystem?," Boston Consulting Group, February 20, 2020.

Chapter 7

1. Bernard Golden, quoted in Jason Bloomberg, "Don't Let Blockchain Cost Savings Hype Fool You," *Forbes*, February 24, 2018, https://www.forbes.com/sites/jasonbloomberg/2018/02/24/dont-let-blockchain-cost-savings-hype-fool-you.

2. Catherine Mulligan et al., "Blockchain beyond the Hype A Practical Framework for Business Leaders," World Economic Forum, April 2018, 6; Homan Farahmand, "Planning for Blockchain Solution Adoption," Gartner, June 2018, 13.

3. Steve Odell and Julia Fadzeyeva, "Emerging Technology Projection: The Total Economic Impact™ Of IBM Blockchain," Forrester Consulting and IBM, July 2018, 5.

4. Odell and Fadzeyeva, "Emerging Technology Projection," 33–48.

5. Mike Jones, "A Healthcare Provider CIO's Guide to Accurate EHR Total Cost of Ownership," Gartner, April 10, 2018.

6. Patara Panuparb, "Cost–Benefit Analysis of a Blockchain-Based Supply Chain Finance Solution" (master's thesis, MIT Center for Transportation and Logistics, May 2019), https://ctl.mit.edu/pub/thesis/cost-benefit-analysis-blockchain -based-supply-chain-finance-solution.

7. Bloomberg, "Don't Let Blockchain Cost Savings Hype Fool You."

8. Panuparb, "Cost–Benefit Analysis."

9. Satoshi Nakamoto, "Bitcoin: A Peer-to-Peer Electronic Cash System," bitcoin. org, 2008, https://bitcoin.org/bitcoin.pdf.

10. Leslie Lamport, Robert Shostak, and Marshall Pease, "The Byzantine Generals Problem," *ACM Transactions on Programming Languages and Systems* 4, no. 3 (1982): 387–389.

11. Ivica Nikolic et al., "Finding The Greedy, Prodigal, and Suicidal Contracts at Scale," Arxiv, last revised March 14, 2018, https://arxiv.org/abs/1802.06038.

12. "DTCC Enters Test Phase on Distributed Ledger Project for Credit Derivatives with MarkitSERV and 15 Leading Global Banks," DTCC, November 6, 2018, https://www.dtcc.com/news/2018/november/06/dtcc-enters-test-phase-on -distributed-ledger-project-for-credit-derivatives-with-markitserv.

13. Sukand Ramachandran et al., "Digital Ecosystems in Trade Finance: Seeing beyond the Technology," Boston Consulting Group, September 2019, 7.

14. "The Trust Infrastructure for Cooperative Ecosystems," evan.network, accessed February 18, 2022, https://evan.network.

15. Litan et al., "Cool Vendors," 2020.

16. Ramachandran et al., "Digital Ecosystems in Trade Finance," 11.

17. Nicky Morris, "Blockchain Trade Finance Consortia Face Challenges as They Go Live," Ledger Insights, May 24, 2019, https://www.ledgerinsights.com /blockchain-trade-finance-consortia-challenges/.

18. Avivah Litan and Adrian Leow, "Blockchain Future. Comparison China and US," Gartner, May 7, 2020.

19. Clara Walsh et al., "Understanding Manager Resistance to Blockchain Systems," *European Management Journal* 39, no. 3 (2021): 353–365, https://doi .org/10.1016/j.emj.2020.10.001.

20. Linda Pawczuk, Rob Massey, and David Schatsky, "Breaking Blockchain Open: Deloitte's 2018 Global Blockchain Survey" Deloitte Development, 2018, 24, https://www2.deloitte.com/content/dam/Deloitte/us/Documents/financial -services/us-fsi-2018-global-blockchain-survey-report.pdf.

21. Jesus Rodriguez, "Five Challenges of Permissioned Blockchain Solutions and the Tools and Protocols That Can Help You," Hackernoon, February 10, 2019, https://hackernoon.com/five-challenges-of-permissioned-blockchain-solu tions-and-the-tools-and-protocols-that-can-help-you-d3e9cf49818a.

22. Sarah B. Mills, "Designing for Blockchain: What's Different and What's at Stake," Consensys, March 22, 2018, https://media.consensys.net/designing -for-blockchain-whats-different-and-what-s-at-stake-b867eeade1c9.

23. Llewellyn D. W. Thomas, Erkko Autio, and David M. Gann, "Architectural Leverage: Putting Platforms in Context," *Academy of Management Perspectives* 28 no. 2 (2014). 190–219, Wareham, "Technology Ecosystem Governance," 1203–1205.

24. Kevin Rutter and Georgio Mosis, "Successes and Failures of Blockchain Proofs of Concept," *Asia Insurance Review*, February 2019, 58–59.

25. Dirk A. Zetzsche et al., "The ICO Gold Rush: It's a Scam, It's a Bubble, It's a Super Challenge for Regulators," *Harvard International Law Journal* 60 no. 2 (2019): 267–315.

26. "Telegram to Return $1.2 Billion to Investors and Pay $18.5 Million Penalty to Settle SEC Charges," Securities and Exchange Commission, June 26, 2020, https://www.sec.gov/news/press-release/2020-146.

27. Raina S. Haque et al., "Blockchain Development and Fiduciary Duty," *Stanford Journal of Blockchain Law and Policy* 2, vol. 2 (2019): 139–187.

28. Eliza Mik, "Smart Contracts: Terminology, Technical Limitations and Real-World Complexity," *Law, Innovation and Technology* 9, no. 2 (2017): 269–300.

29. "Beyond Theory: Getting Practical with Blockchain," Federal Reserve Bank of Boston, February 2019, https://www.bostonfed.org/publications/fintech /beyond-theory-getting-practical-with-blockchain.aspx.

30. "About the FedNow Service," Federal Reserve, accessed February 18, 2022, https://www.frbservices.org/financial-services/fednow/about.html.

31. "Beyond Theory," Federal Reserve Bank of Boston, 18.

32. David Yoffie and George Gonzalez, "Ripple: The Business of Crypto," Harvard Business School Case 719–506, February 2020.

33. Furlonger and Kandaswamy, "Understanding the Gartner Blockchain Spectrum," 11.

34. "EIB Issues Its First Ever Digital Bond on a Public Blockchain," European Investment Bank, April 28, 2021, https://www.eib.org/en/press/all/2021-141 -european-investment-bank-eib-issues-its-first-ever-digital-bond-on-a-public -blockchain.

35. James T. Areddy, "Beijing Tries to Put Its Imprint on Blockchain," *Wall Street Journal*, May 11, 2021.

36. "Building Value with Blockchain Technology: How to Evaluate Blockchain's Benefits," World Economic Forum, July 2019, 4, https://www3.weforum .org/docs/WEF_Building_Value_with_Blockchain.pdf.

37. Silvio Micali, "Algorand's Approach to the Right to Be Forgotten," Algorand, accessed February 18, 2022, https://algorandcom.cdn.prismic.io/algorand com/1206553b-fd57-48be-81be-77f2b82fd0e6_Approach+to++the+Right+to+Be +Forgotten+-+Silvio+070120.pdf.

Index